Change & Renewal
The Essence of the Jewish Holidays,
Festivals & Days of Remembrance

Steinsaltz Center

מגיד
MAGGID

Rabbi Adin Even-Israel
Steinsaltz

Change & Renewal

The Essence of the Jewish Holidays, Festivals & Days of Remembrance

TRANSLATED BY

Daniel Haberman

EDITED BY

Yehudit Shabta

Steinsaltz Center
Maggid Books

Change & Renewal: The Essence of the Jewish Holidays, Festivals & Days of Remembrance

Maggid Edition, 2015

Maggid Books
A division of Koren Publishers Jerusalem Ltd.

POB 8531, New Milford, CT 06676-8531, USA
& POB 4044, Jerusalem 91040, Israel

www.korenpub.com

Please send corrections to: tikunim@steinsaltz-center.org

https://steinsaltz-center.org

Originally published as *Ḥayyei Shana* (Hebrew)

ISBN 978-1-59264-742-2, *paperback*

A CIP catalogue record for this title is available from the British Library

Printed and bound in Turkey

This book is dedicated to the memory of the late

Maurice and Vivienne Wohl z"l

Lifelong supporters of Torah Study
and Rabbinic Teaching

Contents

SUKKOT

THE MONTH OF ḤESHVAN

YOD-TET (19TH) KISLEV

ḤANUKKA

TU BISHEVAT

PURIM

PESAḤ

TISHA B'AV

ELUL AND TESHUVA

Editors' Introduction

This book is a collection drawn from Rabbi Adin Steinsaltz's writings and oral discourses on the festivals and special times of the Jewish year. The purpose of these essays and talks is to reveal the meaning and essence of the holidays so that we may better prepare for them, celebrate them properly, and attune our lives under their influence.

The preparation for a mitzva is almost as important as the mitzva itself, and this is particularly true of mitzvot connected to the sequence of time. When one prepares himself for an experience through study and spiritual elevation, he can internalize the event to a greater extent. Emphasis on the central idea of each holiday guides us to focus on the character of the day and how to properly receive it.

The book was not written as one work, but rather constitutes a collection of individual chapters. Most of these chapters are essays written under various auspices and for a variety of forums and audiences, appearing in the press and various philosophical works and collections. A smaller part is drawn from talks, lectures, and interviews. As a result, the chapters differ from one another in style and degree of complexity. Although the editorial work aimed at minimizing the stylistic disparity between the chapters these essential differences remain discernible.

We attempted to avoid including more than one essay dealing with the same topic, but if the same topic is treated briefly in one essay and at length and in detail in another, we included both treatments, as "words of Torah are terse in one place and expansive in another."

The entire editing process was carried out under the guidance of our teacher, Rabbi Adin Steinsaltz, who reviewed the manuscript and added a preface.

We thank all those who helped us in the editorial preparation of this book, including the staff of the Israel Institute for Talmudic Publications and our colleagues at Yeshivat Tekoa, who assisted us in collecting the material, transcribing tapes, reworking and proofreading the material, and adding helpful comments. May they all receive their due reward.

The Editors

Preface

The word "*shana*" (year) contains within it two meanings that at first glance appear almost contradictory.

On the one hand, a *shana* denotes something that repeats itself again and again. It appears to be a fixed cycle of recurring patterns – day and night, summer and winter.

On the other hand, a *shana* also denotes change, as days and months bring forth new realities and new experiences, changes relative to the past.

Every year of life thus has dual significance. On the one hand, there is a continuous, regular course of life, which generally follows a trajectory of sequential and consequential elements. On the other hand, there are always changes, variability and renewal, which are not truly part of the annual cycle, but rather unique events that lend nuance to the year and give it color and a distinct character.

As human beings, we are constrained by our physical and spiritual limits. Our physical lives follow a fixed pattern, and our internal spiritual limits constrain our ability to attain completely new experiences. Events, feelings and experiences arise and take place against the same background – that of a consistent personality that maintains the continuity of existence.

Despite its continuity and consistency, however, even the regular course of life has a degree of changeability. We each experience distinct and unique events from time to time – joyful experiences as well as emotional and physical pain. Sometimes, we recognize changes while they take place; other times, we recognize them only after a considerable amount of time has passed. Often, we fail to notice periods of growth and blossoming or the changes of aging and withering, which may occur over an extended period of time. We often discern them only in retrospect, as hindsight provides a clearer picture. Since the world remains basically stable, the elements of change and rejuvenation are swallowed up in the overall structure of ongoing existence.

Our festivals and holidays, remembrance days and special occasions, ensure that the paths of our lives do not remain merely dusty roads lacking meaningful points of distinction, like mud into which we sink, unable to extricate ourselves. These special days are the landmarks, signposts, and lights along the way. While they are part of the annual cycle, they are also openings through which we may emerge from the stagnancy and rut of life's routine. They provide us with opportunities not only to celebrate and mourn, but also to renew and change ourselves.

Nevertheless, the holidays and festivals are cyclical, as well; they, too, are liable to be swallowed up in the routine. Just as the days of the week merge into an indistinct succession, the same is liable to happen to the festivals – this Rosh HaShana is like every other Rosh HaShana, and this Pesaḥ like every Pesaḥ that came before.

Still, the cessation from work – the external change and the marking of the event – offers the opportunity of a different perspective, a different outlook on the course of life and even our aims and goals. They are opportunities for soul-searching, for joyous inspiration or for feeling pain, but ultimately for an enhancement of life.

Adin Steinsaltz

Rosh HaShana – The New Year

A New Year

AWAKEN FROM YOUR SLUMBER

The Hebrew phrase *shana ḥadasha* (new year) is itself a contradiction – a *shana* (year) denotes something that repeats itself again and again, whereas *ḥadasha* (new) denotes change, emergence from a cycle of repetition.

Each year is essentially a repetition of the same basic structure. Once again, we experience fall, winter, spring, summer; once again, there are shorter days and longer days, rainy season and dry season, cold and heat. The constant repetition is not limited to the weather or to the annual seasons; recurrence and routine are the pattern of all of life. Every person's life, with the exception of rare incidents, essentially flows in a routine cycle. Even events that involve change or upheaval – birth, marriage, death – quickly fall into set molds. Indeed, the events of most people's lives are so similar that it often appears as though we experience these events not as different people, but as one anonymous figure. It is as if a form of a human being, invested with life-like mobility, moves from place to place, constantly changing its garments, rushing from one ceremony to the next, repeating over and over again the same motions and the same words and going through the same emotions…

And the people themselves, the living people who, after all, have their own character and their own lives – what are they doing? They seem to be sleeping, leading a vegetative existence, looking forward to a "new year," anticipating something that will bring change and awaken them.

Rosh HaShana is the day on which the new year begins, and the central event of this festival is the blowing of the *shofar*. The *shofar* is not and never was a musical instrument. In fact, the shofar's sound, particularly when broken into the tones of *shevarim* and *terua*, is the sound of a cry, of sobbing and moaning. It is a sound that is threatening, agitating, and alarming. Maimonides writes:

> In the blowing of the *shofar* on Rosh HaShana there is an allusion, as though saying: Awake you sleepers from your sleep, and slumberers arise from your slumbering… All who forget the truth in the follies of the times and err the whole year in vanity and emptiness that cannot benefit or save, look to your souls, improve your ways…[1]

The sound of the *shofar* is not meant to be pleasant to the ear; its purpose is to arouse and to shock, to awaken those who slumber in the endless routine of life and guide them towards *teshuva*.

RELIGIOUS LIFE – INTERRUPTING THE ROUTINE

The essence of *teshuva* is the process of stimulating the ability of self-renewal, one's ability to again become oneself instead of being merely a copy – a copy of a newspaper advertisement, a copy of one's neighbors, or even a copy of one's younger and more authentic self.

Perhaps one might argue that *teshuva*, returning to a more religious way of life, is by no means the proper way to renew one's selfhood. After all, isn't religion, with its thousands of fixed details, commandments, duties, and prohibitions, part of the endless repetition and routine, only redoubled?

In truth, religious obligation does not constitute further routine, but rather escape from it. There is certainly a routine of prayers, commandments, and good deeds, but this system does not go hand in

1. Rambam, *Hilkhot Teshuva* 3:4.

hand with the other, ordinary routine of life. On the contrary, it clashes with that routine constantly. It interrupts the ordinary course of eating, drinking, and working, and that interruption of the uniform sequence stimulates change.

It is this "trivial" intervention of the halakha in all the small details of life that saves us from sinking into the mire of animalistic action. The halakha tells us: "Let us desist for a moment from this race! Let us switch for a moment to another system – a system of blessing, of prayer, of washing the hands – a system that is not connected to and does not flow from the daily course of affairs."

There is an additional renewing aspect of religious life that is worthy of consideration. In any other realm, a person can carry on his activity like a robot for years on end, without feeling obligated to give more of himself than that. One may be a talented and successful worker in the office, an outstanding educator, a spiritual leader, a reliable husband, a loving father – and all this may be nothing more than a mask. Even worse, there may be nothing behind that mask!

This is not possible within the world of Judaism, however. One can lead a life of routine, but he cannot escape the knowledge that what he is doing is not right and proper, that he is deceitful. Although one may be absorbed in a routine of mitzvot, he is bound by the basic duty to direct his mind to what he doing. He may certainly fool other people in this regard, but he cannot fool God, and therefore cannot take comfort in the thought that no one knows the truth.

Because the Jew maintains the feeling that he can and should lead a more meaningful life, he has a chance – at rare moments – to relive the primal experiences of *Ma'amad Har Sinai* (the revelation at Sinai) and *Zikaron LeYom Rishon* (remembrance of the first day of Creation).

HARD TO HAVE FAITH

Many people think that true faith is unattainable in our day. "Perhaps it was possible once, in past generations, in the small Jewish towns of Poland, in the ghettos of Morocco, in the immigrant neighborhoods in the far corners of the world. But nowadays, in our wise and discerning era, who can be a true believer?"

The story is told that when King Solomon, in his wisdom, set down in his book of proverbs, "A simple person will believe anything,"[2] all the fools in the world became very agitated. They convened a grand World Congress to deal with a pressing issue: Until Solomon revealed that "a simple person will believe anything," it was impossible to discern the wise person from the fool, and the fools could escape the attention of others. But now what was to be done? The fools concluded that in order to avoid detection, they would do just the opposite. From now on, they must not believe in anything. And, indeed, that is the practice of fools to this very day…

When people, simple or scholarly, speak of the inability to have faith in our day, of the absurdity of faith, one is tempted to ask them: "Were you perhaps a participant in that Congress?"

Of course, the way to faith is not an easy one. It is not easy for a person who grew up in a "religious" home, and not for one who grew up in a non-religious environment. The way of faith is a "long shorter" way; it is not a wide highway, traveled in the same way by all, but rather a narrow and winding path, personal and private.

The words of one *tzaddik* who spoke on this matter are simple and profound. On the words, "For I know that God is great,"[3] he commented, "For I know – I alone know, and no other person can know like me!"[4] Another person may know more than me, or in a deeper, broader, or more complete manner, but knowledge of God is ultimately a private, personal experience that cannot be communicated.

It is possible to recount to another person what you ate through all sorts of descriptions and explanations, but it is impossible to convey the taste. Taste can only be perceived in one way – through actual experience. This is the meaning of the verse, "Taste and see that God is good"[5] – taste Him for yourselves!

---

2. Proverbs 14:15.
3. Psalms 135:5.
4. *Siḥot HaRan* 1.
5. Psalms 34:9.

NEITHER IN HEAVEN NOR BEYOND THE SEA

But who can reach that level? Who can taste "of the fruit of the tree of life"? Isn't it necessary to be great and exalted, an eminent scholar, pure of heart and pure of mind, in order to attain a "religious experience"?

This question has no clearer answer than the words of the Torah that are read communally on the Sabbath preceding Rosh HaShana:

> It is not in heaven, that you should say, "Who will go up to heaven and bring it to us, so that we hear it and do it?" It is not beyond the sea, that you should say, "Who will cross the sea and get it for us, so that we can hear it and do it?" It is something that is very close to you, in your mouth and in your heart, so that you can do it.[6]

Where can faith be found? Neither in heaven nor beyond the sea. It is very close, "in your mouth and in your heart." Both theology and personal experience attest that every person utters words of faith and trust, although he may not be aware of the subconscious thoughts that emerge from his mouth, and he fails to discern what his heart truly believes. In every ordinary statement of "It will be all right," there is a true expression of faith. The comforting words spoken to a crying child, the awareness that somehow it is possible to get through life despite all the obstacles – these and the like are expressions of belief in God.

There are people who deny God's existence and yet believe with all their heart in the "eternity of Israel." There are people who are unwilling to accept anything that is part of the religion, of the tradition, of the heritage of our ancestors, and yet they stand and fight for things they think are good and right. These may be intellectual or simple people, they may have lost their way or they may be on course – but they have a wealth of true faith "in their mouths and in their hearts." There are hindrances and obstacles that lead them to think that they have no share in their heritage; they think that true religious faith is found somewhere far away in the high heavens, inaccessible to them, and so they do not search for it in the closest place possible. They do not nurture and develop the kernel that is found in their own selves.

---

6. Deuteronomy 30:12–14.

The word *emuna* (faith) is related to the word *omen*, one who raises and nurtures an infant. The seedling of faith must be tended like a child. The authentic experience must be developed and given room to grow; it must be given the opportunity to find expression. We must stop being afraid of ourselves, stop worrying about the approval of the Congress of Fools. We must find and nurture the thing that is so close, which needs only "to be done" – to be carried out and actualized.

THIS YEAR WILL BE A NEW YEAR

One year follows the other; "What *has* happened is what *will* happen."[7] A person can spend his whole life repeating externals, never questioning them. For such a person, every year will be another old year, the very same thing again – an endless dream, a closed circuit from which there is no exit.

For this reason, the *shofar* is sounded! Its unpleasant sound is a cry without words, for there are no words that would convey the message to disparate people. This sound simply cries out. Sometimes, it is a blast of broken sobbing over what has happened, over what has been lost, while other times it is a blast of warning against further pitfalls and sources of decline. And sometimes it is the sound of victory, of assurance that this year, in spite of everything, it is indeed possible that life will not be merely a repetition – that in the midst of the cycle of the seasons, there is a door of hope that this year will truly be a new year.

7. Ecclesiastes 1:9.

A Reckoning of This World

IN WHAT DIRECTION IS THE WORLD PROGRESSING?

An assumption widely accepted throughout the world – both as a practical basis for various religions and as a tacit assumption in many intellectual or "scientific" approaches – is that the world is of necessity progressing steadily, and that with time, everything must necessarily become better, improved, and more perfected.

This outlook has not always been the most widely held one. On the contrary, many considered it naive, unrealistic, and meaningless optimism.

The Greek myth about the world's different eras – the first of which was a happy and perfect Golden Age, and the last of which is a hard, cruel, and base Iron Age – is an example of an essentially different world-view, a pessimistic outlook on the future of the world and the direction in which it is going. An even gloomier outlook is found in the Norse myth that concludes with the "decline of the gods," with whom the whole universe declines as well.

A world-view in this spirit can be found in our own time as well – for example, among many scientists who see how the world's population is increasing out of all proportion, and who observe with alarm how the universe draws ever closer to its inevitable decline, even if not in the immediate future.

According to another view, human history is a succession of ever-recurring cycles: "What *has* happened is what *will* happen, and what *has* been done is what *will* be done. There is nothing new under the sun."[1] This approach is also fundamentally pessimistic, for it assumes that all the efforts people make in their lives will ultimately fail to effect real change or advancement.

The Jewish view of world history is more complex, but the essence of it may be encapsulated in the following simple structure: Man begins his journey in the Garden of Eden, from which he progressively descends, falling step by step. This descent, however, is only one side of what transpires. At the very same time another, reverse movement, is active in the world – that of rectification and redemption. Stage after stage, at times openly and at times secretly, an inevitable, unstoppable process advances, ultimately culminating in redemption. Like the process of pregnancy leading to birth, man and the world are slowly elevated even above their starting point.

ILLUSORY PERFECTION

The conception of a world destined to be redeemed, a view of history as progressing towards "the end of days," evolved from Judaism and became a basic element in the thought of the entire modern world. Through the teachings of Christianity (and to a certain degree those of Islam), this concept is well-known. Even the Communist "religion" promoted this belief as the basis of a way of life and a course of action on both the ideological and tactical levels. Communism based itself on the heartfelt certainty that the messiah (in other words, the revolution) would come, although he tarries.

The very same assumptions emerge from views and approaches maintained in the democratic and capitalistic western world, conceptions that seem to be far removed from any kind of faith. The theory of evolution, for example, through a slight change in meaning, metamorphosed from an explanation of the process by which animals adapt

1. Ecclesiastes 1:9.

to certain conditions to a schema outlining how, in every generation, things progressively improve and become more and more perfect. This is the source of the assumption that if we would only let reality operate on its own, with time, it would produce the good and desirable. If we do not stand in the way of progress, if we simply give the forces of the marketplace the freedom to operate, this would result in the constant improvement of human society.

The assumption that the world is getting better rests, among other things, on so-called proofs, such as the advance of technology or science. Yet these assessments are often based strictly on preconceived notions, according to which anything that is more complex or more artificial is also better.

People who think this way may remark indignantly, "Is something as base and primitive as this worthy of our era?" – as though our era is necessarily better, purer, more perfect than the preceding centuries, and accordingly is also incomparably nobler than any preceding time. Characteristically, the essentially neutral word "modern" has become synonymous with "good," "desirable," and "useful;" saying that something is "progressive" has come to mean that it is superior.

AN OBJECTIVE CRITERION OF PROGRESS

Closer consideration of these phenomena reveals that something has changed in the original concept, not only in the idea's external forms, but in the idea itself. In the course of secularization, the idea has lost one of its vital dimensions – accountability, the criterion for and sense of something's value.

The religious belief in the future redemption incorporates a system of reckoning, an evaluation that each year and even each act must undergo. The new year is not necessarily a better year; rather, it must first be subjected to the crucible of judgment. It must prove that man, the era, and the way of life are indeed worthy of continuation.

When people content themselves with the statement that such-and-such is "progressive," thinking that thereby they have justified its existence, they have at least an equal chance of progressing toward hell in this world. When God (and with Him, the acceptance of absolute values) is "banished" from the seat of judgment, a substantial change is made in one's whole outlook, not just in matters of faith and religion. When "man is the criterion," then not only is the criterion reduced, but it ceases to set any standard; the smallest dwarf will always be the equal of the greatest giant. By this criterion, one cannot tell if he has grown; what is worse, one cannot be set straight when he is shrinking!

Restoring Heaven's standard, restoring the values that do not originate within man himself and are not measured by man himself and for himself, is the basic idea of the "Day of Judgment" of the Heavenly Court.

The whole world is very much in need of Heaven's standard, which gives real direction. Any doctrine of general relativism of all values advances steadily toward the Deluge, whereas grasping the "finger of God"[2] is a true return to the conception of possible redemption.

2. Exodus 8:15.

Rosh HaShana: The Head of the Year

THE CENTER OF LIFE

The term "*Rosh HaShana*" is a strange expression; it is only because of our familiarity with it that we fail to notice its strangeness. The more precise designation for the day on which the year begins is "*Reishit HaShana*," the beginning of the year, as the term actually appears in Scripture.[1] *Rosh HaShana* means the "head" of the year (similar to *Rosh Ḥodesh,* the "head" of the new month). But "*rosh*" is the designation of a part of the body and does not denote the beginning of something!

It seems that just as living creatures have a head, so does the year. Rosh HaShana is not simply the point from which the year starts; it is a day that is connected to the year in the same way that the head relates to the body.

Several organs play vital roles in the body, as among them "the three kings" – the brain, the heart, and the liver. The brain is the center of thought, the heart is the center of circulation, and the liver is the center of digestion. To be sure, the body cannot survive without even one of these three, but even among them, there is a hierarchy – and the mind is clearly at the top of the ladder.

1. Deuteronomy 11:12.

The brain, which is in the head, is man's center. In a certain sense, all of man's knowledge of the world – including knowledge of himself – is no more than cerebral experience. When a person sees that something is in front of him, all that he has at that moment is an experience of that thing as perceived in his brain. We have experiences of objects, of people, of the world, of the sun rising – yet they are all "in our head." We do not know with certainty whether all of this is real or not.

The brain contains all of man's being, the whole experience of his existence. Besides the various senses of pleasure, pain, heat, or cold, the brain is the source of one's sense of his own existence.

THE YEAR AS AN INDEPENDENT ENTITY

Rosh HaShana is regarded as a "head" because the year itself is a "body," a complete being with its own actual existence. The year, like every unit of time, is not simply a measure of set duration. It is a being – with beginning and end – that is distinct and distinguished from all others.

If we were to equate two parcels of land of equal measure, we could easily discern that although each one is equal to the other quantitatively, each one differs from the other in nature and character. Every centimeter in the world is unique, and it is impossible to find even one speck of dust that is exactly equal to another.

The same is true of units of time. To be sure, time can be measured in external units, and there would appear to be no difference between its various parts, between one minute and the next, between one hour and the one that follows. But the truth is that each unit of time is distinct; every single moment is new and different.

Such an outlook engenders a serious attitude toward accounting for time and toward the utilization or waste of time. Since every minute is unique, if it is wasted, that minute is no longer rectifiable; the time of rectification is already a different time.[2] Two successive moments may,

---

2. In kabbalistic literature, there is discussion of how the coordinate system of time and place is arranged according to the system of the *Sefirot*. Each point of time is a one-time intersection of time and place – reality. According to this definition, every moment has its own designation, which is not to be found, and will never be found, in any other moment.

perhaps, be similar, but they will never be identical, and they may even be totally dissimilar. If a mitzva is performed at a certain moment, that moment is adorned; in contrast, a moment in which a transgression is committed is defiled.[3]

The same applies to larger units of time – years. The consecutive numeration of the years is not an insignificant successive numbering. The number assigned to a particular year is like a library serial number, which signifies a book's type and subject. Each year has its own character, uniqueness, and array. The new year is analogous to a newborn child, who may be like his older sibling – or significantly worse or incomparably better. A new year can be an ordinary year, and it can also be a year that will bear a special increase in blessing and life.

LIFE FOR THE YEAR

The *rosh* of the *shana*, because it is the "head" of the unique "body," contains within it, as in a single thought, all the days of the year. For this reason, good spiritual work on Rosh HaShana forms a better inner picture of the year's shape and character.

This does not mean, however, that on Rosh HaShana one should make plans for the whole year. That would be impossible, for an entire year is multidimensional and is connected to many different worlds. What one should do on this day is form a general picture of what ought to be the character and direction of this year. One should place on the head of the year a "crown of kingship," and thereby transform the year into a completely different form of being.

This spiritual work must be done not only in honor of the day, but also because of the influence that the "head" of the year exerts on the entire "body" of the year.[4] On Rosh HaShana, a person has it within his power to impart life-force to the whole year.

3. Through *teshuva*, it is possible to retroactively rectify what was done at a certain time, but that path transcends the natural reality. True repentance is inherently supernatural.
4. This is the reason for the custom not to sleep during the day of Rosh HaShana, as cited in the halakhic literature in the name of the *Yerushalmi*: "One who sleeps on Rosh HaShana, his *mazal* will sleep." Sleep on Rosh HaShana puts the whole year to sleep!

In general, dead things belong to the "not good" aspect of the world. In fact, all forms of impurity take effect upon death, and it makes no difference whether it is a great death or a small death. The opposite of impurity is life; hence the expression "the living God." Thus, we read: "See, I have set before you today life and good, death and evil."[5] The conclusion of the passage is not, "Choose good," but rather, "Choose life."[6] Choosing life is of primary importance because life, by its very nature, presents an advantage; a living thing is better, even when the life is not on the side of holiness.

On Rosh HaShana we are to build a new year. We are to instill in the year life and goodness, and thereby fashion a new and different year. If one merits it, he can revitalize many others; at the very least, he can revitalize himself and cause the whole body to follow him, to follow the head.

5. Deuteronomy 30:15.
6. Ibid. 30:19.

To Hear the Sound of the Shofar

SHOFAR OF REMEMBRANCE AND SHOFAR OF CORONATION

Rosh HaShana is not only the beginning of a new year; it marks the conclusion of the old. This conception of Rosh HaShana as the conclusion of a period of time results in the need to review what has happened in the course of the year that has passed and to remember the events that have occurred. This remembrance and review incorporates retrospection and evaluation of deeds, thus turning Rosh HaShana into the Day of Judgment.

The sound of the *shofar* signifies that Rosh HaShana is the Day of Remembrance and Judgment. It is a sound of warning, a sound of alarm. Man is called upon to awaken from his sleep of habit, to reassess his situation, and to consider his ways before the new year. As Maimonides says:

> Although blowing the *shofar* on Rosh HaShana is a Scriptural decree, it contains an allusion, as though saying: "Awake you sleepers from your sleep, and slumberers arise from your slumbering. Search your ways, return in *teshuva*, and remember your Creator."[1]

1. Rambam, *Hilkhot Teshuva* 3:4.

This sound addresses every human being, warning him of consequences and pointing out to him that changes must be made in preparation for the coming year.

In addition to its meaning as a Day of Judgment, Rosh HaShana is also a day of accepting God's kingship, and in this, too, the *shofar* plays a role.

Since the meaning of the new year is renewal of time, the year that begins on Rosh HaShana is like a new creation. As we say in the Musaf Prayer of Rosh HaShana, "This day, the beginning of Your work" – this is the day on which the new time of the new year is created. The world's renewal on Rosh HaShana is not renewal in the sense of formation of new forms of life, but is rather inner renewal – renewed acknowledgement of God as king over His world.

The blowing of the *shofar* marks the proclamation of a king's rule, as we find in the Prophets in the narratives about the coronations of Solomon, Jehu, and others. Rosh HaShana, the day of creation, is the day of acknowledging God's kingship over His world, and the sounding of the *shofar* on this day is the blast that trumpets His coronation.

ISAAC'S RAM

> R. Abahu said: Why do we sound [the *shofar*] using a ram's horn? The Holy One, blessed be He, said: Sound before me a ram's horn, so that I will remember in your favor the Binding (*Akeda*) of Isaac, son of Abraham, and account it to you as though you bound yourselves before me.[2]

On an external level, the *shofar* "reminds" God of the commitment and self-sacrifice of our forefathers, and He takes their merit into account on our Day of Judgment.

There is a deeper connection between the Binding of Isaac and Rosh HaShana, however. The essence of the *Akeda* was change – becoming someone different than who one once was. This was true in the case of Abraham, and even more so for Isaac. A number of sources refer to

2. *Rosh HaShana* 16a.

"Isaac's ashes,"[3] as though Isaac himself was sacrificed, and not the ram that was sacrificed as a burnt offering in his stead. After the *Akeda*, it was as if Isaac no longer existed, for he nullified his own will to such a degree that he became like ashes. This is alluded to by Scripture itself, which states that "Abraham returned to his servants,"[4] but makes no further mention of Isaac in the *parasha*. The Isaac who carries on after the *Akeda* is a different Isaac; out of the *Akeda*, a new and different will came to life.

For both Abraham and Isaac, the *Akeda* entailed complete nullification of all desires. The Binding of Isaac symbolizes the breaking of all rules, not only of customs and regulations, but of all moral law – the bond between father and son, the prohibition of murder, and even the abomination of human sacrifice. The trial in the *Akeda* was to attain the highest level of nullification, wherein all laws cease to operate except for the supreme first Will. Thus, after the former world was nullified to the utmost, a new Isaac and a new world were born.

The *shofar*, which brings the memory of the *Akeda* before God on Rosh HaShana, also reminds man "to bind himself before God," to reach the highest level of nullification – the nullification of the desire to carry on with one's former existence. As a result, within man himself, there awakens the divine will to create a new world.

THE SHOFAR OF THE MESSIAH

Blowing a ram's horn recalls not only the deeds of Abraham and Isaac at the *Akeda*, but also the ram that was ultimately sacrificed as a burnt offering. According to the Midrash, the various parts of this ram accompany Israel throughout the course of history and testify to our merit:

> R. Ḥanina ben Dosa says: From that ram, which was created at twilight,[5] nothing came forth that was useless. The ashes of the ram were the base of the inner altar. The sinews of the ram were ten, corresponding to the ten strings of the harp on which David played. The ram's skin was the girdle of Elijah, may he be

3. *Vayikra Raba* 36:5; *Bereshit Raba* 56:9.
4. Genesis 22:19.
5. That is, at the twilight of the last day of Creation; cf. *Avot* 5:6.

> remembered for good...The horns of the ram – of the left side [was the one] He blew on Mount Sinai... [The horn] of the right side, which is larger than that of the left, is destined to be sounded in the days to come.[6]

The ram's two horns figure prominently in Jewish history: the left one was the *shofar* blown at the revelation at Sinai, while the right one will be the *shofar* of the future redemption, when "a great *shofar* shall be sounded."[7] Both the great revelation and the great renewal stem from the Binding of Isaac, and the sound of both is the sound of the *shofar*.

In days to come, a new world will be born; "the new heaven and the new earth"[8] will be formed. Similarly, every Rosh HaShana, a new heaven and a new earth appear. The heaven and earth of the previous year are not the heaven and earth of the new year. The world is new, the laws are different, and the past is no longer a part of the new reality.

The sounding of the *shofar* relates both to the day of "remembrance of the first day," in which we recall past events and coronate God as king, and "remembrance of the final day," the time in which God's kingship will be manifest in its most complete form.

Rosh HaShana, the year's beginning, is, by its very nature, also *aḥarit shana*, the year's end. Just as every new year contains within it the essence of the eternal recurrence of Creation and of God's first kingship, it also contains the essence of the conclusion and summation – not just the summation of the year that has passed, but of all the time that has passed from the beginning of the world's existence. Rosh HaShana marks the whole duration from the beginning until the end of time, the "end of days."

Rosh HaShana, the day of "remembrance of sounding,"[9] recalls all the soundings, from the sounding of Creation to the great *shofar* of the future redemption.

---

6. *Pirkei DeRabbi Eliezer*, ch. 31.
7. Isaiah 27:13.
8. Ibid. 66:22.
9. Leviticus 23:24.

The Beginning of Kingship

RENEWAL OF TIME

Rosh HaShana's definition, which is mentioned in the Talmud and which appears in the *Zikhronot* prayer,[1] is: "*Zeh hayom teḥilat ma'asekha, zikaron leyom rishon.*" According to the simple meaning, this means: "This day, on which was the beginning of Your work, is a remembrance of the first day."[2]

According to the teachings of Hasidism, however, the meaning of "*yom teḥilat ma'asekha,*" "the beginning of Your work," is not simply that on this day the world was created in the past. Rather, the meaning is that this is the day on which the world is created each and every year. This day is the beginning of the year not because it marks the beginning of a year that is assigned a certain number, but rather because on this day, the year begins as a phenomenon. On this day, the world is created anew.

This conception of Rosh HaShana stems from a general approach to the world's creation and existence, the notion that creation was not a one-time event, but is a constant process that repeats itself regularly. Creation does not steadily progress, but rather has points of recurrence,

1. *Zikhronot* is one of three special blessings added to the Musaf prayer of Rosh HaShana. It deals with historical events and divine memory.
2. *Rosh HaShana* 27a.

of renewal of the process from its beginning. This renewal is constant – in every season and at every hour. There is daily renewal with the cycle of sunrise and sunset, monthly renewal with the appearance of the new moon every *Rosh Ḥodesh,* and annual renewal on Rosh HaShana.

There is a significant difference, however, between the renewal of the smaller units of time and the renewal that occurs on Rosh HaShana. The constant renewal resembles heartbeats, which, although separate and independent of one another, appear to be continuous and ongoing because they are a continuity of one movement. This is the constant cycle of time expressed in the very existence of reality. In the language of the Kabbala, this cycle is called "*ratzo vashov,*" "advance and retreat."[3]

On Rosh HaShana, there is renewal on a higher level. On Rosh HaShana, time not only returns to its starting point, it completely disappears. Last year's time ended and no longer exists. Last year's world has come to an end; existence has returned to the pre-world point. From this point on Rosh HaShana, new time is created – a new year is born.

The designation *Rosh HaShana,* literally, the "head of the year," compares the day to the head of the human body. Just as will and consciousness are found in the brain, from which instructions are relayed to the various limbs, the days and the events that will occur over the course of the year are similarly the realization of what takes place on the "head" of the year.

MALKHUYOT – THE ATTRIBUTE OF KINGSHIP

The world that is created at the beginning of the new year is not a direct continuation and obvious corollary of the world of the preceding year. Before the world is recreated on Rosh HaShana, there is a return to nothingness, to the *Ein Sof* before the world's creation. From out of nothingness and nonexistence, it is necessary to rebuild the relationship between God and the world that is to be created.

The re-forging of this relationship takes place through the renewal of the attribute of divine kingship. Thus, Rosh HaShana is a "remembrance of the first day," the day on which the world was first created as a result of the attribute of kingship.

---

3. Based on Ezekiel 1:14. See *Ḥagiga* 13b; *Sefer Yetzira* 1:7; *Tanya,* ch. 41.

Kingship can exist only if the king has subjects; it has no independent existence. By its very nature, kingship depends on the existence of an object and on the possibility of communication and relationship with that object. There is a mutual dependence of king and subjects, a dependence so definitive that "there can be no king without a nation."[4]

This mutual dependence exists between God and His world as well. Commenting on the verse in *Isaiah*, "You are My witnesses... and I am God," the Midrash writes, "When you are not my witnesses, then I, as it were, am not God."[5] If the people do not accept God's kingship – if the witnesses do not continue to testify – they thereby nullify the King of world.

On Rosh HaShana, the Jewish People are not bystanders to the recreation, but rather play an integral role. Our task is to establish God's kingship by being the people who acknowledge the king. The prayers and the sounding of the *shofar* on Rosh HaShana are the coronation ceremony in which we proclaim God's rule and our allegiance to Him.

It seems that many Jews unconsciously sense this obligation despite the fact that they are ordinarily disconnected from their tradition. As a result, they participate in the prayers and mitzvot of Rosh HaShana, even though they do not usually do so the rest of the year. Our sages explain that there are things that a person does not see, but which his *mazal* – the root of his soul – does see. On the eve of Rosh HaShana, the souls subconsciously sense that the world is ending, how its final moments are ebbing at year's end, and how a new year is being born. Even if people do not perceive this as a full-fledged emotional and conscious experience, they have a dim, unarticulated awareness that they, too, must be present at the proclamation that God is king. They, too, must participate in the birth of the new year.

---

4. *Sha'ar HaYiḥud VeHaEmuna*, ch. 7: "It is known to all that the purpose of the creation of the world is for the sake of the revelation of His kingship, may He be blessed, for 'there is no king without a nation'. Only 'in a multitude of people is the glory of the king.'"
5. *Sifre Devarim* 346.

KINGSHIP AND FATHERHOOD

Kingship is not an intimate relationship, but rather one that is built on distance and hierarchy. The world is built on the foundation of this relationship between those who accept upon themselves the kingship and the one who takes it upon himself to be the king. In this tripartite dependence – the Jewish People, the world, and the Creator – there is no intimacy. On the contrary, it is based precisely on the recognition of the majesty of the King-Creator, Who is exalted above and removed from the creation, for only thus does He in fact sustain the creation that, as it were, is separate from Him.

On Rosh HaShana, every individual stands before the King. When one stands before the King, it does not matter how one came to stand there – whether he prayed and kept mitzvot throughout the year or did nothing of the sort. In any case and for every person, standing before the King on Rosh HaShana is problematic, because it poses a painful question: Where have you been all year? Why do come only now?

One Rosh HaShana, it is said, the great Rabbi Aharon of Karlin was leading the prayers, and when he reached the point in the service that begins "*HaMelekh*" ("The King"), he fainted and could not continue. After he was revived, he explained that he had been reminded of Vespasian's question to R. Yoḥanan, who had referred to him as the emperor: "If I am the king, why have you not come to me until now?"[6]

This question is the constant terror of the servant. Man cannot bear to face it, for his whole existence hinges on it. Moreover, the existence of the whole world depends on it – for if there is no king, there can be no people.

Yet an intimate relationship is also present on Rosh HaShana. God's relationship with Israel is compared to a father's relationship with his children, a close personal relationship. This dual relationship appears in the Rosh HaShana prayers in the prayer *Avinu Malkenu*, "Our Father, our King," and in a line of the hymn recited following the *shofar* blasts, "Whether as children or as servants." Our relationship with God is not strictly a master-servant relationship, nor is it strictly a father-child rela-

6. *Gittin* 56a.

tionship; rather, both aspects are always together. On Rosh HaShana we indeed relate to divine kingship, its establishment and its renewal, but in both ways – "whether as children or as servants."

Servants cannot possibly meet the test of the king, but a child always remains a child. Even if he was not at home all year or did not behave properly, the child's bond with his father cannot be broken, just as a father cannot disavow his fatherhood. Similarly, although it is possible to commit severe offenses and rebel against God's kingship, it remains impossible to detach oneself from the paternal bond. It is precisely through such a bond that the beginning of a new relationship can be formed, which can influence the new year and from which a new world can emerge.

TESHUVA ON ROSH HASHANA

Rosh HaShana is the day of the world's "macro-accounting," the day on which we attempt to "persuade" the Holy One, blessed be He, that it is worthwhile for Him to recreate the world. On Rosh HaShana, it is the task of the Jewish People to provide God with desire to do so, and this is the purpose of all the magnificent prayers and themes of the day.

In this sense, the judgment of Rosh HaShana does not focus on transgressions, but primarily on the essence of man and his soul. Although Rosh HaShana is the Day of Judgment, sins and iniquities are not mentioned on this day at all; it is loftier and more exalted than the consideration of any specific defects. It entails not just weighing good deeds against bad deeds, but contemplating the totality of man's actions and the totality of his being against the background of a standard that transcends the fleeting and the transient.

Although Rosh HaShana is not the time designated for *teshuva*, *teshuva* is nevertheless the backdrop for its entire essence. There is not a day of the year that can exist on the basis of the attribute of strict justice, exclusively according to the law and within the bounds of its framework. Surely this applies to Rosh HaShana as well, the day on which matters are set on the larger scale of the entire year.

In the natural world, which operates in a completely causal

manner, the consequences of behavior that contravenes the attribute of strict justice are disastrous. As implied by the verse, "Evil shall kill the wicked,"[7] the evil itself is what kills the wicked – not as an act of punishment for the evil, but as a consequence, like swallowing poison. The wicked man dies because that is the natural-causal result of his action.

In principle, we deserve to die for any evil act, speech, or thought; the world should return to an unformed state. The only way it is possible to continue to a new stage, to a new year, is by returning – momentarily, for one day – to the original source that preceded the beginning. On Rosh HaShana, although we do not speak of *teshuva* from sins, *teshuva* is done in an all-encompassing sense by returning to the source of the soul, the source of life and of the world.

On Rosh HaShana, we rise above the world of causality to a place where there is no cause and effect, and from there we once again receive new life. We return to the boundless flowing spring and draw new days for the coming year as if on credit. From there, we draw new life into the vessels, into the days of the coming year.

7. Psalms 34:22.

The Day of Remembrance

CHAPTER HEADINGS

In European languages, a new sentence always begins with a capital letter. The Jewish People begin periods of time with a "capital" day: Rosh Ḥodesh (the first day of the new month) and Rosh HaShana.

The purpose of grand beginnings is to draw our attention and remind us that the previous sentence or chapter has ended, and that now something new begins. The new element may be the continuation of what preceded it, or it may be entirely different or even contradictory. In either case, it must be clearly noted and recognized.

In life, there is continuity and regularity. The stream and flow of daily life automatically establish certain frameworks and patterns. Today is like yesterday, and tomorrow is nothing but the continuation (or even repetition) of the day that has passed. Life goes by and often melts away under the force of constraints that a person assumes willingly or unwillingly. The framework in which one lives, the things that one does, the profession in which one engages, and even the pastimes that one takes up to break the routine – all these become routine.

There is no free time in which to ask basic questions, because everyone is too busy solving secondary problems that arise. The important questions – "for what reason?" and "for what purpose?" – are pushed aside. Everyone runs, and the individual runs along with them. He is pushed and shoved and competes in the race, to the point that he has no spare time in which to clarify where all this running actually leads to.

Kohelet (Ecclesiastes) expresses this as follows: "He also preoccupies them with the world, so that man fails to find out the [nature of] things ... from beginning to end."[1]

The "chapter headings" in time are intended for such clarification. They serve not only to mark the end of the preceding period, but also to point to the beginning of a new chapter. But before beginning, one must sort through, clarify, and summarize. A new year cannot begin for a person unless he can conclude the previous one.

REMEMBERING THE FORGOTTEN THINGS

Before any deliberation and drawing of conclusions can take place, it is necessary to remember. In the prayer book, Rosh HaShana has one designation: "This Day of Remembrance." Before making an accounting and before rendering judgment, there is a prior duty of retrospection.

It is well-known that memory is selective by its very nature. There are things one remembers easily, there are things one would like to remember, and there are quite a few things one would like to forget. What a person remembers is, to a large degree, a true indicator of his essential nature and character. It is told of one sage that he would ask those who came to him only this question: "What do you remember?" According to the answer, he would evaluate the person's nature.[2]

One of the problems with memories of any kind is that they tend to distort the past in order to compare it to, and bring it into line with, the present. For this reason, absorption in and reflection on memories are not necessarily beneficial to one's personal development. Not infrequently, the "wisdom of hindsight" enlightens and clarifies nothing.

However, memory can indeed become a source of greater understanding if one emulates the Holy One, blessed be He, who "remembers all the forgotten things."[3] As our sages explain, God remembers the

1. Ecclesiastes 3:11.
2. See also "The Seven Beggars" in *The Tales of Rabbi Naḥman of Bratslav.*
3. From the *Zikhronot* in the Musaf prayer of Rosh HaShana, based on *Ta'anit* 16b.

things that man forgets. If one forgets his sins, God remembers them for him; and if one forgets his merits, God remembers them, too. In other words, there are things that, for various reasons, a person does not wish to remember – errors in judgment, errors of commission, mistaken conceptions. It is precisely these things that one must remember especially! Conversely, people tend to remember important things that happen, momentous and shocking events. However, it often turns out that one should search especially among the forgotten things and recall the minor details of which life is woven.

This process of recollection opens the way to a reassessment of the past and thus also to the possibility of a different view of the future. The tendency not to remember mistakes and stumbles (except, of course, those of others) perpetuates the present path. Only a reexamination of the things that slip from memory, of the matters that one does not wish to recall, creates a new opening and allows one to choose a different path.

A TRUE STANDARD

Opportunities for remembering present themselves at various times, both for the individual and for the community, but they often fail to lead to any change or turnabout. Memory alone is insufficient; what is also required is a suitable background and, even more so, a standard against which to measure things.

As long as a person serves as his own sole standard, he cannot extricate himself from his basic problems. As in other areas, in the realm of personal development, a standard that is not fixed fluctuates along with the system of coordinates. Only in a system that has a constant point of reference does the measure always remain accurate, even if the actual proportions incessantly change.

Stagnancy, routine, and repetition of the very same mistakes do not stem only from a failure to examine the past. They have a deeper cause. When people cling to the same old conceptions, when aims and goals are determined by past habits, there is no chance for renewed vision. At most, one can discern various tactical errors that one has made, but the basic strategy remains the same.

Real renewal, a truly new chapter, can spring only from a reassessment of standards. Only through that is it possible to raise the level of the questions that one asks from the likes of, "What were the mistakes that I made in attempting to reach such-and-such a goal?" to the fundamental question, "What, truly, should I do?"

Toward this end, one must view things from a much wider perspective. Variables must be considered against the background of truly constant standards; goals must be considered in the light of fundamental assessments. Policy must be assessed against the backdrop of the nation, and – on a grand scale – the world must be considered in the light of eternity.

Viewing things in this way is likely to be regarded as an escape from the world's concrete problems of existence to abstract intellectual detachment. But that is not so. To be too anchored in practicality not only does not uplift man; it is not even practical. Experience has demonstrated that in all fields and realms, the inability to devote time and resources to the investigation of fundamental questions, to the examination of accepted principles, ultimately leads to destruction by blindness and degeneration. These questions must be examined regarding factory equipment and army training methods; all the more so must they be asked regarding the aims of life!

STANDING BEFORE DIVINE KING

It goes without saying that not everyone can be expected to make such a basic and fundamental reckoning every day, and that is precisely why it is important that there be "chapter headings" in time that are devoted to essential and fundamental inquiry.

This inquiry can be conducted properly only when it is placed against the background of the majestic, true Expanse. Hence, the *Zikhronot* must be preceded by the *Malkhuyot*. In other words, only after an individual confronts himself (or an entire nation confronts itself) with divine kingship can he (or it) examine their remembrances.

Thus, at least once a year, the question of "How is it good for me?" should be replaced with a question of a different kind, namely, "How am I, are we, good for the totality of existence?"

For this reason, although Rosh HaShana is the Day of Judgment, sins and iniquities are not mentioned on this day. This is not because we have no sins, but because the Day of Judgment is far loftier and far more exalted than the consideration of personal defects or sins. It entails not just weighing good deeds against bad deeds, but contemplating the totality of aims and goals against the standard that transcends the fleeting and the transient.

The Day of Judgment is, in effect, the posing of a basic question – not "What am I entitled to?" but "What is required of me?"

Standing before divine kingship is by no means easy. The awesome aspect of the Days of Awe is the very attempt to look at oneself as though from above. Such self-contemplation can be a frightening experience; it can make one feel very small, drastically change one's perspective, and cause a shift of one's center point.

But just as such contemplation has a frightening and unsettling aspect, it also has other elements. When we are immersed in the details of our problems, we cannot perceive fundamental distortions; we likewise cannot discern positive aspects that are all around us. As in aerial photographs, the view from above sometimes reveals the hidden features of underground treasures. Inasmuch as a person's overall attitude is "I am entitled" to this or that, as long as he is caught up in a personal or collective feeling of "I'm okay," he fails to notice or appreciate good and beautiful things that are present in his life. At times, by elevating his perspective, he sees on the surface not just mires, but also points of light.

Remembering the forgotten things can also bring to the fore small or great things whose beautiful side one fails to see as a result of habituation or pretentiousness.

SHOFAROT

The contemplation of *Malkhuyot*, Heaven's perspective, as it were, is necessary not only for a correct understanding of the *Zikhronot*, for the summary and reconsideration, but also for the future. Moreover, its importance for the future exceeds its importance for an accounting of the past.

The ability to set aims and goals and to bring about an essential change in direction depends on whether Rosh HaShana will truly be a *rosh* (head), a festival marked by the ability to confront what lies beyond day-to-day existence. When the Jewish New Year is turned into just a day on the calendar, it can no longer serve as the crown or heading of the year. The prophet's curse "And I will turn your festivals into mourning"[4] is not necessarily the nadir of decline. Worse than that is when the festival is turned into an ordinary day. Not only do we then lose an opportunity to make a break and start something new, but life is deprived of the "capital letter" of the beginning. When all of life's peaks are merely hillocks, there is no way to view the past or to truly gaze into the future. In the absence of *Malkhuyot*, when there is no will or ability to stand before divine kingship, there is no way for remembrance, nor is there strength to hear the *shofarot* – neither the *shofar* of Mount Sinai nor the *shofar* of the Messiah.

For this reason, not only regular worshipers come to synagogue on Rosh HaShana, but many other people as well. Perhaps not all those who come give an accounting to themselves as to why they come, but they have an inner understanding – it is the will to make of Rosh HaShana a festival, the aspiration (openly revealed or in the secrets of the heart) for a favorable moment of enlightenment, of revelation of God's kingship.

4. Amos 8:10.

Is Creation Justified?

YAMIM NORA'IM

Of all the Jewish holidays, the *Yamim Nora'im* ("Days of Awe") stand out because of the difficulty they present to all those who attempt to grasp their essential nature. Indeed, there appears to be an inherent contradiction in the very nature of these days. On the one hand, they are festivals; on the other hand, they are accompanied by fear of judgment, repentance, and even fasting.

Although "*Yamim Nora'im*" is a rather enigmatic designation, it explains something about the nature of these days. The word *nora* as used in Scripture and in most of Hebrew usage through the ages does not mean "frightening" or "intimidating," but, rather "exalted." The *Yamim Nora'im* are not frightening or full of dread, but days full of exaltation and grandeur. Instead of the joyous intimacy that characterizes other holidays, the *Yamim Nora'im* are imbued with a sense of encountering the majestic and the sublime.

MAN'S JUDGMENT DAY

Rosh HaShana's special standing and uniqueness is rooted in its being the "Day of Remembrance,"[1] identified in an ancient hymn in the Musaf Prayer as "remembrance of the first day."[2] This first day is not the day of the world's creation, but the first day since man's creation. This distinction is certainly not significant as regards the dates, but it has significant implications regarding the meaning of the day. Since Rosh HaShana is considered the day of *man*'s creation, it is man who is placed at the center of the day. The New Year is not a summation point in the course of nature, but it is specifically the date of humanity.

Rosh HaShana is connected neither with an event in Jewish history, nor with the various dates of the agricultural year, nor with one of the special dates connected to the times of the year (the equinox and the like). Its place as "remembrance of the first day" establishes it as the day of man.

From this conception of the "Day of Remembrance" emerges the conception of the "Day of Judgment." A year passes, the first day – the day of man's creation – rolls around again, and the question again presents itself: Should man be created? Is there justification for his existence? The judgment to be rendered, not about a specific individual but about man in general, is always: What is the justification for his existence? Has he, over the course of the year, through the generations, from the day of his creation until now, justified his coming into being?

The judgment is not confined to a reckoning of mitzvot and transgressions alone, rather it applies to the whole sphere of man's worthiness or unworthiness to continue existing in this world.

Finite man put to the test before the Absolute, the Eternal, the exalted transcendent One – this is what makes this day a Day of Awe.

1. "The first day of the seventh month shall be a day of rest for you, a remembrance of sounding, a holy convocation" (Leviticus 23:24).
2. *Rosh HaShana* 27a.

RETURN TO THE CREATION

However, remembrance and "this day, on which was the beginning of Your work" have a deeper meaning as well, which entails understanding the concepts of *Ḥag* (festival) and time in general.

Most Jewish festivals and holidays are "days of remembrance" – in other words, fixed times established in remembrance of specific events that occurred in the past. The Sabbath is primarily "a remembrance of the Creation," the three pilgrimage festivals are fundamentally "a remembrance of the departure from Egypt," and later holidays likewise commemorate particular events.

But the function of these days as days of remembrance, as subjective evocations of objective events that happened in the past, is only partial. From the language of Scripture, it appears that a *Ḥag* is not simply a remembrance but actually a recurrence. In fact, the word "*Ḥag*" literally denotes a circuit or circle. The *Ḥagim* are reactivations of events that occurred long ago. In a certain sense, these events transpire again and again.

In Judaism's conception of time, the past and the events that occurred in the past did not pass away with time; they continue to exist in the present. Judaism's approach to history is not that of relating to what once was. Rather, Judaism conceives of historical events as dynamic elements that continue to operate in all times.

This conception is expressed in various forms in almost all Jewish sources, but it is developed profoundly in several later systems that draw on mystical doctrine. According to these systems (which are rooted in the thought of our ancients), time is not a sequence in which the past may be found way back somewhere. Instead, time should be regarded as a long line of discrete units, each of which constitutes a re-creation. The past serves as a basic pattern on the basis of which the present is formed anew in every moment.

According to this conception, which in a certain sense denies historical continuity, there is a cyclic nature to all phenomena; the past serves as a foundation for the present, and past events reoccur at other times. According to this approach, the essence of a *Ḥag* (festival) is the re-experience of the original event, which becomes operative again.

This conception is all the more significant when it comes to accepting Rosh HaShana as an event that recurs each new year – the re-creation of man. The focus of the Day of Judgment is thus more profound, transcending the reckoning of man's merits and demerits. The focus is on the very question of man's creation and existence. The Day of Judgment is like a recurrence of the legendary debate among the ministering angels:

> When the Holy One, blessed be He, wished to create Adam, the ministering angels split into opposing groups, some saying that he should not be created, and others saying that he should be created…[3]

"WHAT IS MAN THAT YOU SHOULD BE MINDFUL OF HIM?"

In a certain sense, the Day of Judgment reflects a fundamental question, one of the basic questions of all religious belief: What justifies and explains the relationship between eternal, infinite, impersonal divinity and the temporal, limited, and very personal existence of man – of the individual or even of humanity as a whole?

This question is related to other problems of faith – such as the significance of prayer or the reason for revelation – but it is not often articulated. Whenever it is expressed, however, it is asked in all its sharpness.

This question appears in contemplative passages in our prayers, as in the Midrashic segment among the preliminary prayers of the morning service:

> What shall we say before You, God… Are not all the mighty as nothing before You, the men of renown as though they never existed, the wise as without knowledge, and men of understanding as without discernment? For most of their works are void, and the days of their lives are vanity before You, and the preeminence of man over the beast is naught, for all is vanity.

Each year on Rosh HaShana, this question returns, implicitly yet forcefully, when the question of man's standing and role is raised anew. "What

3. *Bereshit Raba* 8:5.

is man that You should be mindful of him, or the son of man that You should notice him?"[4] What is the importance and worthiness of a four-dimensional worm before the Infinite?

THE JUSTIFICATION FOR MAN

The answer to this question is set forth in *Malkhuyot, Zikhronot,* and *Shofarot.* Man's awareness of God's existence and his will to attain connection, relationship, and identification with the Infinite give him his special standing and his human worthiness. The recognition of God's kingship is what attests to the heavenly in man; it is what releases man from the shackles of his physical dimensions and attests to his lofty soul. Thus, the Jew's answer to the question of his worthiness is *Malkhuyot* – the recognition and acceptance of God's kingship.

The response to *Malkhuyot* is *Zikhronot.* The Holy One, blessed be He, recalls, as it were, that in the vast expanses of His worlds, there is one creation – mankind – for whose sake it is worth creating the world, and who is deserving of God's attention. Thus, the world and man merit to be remembered because of man's ability to transcend his own limited physical sphere. This is the justification not of God, but of man.

What follows from this justification is *Shofarot,* descriptions of divine revelation at the Giving of the Torah and in the days of the Messiah. Relating to God, connecting with Him, and God's response, constitute the solution and the answer of the Day of Judgment.

---

4. Psalms 8:5.

You Are My Witnesses, and I Am God

RENEWAL AND THE DAY OF JUDGMENT

Rosh HaShana is a festival, a sacred occasion, but it has elements that set it apart from most of the other holidays. Thus, for example, whereas the pilgrimage festivals are joyous and festive historical remembrance days, Rosh HaShana has a special, weightier meaning – it is the day on which heavenly and earthly creatures stand in judgment before the Creator.

As in most cultures, however, the day on which the new year begins is a day of rejoicing and gladness, a joyous commencement of a new period, in the sense of "the year should end along with its curses."[1] The New Year is an expression of hope that the coming year will be happier and more joyous.

At first glance, these two aspects do not seem to be connected. Nevertheless, there is a profound intrinsic connection between the two perspectives, between the optimism of the new year and the conception of general judgment precisely on this day.

Superficially, Rosh HaShana may be regarded as merely a date on the calendar, an arbitrary reference point in the course of time. Judaism, however, sees a deeper meaning in Rosh HaShana. Rosh HaShana

1. *Megilla* 31b.

is also the day of creation, "the beginning of Your work, a remembrance of the first day." Moreover, the day of Rosh HaShana – ever since the world's creation – marks the beginning of a new time, a re-creation of the world for an additional period. Within the overall conception that God renews the work of creation each day, Rosh HaShana is a more general renewal of the creation, a renewed decision about whether the world should continue to exist.

The Day of Judgment, then, is like a balance sheet for the world of the past, a balance sheet that must answer this question: Did the past year justify its existence? This leads to the more penetrating question: Does the past year justify the continuance of existence? Is it worthwhile to continue the "experiment" for another year? The year's end brings the world's existence to a state of termination, a state of temporary summation. A certain period of creation in the world – with all its problems, its ups and its downs – has lasted until this point. From this point on, does the world deserve to be continued? Rosh HaShana, then, is the point of connection between the past and the future; the judgment and verdict are the link between what was and the conclusion as to what will be.

SOUL-SEARCHING OF THE INDIVIDUAL AND OF THE COMMUNITY

The Day of Judgment is a day of major soul-searching for the summation of the preceding period. To be sure, soul-searching is not confined exclusively to this day, for self-evaluation should be performed every day of the year. Nor does soul-searching pertain only to the community; rather, it pertains to each and every person as an individual. However, Rosh HaShana's uniqueness lies in its all-encompassing nature, in its being a day of overall reckoning, featuring the various combinations of individual and community.

This duality of individual and community is found not only in Rosh HaShana, but in all Jewish holidays and throughout the system of blessings and prayers. In one respect, the prayers are collective; they are prayers of the Jewish People as one unit. But it is a mistake to think that this collectivity must lead to the loss and obscuring of the individual within the communal structure. Almost all Jewish prayers are formulated in the plural and are directed to the needs of the entire Jewish community, but there is room for the individual to offer his private individual prayer whenever he wishes, in any manner of address and in any language of appeal. Moreover, the community's prayer itself constitutes only an overall framework within which the individual can and is even required to integrate his own personal prayer.

Similarly, while it is true that the festivals are days of celebration for the entire community and that they have a fixed time and format, within this inclusiveness there is room for each individual to express his own unique essence. Each person must discover his own singular aspect within the national community's constellation of holidays.

Rosh HaShana should therefore be regarded as a day of national reckoning, a combination and integration of the reckoning of the nation's various individuals, who join together to form the reckoning of the whole of the People of Israel.

Every initiative of an individual within the nation – even though he may be isolated and set apart – also has national significance. Although the individual goes his own way, seemingly without any special connection to the problems of the nation as a whole, when all the seemingly independent individual paths are viewed together, it becomes apparent that all of them are interconnected. In the grand reckoning, all of the individual paths travel in the same general direction.

When the individuals perform their own unique soul-searching, each person on the same day, they are automatically linked to the soul-searching of the nation. Similarly, the nation's soul-searching is not abstract; rather, it has meaning only insofar as it is expressed and individualized in the soul-searching of the individuals, the nation's components.

TO BE OR NOT TO BE

Numerous stories and images depict the Day of Judgment as a day of trial and weighing, as though a person's merits and demerits are weighed on a scale and his sentence depends on the surplus or dearth of merits and demerits.

However, from the profound standpoint of the Day of Judgment, this arithmetic aspect, the "commercial" balance sheet, is only a partial factor. The most fundamental reckoning is not the detailed account of a person's or a nation's surplus of good deeds or sins, but rather the question of justification for continued existence. The question raised about each individual – "Who shall live and who shall die? Who shall finish his allotted span, and who shall not finish it?" – is part of the question about all of existence as a whole: To be or not to be?

In this sense, the question of the balance between merits and demerits is of little significance. Even when the year's balance tips to the side of merit, the more profound and fundamental question still remains. In light of the year that has passed, is it worthwhile to continue bearing such an existence for another year? When it comes to the question of our very existence, there are victories that are equivalent to losses and losses equivalent to victories. Merits and demerits are not measured only by a reckoning of their quantity, but also according to their qualitative weight and in consideration of the connection between them and life as a whole.

When Maimonides describes God's judgment regarding those inscribed for life or for death, he observes that we cannot always determine who is worthy and who is unworthy, nor can we know the nature and value of various deeds.[2] The "important" mitzvot are not always decisive, and we do not know which are the truly fateful transgressions. God's reckoning is no doubt more complex and is surely connected to the question of essential value: What is the relation between various deeds and the person's essential nature? How do the deeds relate to the essential nature of the nation, of the country?

The critical question of Rosh HaShana, then, is not whether the past year was a good year or a bad year, a year of merit or demerit, but, rather: Is it worthwhile to continue? Is it worthwhile to go on in this fashion?

RECKONING AT A TIME OF CALM

These existential questions are certainly not asked on only one specific date. There are days set aside for individual soul-searching, and there are hours of reflection and remorse, but the entire nation experiences times of retrospection, particularly in its difficult times. Nevertheless,

2. *Hilkhot Teshuva* 3:2.

there is a special element in these questions when they are raised precisely on Rosh HaShana.

Generally, making an accounting of one's life is likely to be very painful and even ruthless, but it is not always based on true considerations, and the dimensions of such an accounting do not always reach the proper level. Often, in difficult moments, a person, or even an entire nation, will reconsider his (or its) path, but difficult times are not the right time in which to make such an accounting. Sometimes, the pain and the temporary bitterness overshadow the main problems. These problems should be clarified at a time of relative calm, in a moment of relative repose. At such a time, it is fitting to examine whether there is justification for one's way of life and for one's existence. That is the soul-searching of Rosh HaShana, and that is what distinguishes it from other periods of self-reflection.

This reckoning is expressed in the day's special prayers, the special additions of *Malkhuyot, Zikhronot,* and *Shofarot.* In these blessings, these questions are raised explicitly and implicitly and are given an answer.

TESTIMONY TO GOD'S KINGSHIP

The first blessing is that of *Malkhuyot,* which deals with God's overall kingship in the world. From this blessing emerges a twofold question. First, there is a question that we pose to ourselves: Do we desire His kingship? Do we desire the world's and our own continuance? Then there is the question that God, as it were, asks: Do I wish to be king of this world? Is this kingship worth continuing? What reason is there for, and what value is there in, its continuance?

The verse, "You are My witnesses... and I am God"[3] is boldly interpreted by our sages: "When you are My witnesses, then I am God; when you are not My witnesses, then I, as it were, am not God."[4] Our sages give sharp expression to the special relationship between God and the Jewish People, to our stature and eternal role. The Jews are "God's witnesses," and their existence is testimony before all of mankind to

3. Isaiah 43:12.

4. *Sifrei Devarim* 346.

the existence of God. The very fact that the Jewish People exists is an enduring demonstration of God's kingship in the world.

This conception of testimony has been expressed by thinkers and historians, Jewish and non-Jewish alike, in connection with the enduring existence of the Jewish People. The fact that there exists a people that is "one lamb amidst seventy wolves,"[5] a nation that survives despite all the hardships and despite all the persecutions, constitutes more than a historical curiosity. The continued survival of this people, while in the meantime great civilizations rise and fall and superpowers emerge and vanish, makes the Jewish People "ahistoric." It seems that the general laws of history do not apply to it; it lives and acts according to a system of laws of its own. In this sense, the Jewish People serves as testimony before all mankind to another reality, to a higher form of being.

CONSCIOUS AND ACTUAL TESTIMONY

The understanding that the Jewish People's testimony expresses itself solely through its physical survival throughout the generations stems from a strictly external view, from the viewpoint of an onlooker who does not belong to the Jewish People. For the Jewish People itself, in the way that it sees and perceives itself, the conception of this testimony has a deeper meaning.

There is meaning to the Jewish People's unique existence as long as it is aware of the function of its existence, as long as it regards itself as a witness. The existence of a chosen people is meaningful only when it is a people of choice. In the Talmud, this is expressed figuratively:[6] Just as we put on *tefillin* containing the words, "Listen, O Israel: God is our Lord, God is one,"[7] the Holy One, blessed be He, wears *tefillin* in which it is written, "Who is like Your people Israel, a unique nation on earth."[8]

The Jewish People's existence is a meaningful existence, and its very being is endowed with supreme value. Its existence is bound up

5. *Esther Raba* 10:11.
6. *Berakhot* 6a.
7. Deuteronomy 6:4.
8. I Chronicles 17:21.

with its consciousness of being "God's witness," with its effort to become "Israel through whom I derive glory."[9]

The motto that Israel must be "a light unto the nations" has often been understood as the demand that the Jewish People and its individual members endeavor to teach and instruct others. But a lighthouse fulfills its function not in that it casts light and illuminates the ways through the sea, but in that its very existence provides mariners with a reference point, a direction. Uniqueness, individuality, and chosenness do not require publicity; rather, they need to be actualized within life itself.

The justification of the Jewish People's existence does not result from this or that success, but from the people's unique nature. As long as the Jewish People exists and attests to the existence and kingship of God, it sustains the world, for it thereby indicates that the world can be different, that the world can be meaningful and of value. The Jewish People's existence is bound up with its testimony, with its chosenness and uniqueness.

The Jewish individual, and at times even the entire nation, sometimes tire from this burden of testimony. Habits, imitation of non-Jews, small and great passions, misconceptions, and foolish aspirations pull the Jewish People toward normalization, toward being a nation like all other nations. But for the sake of its own survival and for the sake of the world's survival, it is pushed back, time and again, to its special role. World events force it to be special, even when it thinks that it does not want to be so. A higher force compels it to do much more than others in order to survive and thereby to uphold God's kingship.

REMEMBRANCE OF THE PAST, SHOFAR FOR THE FUTURE

The *Malkhuyot* are the framework and the purpose, the existential question and answer. The *Zikhronot* and the *Shofarot* are the lines that delimit this framework – the *Zikhronot* from the past and the *Shofarot* toward the future.

The *Zikhronot*, like the whole essence of the holiday, are dual: they are the recollections of both God and man. They are the reemphasis of our continuity. Inasmuch as we recall our history from its beginning,

9. Isaiah 49:3.

we are strengthened in our "I;" we receive encouragement and guidance to continue on our path. Reviewing the path we have taken, these *zikhronot* show that despite all the straying and deviation, on the whole we are carrying out the task for which we were created, and that in spite of everything, we will continue doing so.

The *Shofarot* indicate the pathway to the future. Every *shofar* is a blast of revelation of God in the world, from the revelation of God's Presence at Mount Sinai to the revelation of God's Presence in days to come. Every such revelation is, in and of itself, a culmination of remembrance and of kingship, for it expresses the culminating point toward which the present – with its defects, pitfalls, and failures – is progressing. The *shofar* is the promise and the signpost indicating towards what we are headed.

Rosh HaShana is a day of judgment and reckoning, but it is not the conclusion of the reckoning. The climax of the reckoning is on Yom Kippur, which is preceded by the Ten Days of *Teshuva*. On Rosh HaShana, we make an accounting of ourselves, revealing our failings up to now. Thereafter – during the Ten Days of *Teshuva* and on Yom Kippur – must begin the attempt at rectification.

On Rosh HaShana, we review the path we traveled on and discover a bit of the direction in which we must go. From here on begins the real path – to rectify what we have impaired, to do *teshuva* for transgressions we have committed, to repent for mitzvot we have ascribed to ourselves but neglected, and to begin a new year with a clear-eyed view of the past and with resolve to make the future worthier.

The Ten Days of *Teshuva* and Yom Kippur

"Children, Return"

"Return, rebellious children; I will heal your afflictions. 'Here we are, we come to You, for You are God our Lord.'"[1] In the days before the great day of forgiveness and pardon, Yom Kippur, we are all called upon to do *teshuva*. We stand laden with our sins, both small and great, hoping for God's mercy. We stand laden with our suffering and pain, longing for the wellspring of consolation. Knowing that we cannot justify our actions during the past year, we can only hope for mercy, forgiveness, and pardon.

Indeed, that is the role of Yom Kippur – to forgive, pardon, and atone. Only one thing is required of us: to desire forgiveness, to turn our faces to God instead of our backs.

God summons each of us with the call and the promise: "Return to Me, and I will return to you."[2] God calls to each one of us, wherever he is, to return to Him, to draw near to Him, to take refuge under His protecting wings. In *teshuva*, no one is far and no one is near; what applies to the near applies equally to the very distant. God calls out

1. Jeremiah 3:22.
2. Malakhi 3:7.

even to those who gloomily imagine that they are as remote as can be. To them, too, He promises the grace of His emanation, the light of His forgiveness, and the wholeness of unity with Him.

It is not a political party or social body that calls out to those who must return. God Himself is the One who speaks to each and every individual. It is He who calls, and it is He who promises. We should not allow individuals or groups to conceal the true light, the light of God, to which we all must return, nor should we deny the inner will innate in each of us to be a complete Jew. Let us not hold on to excuses and alibis to delay our return.

The accounting and reckoning, penetrating to the depths, must be performed in each of our hearts. Let us not put the blame on others, great or small. Let us not imagine that true rectification can be attained by superficial means, by daubing a little plaster, through false remedies. Let us take off the filthy garments of empty pursuits, of racing after desires, of imitating others, of casting blame, and of evading responsibility. Let us clothe ourselves again in the garments of salvation and adorn ourselves with a crown of true beauty. Our fine clothes are soaked with the blood of generations, but their splendor has not dimmed. They are heavy to bear, but they carry and uplift their wearers.

The crown of the Torah was not given to anyone as an inheritance; it was not handed over to any group or party among us. It is an everlasting heritage for all Jews, and every member of our people is entitled to draw himself near to the Source, to connect himself to the light of God, to adorn himself with the crown of the Torah of truth.

The call to *teshuva* is a call to everyone. It is a call to break through the barriers of remoteness, to disregard concerns about what others might say, to detach one's thought from the influence of foreign cultures. Each individual is called upon to search within the hidden recesses of his heart, to engage anew in soul-searching, to make a grand reckoning of his life, and to return wholeheartedly to God.

It is not a disgrace to reexamine one's way of life; it is not a shame to admit, "We have gone astray, we have led astray." So many of our errors and deviations were rooted in good intentions, in fine aspirations, although the course of life was misleading and led far afield. It is not embarrassing to admit, "We have erred." On the contrary, it is a disgrace to retain, out of feeble-mindedness, a mistaken path.

When there is courage to acknowledge one's error, one still has the opportunity to rectify it. Remember, this accounting and reckoning is not submitted to man, but presented before God. Fortunate are those who return to God, for upon returning they will find the Source of life, the true rejuvenation of their lives.

The path of return is open to all, even for one who never studied and has no knowledge of Judaism. Let him overcome the inhibitions regarding the strangeness – let him break through the barriers of ignorance and illiteracy – and then the Jewish spark in him will reveal itself in all its splendor and grow into a true fire. For all are holy seed, members of a holy people, practiced in self-sacrifice and familiar with the encounter with death as with the major questions of life. In hearts of the learned as well as the unlearned burns a secret fire, a flame of holiness. Each and every one can see for himself and demonstrate that he indeed is "Israel, through whom I derive glory."[3]

The gates of *teshuva* are open, as are the hearts of so many who are ready to welcome those who return. The doors of the *batei knesset* (synagogues) are open for prayer, the doors of the *batei midrash* (study halls) are open for Torah study, and – most importantly – the gates of heaven are open. Generations upon generations of ancestors, holy souls, stand at the gates waiting for each Jewish soul to make this turnabout, the return to its true and original place within Israel's pure essence.

God is the One who calls to us, to all of us, to return to Him – to those who imagine that they are always close to Him and to those who think that they have gone irreversibly far from Him. To all of us He calls, "Return to Me; children, return."

3. Isaiah 49:3.

There Is No Pardon in the World of the Gods

THE PLACE OF SIN

More than any other day of the year, Yom Kippur gives cause for reflection. No matter how it is experienced – whether as an overwhelming event, a day of recollection of fading childhood memories, or merely as a day on the calendar – the very name *Yom HaKippurim* (the Day of Atonement) evokes a series of familiar yet enigmatic concepts: sin, guilt, forgiveness, atonement.

In modern society, Yom Kippur arouses primarily a feeling of perplexity. It recalls the concept of sin, a concept that our permissive society attempts to completely uproot from law, public opinion, and personal conscience. "Sin" implies that there is something that is truly forbidden, that there is something that is intrinsically loathsome and contemptible, that there is something that one cannot possibly do. When the general conception is that everything is permitted, sin is no longer possible, and if there is no God, there is no one to sin against. The world in which we live attempts to present a picture of a free and liberated life, without gods and without sins, without pangs of repentance or remorse – a world entirely free.

In truth, however, this picture is merely a facade that does not reflect the actual reality. This brave new world – no less than the society that it replaces – is bound with hundreds of laws and rules, with thick ropes of basic concepts and thin threads of custom and tradition of its own. Many times, of course, these laws and customs do not resemble those of earlier generations, but like them, they are solid and restrictive. These are substitutes for gods.

Institutionalized religions – both modern and more ancient – produce God substitutes, but secular society does as well. Although they may declare, "There is no law and no judge," or, "Eat and drink, for tomorrow we will die!"[1] they, too, have gods. They are more nebulous and obscured, but no less demanding and controlling.

The reason for this is simple. Man can deny the world's Creator and Director; he can, as it were, topple the Holy One, blessed be He, from His throne. But by his very nature and personality, he cannot leave the seat empty. Someone will have to occupy the high and lofty throne – an idea, a concept, or a human being.

AND YOU WILL BE LIKE GOD

Modern society is founded on the humanistic approach, one of whose basic tenet is God's eviction from His throne and man's placement in His stead. Man is one of the gods of the world of the present – his happiness, his freedom, his satisfaction, and the fulfillment of his desires determine the ideals, laws, and patterns of life.

Naïve and canting beliefs are found to a great extent in the cult that glorifies man's free will. An example of this is the belief that everyone can be satisfied at one and the same time and that the free will of every individual, unrestricted by the law, can coexist with tens of thousands, even billions, of other free wills. A similar naïve belief is that man can live in peace with himself, that all his passions, desires, and aspirations can be reconciled with one another.

When man himself is the measure and gauge of everything, judgment has no real meaning, for there is no objective external standard. What is worse, when man ascends to the seat of authority, he faces the test of being an all-powerful god who establishes what is good and what is evil in accordance with his own will. This god who is called "man" not

1. Based on Isaiah 22:13.

only has feet of clay,[2] points of weakness here and there; he is entirely caught up in a fundamental contradiction between ordered, defined creation (the "Universe of Rectification" in kabbalistic terminology) and the influence of the depths of the soul (the "Universe of Chaos"), whose desire is death, ruin, and self-destruction.

This god not only does not fulfill all of the good, upright, and positive expectations, but he brings about the exact opposite: chaos, confusion, and ruin. Hence, man does not wish to remain seated on this high throne, which is not made according to his size.

THE ANCIENT GODS

As in every place where a new, superficial, and flimsy cult is established (like the worship of the brave, free, rational, and glamorous individual) mankind's ancient gods – Ashtoreth, Baal, Periapis, and Hades, who for so many years were mere shadows – sneak back in.

What began as refined worship of man – man's bowing to the ideal of himself, to a divine image that he discovered within himself – has not continued in that direction. The number of believers in a complete image of "Supernal Man" who is still human is progressively declining. This image is disintegrating into parts more crude and basic. This "god" is no longer a complete image of man, but crude force, which no longer attempts to wrap itself in the cloak of aims and aspirations. It no longer exalts love, but physical relationship devoid of all emotion, which seeks to gratify itself alone and is not connected with love or fertility. Money, too, no longer serves as a means to an end, but has become a vision, dream, and an end in and of itself.

Even murder is no longer committed for a purpose, but is increasingly becoming a pleasure unto itself, a cult of ruin and liquidation!

Some regard these phenomena as external signs of a problematic society's degeneration, or as a chance confluence of various problems. Actually, however, this constitutes nothing less than the reemergence of the ancient gods. The decline of Western civilization has led to the reinstatement of the Greek and Canaanite gods and of nameless idols of earlier cultures. Drugs, sex, unrestrained pursuit of money, prestige,

2. Based on Daniel 2:43–44.

and power – all these are the cult of those ancient gods, the gods of the base instincts, who have reawakened and returned.

The ancient gods have one thing in common – they are merciless and unforgiving. They have no memory of past merits or of promises for the future.

A beautiful young woman can be the priestess of Ashtoreth as long as her body is suitable for the role. Through desperate efforts, she tries to extend the term of this service, forever and ever, to attain eternal youth. But after the final loss, there is no forgiveness or atonement. The body which is no longer useful is thrown into the garbage, for there is no mercy before the Ashtoreth.

Nor is there mercy before the "god of money." One who loses his money does not lose just another asset, for money is already not the man's possession but his master. Thus, one who loses his money loses his essence, his entire personality, and becomes truly nothing.

The same applies to the other cults that have filled the vacuum and empty space of the world. Like the gods of the ancient Aztecs, these gods are claiming more and more victims. These unforgiving gods are gods before whom one sacrifices everything – ultimately even human sacrifices.

THE ROOT OF FORGIVENESS

The absence of forgiveness in a world that has returned to chaos and in which man is everything requires clarification.

The concept of forgiveness – not only in its religious sense, but in its human sense as well – is not at all simple and cannot be understood without positing a metaphysical background.

In the natural (physical and spiritual) world-view, any act that a person performs, good or bad, cannot be taken back. After the act has been performed, it is possible to act differently in the future, but there is no way to change and rectify the past. Forgiveness, in contrast, contains within it the belief in the ability to control the past as well.

Even in the human realm, the ability to forgive is based on the recognition of the possibility to erase past events, to let go of a certain reality in the past. The human concept of forgiveness necessarily draws from an unconscious assumption of omnipotent control over the flow of time. This unlimited control stems from man's connection to the absolute, to God Himself, who is without bounds and limits in time or any other structure.

A DAY OF FORGIVENESS AND PARDON

On Yom Kippur we are called upon to forgive one another. This call is an attempt to arouse in man the holy spark, the "part of God from on high"[3] that sets him above the limits and "laws" of reality. The possibility of forgiveness is the highest expression of man's essential nature, of his being created "in the image of God"[4] and of his attachment to the Almighty.

Through its characterization as "a day of forgiveness and pardon," through the plea to God for atonement and the call to the people to pardon one another, Yom Kippur expresses a connection with the most exalted conceptions of the world of faith. For the essence of faith is a relationship with the eternal and the infinite absolute, which is not subject to any framework of "law" or any definition or structure that man constructs from within himself or through his speculations.

Yom Kippur is "the holy day," which invokes and brings to mind, consciously and unconsciously, not only atonement and sin, but God Himself. By the very fact that it brings to the fore the principles of forgiveness, pardon, and atonement, Yom Kippur reveals the point expressed ages ago by R. Akiva: "Fortunate are you, Israel. Before whom do you become pure and who purifies you? Your Father in Heaven."[5]

3. *Tanya*, ch. 2.
4. Genesis 1:27.
5. *Yoma* 8:9.

For the Sin That We Have Committed

THE CONTENT OF THE CONFESSION

One of the most important elements of the Yom Kippur prayers is the confession that we make for the sins of the individual and the community.

The longer confession, which begins with the words *"Al ḥet sheḥatanu lefanekha"* ("For the sin that we have committed before You"), is recited ten times over the course of Yom Kippur, privately and communally. This extensive repetition on the day intended for thorough and fundamental soul-searching underscores how much attention is directed precisely to this list of transgressions and sins.

While it is true that at the conclusion of the detailed confession there is also a more general confession of transgressions of commission and omission of all degrees of severity, the greater part of the confession is a detailed list of sins, arranged alphabetically with two clauses for each letter of the Hebrew alphabet. This list emphasizes and stresses certain transgressions for which one ought to do *teshuva* with special intensity.

What is surprising about this list is what is included in it and what is missing from it. Seemingly, it would have been reasonable for the confession to be a list of common sins that many people commit during the course of the year, each person according to his situation and way of life. Yet sins such as violation of the Sabbath, eating non-kosher food, adultery, and sexual relations with a woman in the status of *Nidda* (menstrual impurity) are not mentioned. Likewise, sins such as neglecting to pray, neglecting to put on *tefillin*, and neglecting Torah study are not included. While these sins are included in the general summaries of sins under the categories of violation of positive and negative precepts and sins for which one is liable to *karet* (excision) and the death penalty, they are not mentioned specifically.

On the other hand, the list does include an extensive enumeration of sins against one's fellow man, against one's family, against the society in which one lives. It also includes sins that are very difficult to classify inside the 613 commandments or under a particular paragraph of the *Shulḥan Arukh* (the Code of Jewish Law).

INTERPERSONAL SINS

The extensive specification of interpersonal sins reiterates how serious they are. If a person commits a sin against God, he sins against God alone, whereas if he sins against his fellow man, he thereby commits a double sin – against man, as well as against God. Our sages have already stated that Yom Kippur atones for transgressions against God, but to attain atonement for transgressions against one's fellow man, one must conciliate and appease the offended party.[1]

The seriousness of interpersonal sins is known to all; it is stated in the Torah, reemphasized in the words of the Prophets, and reiterated in the Writings and throughout the sayings of our sages. Yet these sins are more common and widespread than sins against God, even among people who all their lives try to follow a good and straight path. Indeed, our sages teach us that "most [people are guilty] of robbery, a minority [are guilty] of sexual offenses, and all [are guilty] of fine shades of slander."[2]

Upon reflection, this phenomenon should surprise us. For when a person sins against his fellow man, no faith or Torah knowledge is required for him to see at least the human consequences of his sin. After all, the stricken and the robbed, the insulted and the slandered, stand

1. See *Yoma* 8:9.
2. *Bava Batra* 165a. "Fine shades of slander" refers to speech that is not actual slander, but rather implied, or instigation to slander.

in full view of the sinner; he can see their suffering for himself. Even if the sinner fails to see this on his own, the society and its courts and prisons help him realize and understand what is worthwhile and not worthwhile for him to do. Nevertheless, people do not refrain from committing such sins.

Many have tried to solve this psychological riddle. One of the explanations of the phenomenon stems precisely from the fact that the sins are interpersonal. Because of interpersonal proximity and contact, one gets the impression that he can decide the fate of other people; he can justify and explain his behavior towards others, even if it harms them physically or emotionally. These justifications may sound different depending on whether the perpetrator is a kindergartener or a national leader, but they are essentially the same. There is the typical, "He hit me first" response – revenge, even self-defense. Or we maintain, "Why should only he have that?" – jealousy or false equality of rights. And, of course, "He deserves it" – we appoint ourselves judge over others and punish them for what they have done, or for what we imagine they have done. In the case of adults or well-educated individuals, these justifications appear in more intellectual forms, but their roots and origins do not differ by much. The justifications simply become "loftier," as one consistently acts "for the sake of Heaven" – for the good of the community or the benefit of the state.

THE RECTIFICATION IS INWARD

To properly rectify one's actions and attain forgiveness, it is not sufficient to change one's patterns of behavior, or even to redress the wrong and appease the victims. One must, to an even greater degree, see to the rectification of his inner life, his character; he must root out the "poison weed and wormwood"[3] that leads to such patterns of behavior.

That is why the *Al ḥet* confession includes many sins that do not pertain to any specific transgression or to any defect with an immediate practical definition. We are called upon not only to repent for overt sins – "forbidden sexual relations," "bribery," and the like – but also to carefully search within ourselves for the root of our sins in our faulty

3. Deuteronomy 29:17.

character – as in "For the sin that we have committed before You out of ignorance" or "For the sin that we have committed before You by folly of the mouth."

Some sins are specific and defined, and one knows that he has committed them – "in business dealings," "by deliberate deceit," "by denying and lying." Other sins are more general and less defined, but they are the primary sources of impurity – "with haughty eyes," "by insolence," "by scoffing," "by throwing off the yoke [of the commandments]."

We list a number of negative traits and qualities to which the human heart is inclined to succumb. We have sinned "with wanton looks," by gazing upon and coveting what does not belong to us; we have transgressed "by association with impurity," by arousing and bringing ourselves to base desires that we truly have no penchant for. We have stumbled by evading responsibility "by confession with the mouth alone," and we have acted "with violence" when we could and should have acted differently. More inwardly, we must ask for forgiveness "For the sin that we have committed before You by ensnaring our neighbor," "by envy," "by causeless hatred."

In committing all of these sins, we have justified ourselves "by playing the judge," by hastily condemning others and by "hardening the heart," refusing to recognize and admit our sins.

For all of these, we are given one day, a day that transcends the ordinary days of the year, so that we may look inside ourselves and feel anguish, remorse, and shame. Not everything can be changed and rectified at once, but a person can resolve and aspire to be different and better in the coming year.

The Service of the Holy of Holies

ATONEMENT FROM ABOVE

Yom Kippur, as its name implies, is a day on which *kapara* (atonement) is effected for the Jewish People's sins, a day that is centered around the basic idea of atonement.

The idea of atonement is not identical to the idea of *teshuva*. Although they have a common element – recollection of sin and its renouncement – there is a vast difference between the two concepts, both in their content and in man's attitude toward them.

The essence of *teshuva* is the effort of man turning back from his evil ways and attempting to rebuild a connection with God. *Teshuva*, therefore, is the glory of man, and the days of *teshuva* are the great and sacred days of man.

By contrast, atonement is an act of Heaven. Man serves only in an instrumental capacity, embracing *teshuva* and good deeds, so that the atonement may apply to him. But the essence of atonement is always and in every case God's grace coming from above.

The difference between *teshuva* and atonement can be discerned in man's moods. The *ba'al teshuva* is in a state of sorrow, and the memory of his sin is before him: "My sin is ever before me."[1] Hence, *teshuva* is accomplished through weeping and bitterness. Atonement, on the other hand, is in every respect a joyous event. Although it is connected with a past sin, the granting of atonement involves only the joy of purification and refinement.

Although the atonement of Yom Kippur depends on the *teshuva* that precedes it (in accordance with the halakha that Yom Kippur atones only for those who return in *teshuva*),[2] this *teshuva* is not an integral part of Yom Kippur itself. That is why, according to one opinion, the main confession of Yom Kippur is made just before, not during, the holiday.[3] The time for *teshuva* is primarily *before* Yom Kippur; Yom Kippur itself is purely the time of forgiveness and atonement for sin.

THE HOLINESS OF THE DAY

An examination of the verses in the Torah dealing with Yom Kippur reveals that it includes two motifs. In *Parashat Emor*, amidst the descriptions of all the holidays, we find one aspect of Yom Kippur: "It is a Day of Atonement, on which atonement is made on your behalf before God your Lord."[4] Yom Kippur is a day of fasting and expiation. The second motif appears in *Parashat Aḥarei Mot*. There, atonement is also mentioned, but the *parasha* principally deals with the Service in the Sanctuary, climaxing with the High Priest's entry into the innermost chamber of the Temple, the *Kodesh HaKodashim*.

In terms of its character as a day of fasting and atonement, Yom Kippur is a day of complete passivity. Refraining from work and eating are not forms of activity that bring about atonement; they are the very opposite – forms of refraining from activity. Regarding atonement, man's actions are certainly not the decisive factor, but rather, "the essence of the day effects atonement."[5]

By contrast, in terms of the day's Service in the Sanctuary, Yom

1. Psalms 51:5.
2. Rambam, *Hilkhot Teshuva* 1:3.
3. See *Shulḥan Arukh HaRav* 607:2.
4. Leviticus 23:28.
5. Rambam, *Hilkhot Teshuva* 1:3.

Kippur is filled with activity; there is no day whose activities are more numerous and complex than those of Yom Kippur. The preparation and purification of the High Priest, followed by his entry into the Holy of Holies, distinguish the day not only as *Yom HaKippurim* but also as *HaYom HaKadosh* ("the Holy Day").

Thus, the principal and central element of the day is one specific and defined point – atonement – which is flanked by two other elements: confession and *teshuva* on the one hand and the holy Service in the Sanctuary on the other.

ATONEMENT AND HOLINESS IN THE PRAYERS OF YOM KIPPUR

The overall framework of the Yom Kippur prayers is arranged in accordance with this scheme. In the *Amida* prayer, besides for the first three and last three blessings that are fixtures throughout the year, we include a blessing that expresses the day's themes, as on all other holidays. This simple blessing reiterates the day's essential point – the atonement and the trust that God pardons and forgives sins on this day. As we noted, the atonement is essentially marked not by the mention of sin or by anguish over it, but, on the contrary, by the joy of purification and the elation of renewal: "I wipe away your sins like a cloud, your transgressions like mist; return to Me, for I redeem you."[6]

However, *teshuva*, the necessary prerequisite for atonement, cannot be absent from the order of prayers. For this reason, although it is not part of the *Amida* itself, attached to each and every one of the day's prayers is the recitation of the longer confession, which begins with the words "*Al ḥet*."

The confession, the *teshuva*, and the atonement that follows them, express the day's content and meaning for every man at all times. But there is, as we have said, another aspect of Yom Kippur as a unique day in the Sanctuary with its special Order of Service (*Seder HaAvoda*). Although there is no special section of the *Amida* dedicated to the Yom Kippur Service, many hymns describing the Service have been added from the very inception of the prayer book.

6. Isaiah 44:22, cited in the central blessing of the Yom Kippur *Amida*.

Our description of the Service on Yom Kippur does not play a minor role in our prayers, merely adding spice as a hymn. In fact, it has become a central part of the day's liturgy, and in a certain sense, it serves even as the preeminent part of that liturgy. This centrality is expressed in the great deal of time devoted to the description of the Service, in the emotional value ascribed to it, and in the unique and striking ceremony of bowing and prostrating oneself that is included in it. Although there is prostration in the liturgy of Rosh HaShana as well according to Ashkenazic custom, it is not invested with the profound significance that is attached to the prostrations in the description of the Service on Yom Kippur.

THE DIMENSION OF SANCTITY

At first glance, it seems that the great importance ascribed to the Order of the Service and its emphasis as the central theme of Yom Kippur are a distraction, a diversion of our attention from the central point of the day. The day's prayers themselves focus primarily on the idea of atonement, whereas the liturgical hymn "The Order of the Service" appears to replace the primary with the secondary. While the principal element of this day is atonement, the Order of the Service emphasizes the day's aspect of sanctity.

We could offer a simple and rather technical answer, explaining that, unlike other holidays, Yom Kippur is devoted entirely to prayer, and there is therefore sufficient time during the day to elaborate on the element of sanctity as well.

But there is also a more fundamental explanation. Although from the halakhic standpoint, Yom Kippur is of lesser sanctity than the Sabbath,[7] throughout the generations and in all Jewish communities, Yom Kippur was regarded as the most sacred day of the year. Yom Kippur's uniqueness and preeminence are implicit in the words of our

7. Yom Kippur's comparatively lesser sanctity is attested to by the less severe punishment for violation of the day. The punishment for violation of the Sabbath is more severe than for the violation of Yom Kippur. It is similarly expressed by the halakha that more individuals are to be called up to the Torah on the Sabbath than on Yom Kippur.

sages, and to an even greater degree, the supreme sanctity of Yom Kippur is expressed in the Torah itself in *Parashat Aḥarei Mot*. From the standpoint of the Service in the Sanctuary, Yom Kippur is the pinnacle of sanctity, man's closest contact with God.

On closer inspection, we discover that the concept of atonement and a day designated for the purpose of achieving it is connected to the highest level of sanctity. The atonement of Yom Kippur is an expression of an exceedingly lofty revelation. On Yom Kippur, the second Tablets were given to the Jewish People,[8] representing that the Torah is an eternal gift to Israel. At that time, God revealed the Thirteen Attributes of Mercy, the pinnacle of revelation to man and the root of all forgiveness. In other words, Yom Kippur is a day of revelation of sanctity, and therefore a day of atonement.

Yom Kippur is not simply a day that has sanctity, but rather the day of sanctity, the day designated for drawing near to, understanding, and identifying with the sacred and the holy. Although this idea is concealed in the formal conception of the holiday, it is present in the foundations of all the day's ideas, laws, and customs, and in the aspiration – conscious or unconscious – to dedicate the day to holiness.

Indeed, most of the hymns and additional prayers that we recite on Yom Kippur, despite the differences in style, expression, and ideas, aspire to one and the same goal: to intensify the experience of the sacred and the holy on this day. Indeed, a vast distance separates the expressions and conceptions that appear in *Keter Malkhut*,[9] which the Sephardim recite on the night of Yom Kippur, from those of *Shir HaYiḥud*, which most Ashkenazic communities recite at that time. Yet their common denominator is this emphasis upon the sacred and the conception of holiness.

Even the hymn about the *Aseret Harugei Malkhut*, the Ten Martyrs,[10] is not an expression of mourning and grief, but rather a statement

8. *Ta'anit* 30b.
9. A major poetic-philosophical composition by R. Shlomo Ibn Gabirol (1020–1058).
10. "The Ten Martyrs" were ten of the greatest scholars of the Mishnaic period who were tortured and executed by the Romans for their insistence on continuing to teach Torah.

regarding the sanctity of the martyrs and their glorification of the divine name through their willingness to sacrifice their lives for the sake of Torah and Judaism. Additionally, the mention of the martyrs continues the point mentioned in the day's Torah reading – the death of Aaron's two sons, who died holy deaths "when they drew near to God."[11]

Hence, our people were right in feeling that the Order of the Service, and particularly those moments when the High Priest would utter the name of God, are the day's most exalted moments, for they express the essence of Yom Kippur's tripartite sanctity of time, place, and man.

The inclusion of the Order of the Service and the sacred hymns in the Yom Kippur prayers expresses the people's sense throughout the generations of the need for ascent towards the holy on this day. For although atonement is the day's principal element, it is not in man's hands; man can only prepare the ground for it. Hence, our people have added to it an aspect of human initiative and activity, the preparation and vehicle for forgiveness and atonement – the ascent and attachment to the conception of holiness.

11. Leviticus 16:1.

The Day of Atik Yomin – Teshuva and Yom Kippur

BEFORE HASHEM

Yom Kippur is a singular and unique day in the year, a day of forgiveness and atonement, of *teshuva* and purity: "For on this day, atonement shall be made for you, to purify you of all your sins; before *HaShem* you will be purified."[1] The essential nature of this day is that it is "before *HaShem*," before the name of God.

Every name is a definition, and every definition is a reduction. Just as the name of a person – or the name and definition of anything – is only a very partial revelation and illumination of the essence, the name of God is similarly only a slight illumination and revelation of the Divine Essence in the world. However, unlike the name of a person, the name of God does not only reveal itself through a thing; through its revelation, it constitutes the thing's very existence.[2]

In general, we experience two names of God. The name *Elohim* signifies the divine that reveals itself in nature; the Tetragrammaton

1. Leviticus 16:30.
2. See *Sha'ar HaYiḥud VeHaEmuna*, ch. 1.

signifies the divine that transcends nature, sustaining and granting existence to the world, but not revealing itself in it.[3]

The name *Elohim* contracts and conceals the divine light, while the Tetragrammaton brings the world into existence and gives it life. However, although the Tetragrammaton represents the true essence of the Creator that does not constrict itself in its revelation, that is only the Creator's essence as it relates to the product – the world. The "Name," on all levels, represents the divine's connection to the world, and in a certain sense, it also represents the essence of the world and the world order.

By contrast, the idea of *teshuva* and forgiveness is not part of the natural system of the world order; on the contrary, it is in complete opposition to it.

The laws of physical nature, like all the laws of reality, maintain that we cannot go against them without being harmed. One cannot put his hand into a fire without being burned; one cannot walk in snow without freezing. Within this system, one cannot say, "Sorry, I made a mistake." A person who jumps off the roof cannot become remorseful half way down, arguing, "I didn't mean to do it! I take it back!"

Like the rest of the laws of nature, there is also a law that says that a person cannot sin without the sin making a difference in his world, without it cutting off part of his soul, without it leaving a stain on reality. By the laws of nature, there is no room for remorse and forgiveness in the case of sin.

Nevertheless, there is the possibility of *teshuva* and atonement. A person *can*, in fact, say, "I am sorry. I have remorse." One can turn back the clock and erase the sin as though it never existed.

By definition, this possibility derives from a higher level which is not bound by laws of physical or spiritual nature.

---

3. Ibid., ch. 6: "Now, the name *Elohim* is the name of the attribute of *Gevura* and *Tzimtzum*; hence, it is also numerically equal to *hateva* (nature), for it [*Elohim*] conceals the supernal light which brings the world into existence and gives it life, and it appears as though the world exists and conducts itself in a natural way. And this name *Elohim* is a shield and a covering for the name *Havayah* [the Tetragrammaton], to conceal the light and life-force which flows from the name *Havayah* and brings creation into existence from nonexistence, so that it [the light and life-force] should not be revealed to the creatures, who thereby would be absolutely nullified."

For this reason, Yom Kippur, the day of *teshuva* and atonement, is the day "before *HaShem*," before the Tetragrammaton, before there existed a name. It is a day of ascending above the world's fundamental laws to the Holy One, blessed be He, Himself – rising towards the *Ein Sof*, the Infinite Being who is not defined by any name or by any constricting framework of necessity and law.

The Tetragrammaton is the source of life and existence, the channel from God's essence and being to the world. When we are "before *HaShem*," we refer not to the Source of life, the Creator, but the Being itself, existence itself, that which is beyond all definitions. This is the level that is termed "*Atik Yomin*" in kabbalistic literature – that is, removed (*ne'etak*) from the times (*yomin*). God is beyond the level of time-bound definitions;[4] the *Atik Yomin* is existence itself, to whom no definition of reality and time is applicable:[5] "I was the same before the world was created; I have been the same since the world was created."[6]

On this level of relationship, God bears patiently with everything. Everything that happens in the world – for good or for bad – makes no difference whatsoever. Thus, this level is the source of atonement.

This aspect of God's behavior – when the Holy One, blessed be He, bears patiently with the whole world, declaring, "I have made, and I will bear; I will carry and will deliver"[7] – is called "*Sovev kol almin*" ("He who surrounds all worlds"). He is unchanging, treating small and great alike. All of the world's beings and doings are equal before Him and insignificant in relation to Him. When man touches this level, everything that happened is as though it never happened, and everything can receive a different form.

---

4. The Tetragrammaton consists of the four letters *yod* (י), *heh* (ה), *vav* (ו) and *heh* (ה) and is related to the past, present, and future tenses of the Hebrew verb "to be": ⊠⊠⊠ (was), הוה (is) and יהיה (will be).
5. *Likutei Torah, Vayikra* 29a: "Yom Kippur, the day of *teshuva*, is the revelation of *Atika Kadisha* (the Ancient Holy One), the Hidden One of all the hidden, which is above the aspect of Skull and Crown of *Arikh Anpin* (Long Face).
6. *Yalkut Shimoni, Va'etḥanan* 836.
7. Isaiah 46:4.

CHANGING THE PAST

Teshuva "before *HaShem*" constitutes not only rectification of the future, a commitment that henceforth we will sin no more (an analogue of which is found also in the natural world), but also rectification of the past. We ask that the sin we committed disappear from the past, as if it had never happened at all.

Erasing the past is possible, but it is not easy. Although *teshuva* constitutes "return," it is not simple repetition, whereby we repeat a certain phase of life. Such a repeat is possible in a game; when shooting a movie, a director can say, "cut," and film the scene afresh. In our reality, however, it is impossible to simply erase what happened. One must relate to every detail of what took place and change it – not in the present, but in the past. Sins, like all our deeds, are not simply subjective, inner events. When we sin, we affect and change reality; when we wish to do *teshuva*, we must also change the reality around us, in the past as in the future.

All *teshuva* is thus a rewriting of the world and of history. More than just redoing yesterday, we must change yesterday itself, the day before yesterday, the past year, and the year that preceded it by thirty years. What was done will be as not done, and what was not done will be as done. That is the paradox, the wonder of *teshuva*; a person can change the course of his life not only prospectively through resolutions for the future, but also retroactively.

For this purpose, we need a day that is "before *HaShem*," a day that transcends the physical and spiritual laws of reality and on which it is possible to manipulate that reality.

"YOU WILL BE PURIFIED"

One's personal *teshuva* is a return home – not the parental home, nor the family home, nor even the nation's ancestral home, but the home of the soul. As the *Song of Songs* describes, "Draw me, I will run after You."[8] The soul pleads: "Draw me," because once, in the past, "the King brought

8. Song of Songs 1:4.

me to His chambers."[9] Originally, the soul was in "His chambers," and it can therefore recall it and once again be drawn home.

When the soul returns "home," it leaves all the foreign, remote places and returns to the starting point, where everything is still possible. There, the whole reality of life, the reality of time, place, and deed, is as yet intangible and undefined, like an embryo at the initial stage of its formation. From this point, it is possible to rewrite the past.

It is the universal custom to immerse oneself in a *mikveh* (ritual bath) on the day before Yom Kippur.[10] Immersion in a *mikveh* is also connected to *teshuva*, forgiveness, and atonement. When one enters the living waters, the primal source, he disappears and nullifies himself in it. When he emerges, he emerges not only to a new beginning from this point on, but as a man reborn; he is not a changed man from now on, but the infant he was twenty or fifty years before. This is the basic point of *teshuva* – the return to the original source.

Yom Kippur is a day of purity: "For on this day, atonement shall be made for you, to purify you of all your sins; before *HaShem* you will be purified." This exalted purity is the level of the soul in and of itself,

---

9. Ibid. See *Likutei Torah, Bemidbar* 44a: "'Draw me' refers to the future, whereas 'brought me' is past tense, and one would think that Scripture would have said 'May the King bring me to His chambers.' Rather, [Scripture's] meaning [is as follows:]... The past tense, 'brought me,' refers to [the time] when the soul was above, before its descent into the body, when it was taught the Torah in its entirety. That is [the significance of] 'His chambers.' Hence, as a result, later, too, when [the soul] is clothed in the physical body, [it] nevertheless [can say] 'Draw me,' for the King has already 'brought me.'"
10. *Tur, Oraḥ Ḥayyim* 606: "The custom is to immerse oneself [in a *mikveh*] on the day before Yom Kippur." See the *Siddur im Divrei Elokim Ḥayyim*, "*Kavanot HaMikveh MeHaBesht z"l*" (Meditations for [immersion in] a *mikveh* from the Ba'al Shem Tov), p. 159d: "The meaning of the immersion is as follows... For when anything returns to its source and origin, from there it can undergo metamorphosis... This also explains the meaning of immersion in the *mikveh*. As is known, the difference between sea and land is that the sea is called a concealed world, whereas the land is called a revealed world... This being the case, when man, who comes from the revealed world, from the earth and so forth, immerses in the waters of the *mikvehmikveh*, which are a concealed world, this also constitutes the integration of the revealed world in the concealed world, so that [man] thus is integrated into and returns to his source, from which he can undergo metamorphosis, as stated above..."

before it descends and is clothed in the body.[11] "For on this day, atonement shall be made for you, to purify you," no matter what the situation – even when the mitzvot are not carried out.

In a certain sense, this level of purity is even higher than the sacred level of "Who has sanctified us with His commandments," the level achieved through fulfillment of the mitzvot. To be holy means to belong to a state of being that is different, distinct, and more exalted, but which still has its own independent existence. Purity, in contrast, is the nullification of existence vis-à-vis God. It is therefore associated with the color white, which has no hue and no defined cast or appearance because it contains within it all the appearances, the integrity of the whole before it divides into parts.[12] There is a high level at which everything is in harmony, and a still higher level at which things do not exist at all, at which even harmony does not exist – a level at which there is only the one thing before it begins to be divided. This is the level of Yom Kippur "before *HaShem*."

THE LOWER WATERS WEEP

Teshuva on the highest level relates not only to the state of the individual who confronts himself and faces up to the things he did and did not do, but also to the existential state of man as man, as part of the state of the world as a world. Here, the question is not simply whether I was a good man or a bad man, but why I was merely a man.

This deficiency is a "sin" in the broadest sense of the term. The word *ḥet* (sin) stems from the word *ḥata*, to miss; when one's very existence falls short of the perfection of a divine being, he has missed his

---

11. As we say in the Morning Blessings: "The soul that You gave me *tehorah hi* (is pure)." See *Torah Or* 77a: "The meaning of *tehorah hi* is in the sense of what is stated here, 'the like of the very heaven *la'tohar* (for clearness)' (Exodus 24:10), where '*la'tohar*' signifies the clarity of light…That is [the meaning of] *tehorah hi* – that it [the soul] flows from the aspect of *tehiru ila'ah* (supernal clearness) mentioned in the holy *Zohar*… This is the aspect of clearness, meaning that it is not something in its own right…"
12. Indeed, it is customary to wear white clothing on Yom Kippur, and the High Priest wore special white garments during his Service on the day. See *Likutei Torah, Vayikra* 28b–c.

target. This failure is not connected to a certain way of life or anything in particular that one has done or impaired, but to life itself. It is not connected to a certain form of existence, but to existence itself.

This is the most basic conception of deficiency, which is connected to the fundamental, impassable, unbridgeable gulf, the *ḥalal hapanui* (vacuum) between God and the world. This intrinsic deficiency and its ramifications are found on all levels of creation qua creation, from the lowest level to the highest.

Since this deficiency is a universal problem, it is felt less as a personal problem. Nevertheless, on the personal level as well, we occasionally sense it at times of inspiration; we sense that our problem is not simply the particular flaws of our individual lives, but rather the problem of our lives in general. At such times, we are no longer satisfied with our portion and lot.

On the second day of Creation, God separated the upper waters from the lower waters. The waters, like all of reality, were divided into two: "The waters above the firmament,"[13] which is the part that is near God and feels God, and the lower waters.[14] The *Zohar* teaches that ever since this division, the lower waters have been weeping, "We, too, wish to be before the King!"[15] This weeping is not the result of an aberration or deviation in the world, but of the world itself. The lower part of the world bitterly complains, "Why are we not in heaven?"

When Pharaoh's daughter finds Moses, she opens the ark and sees "a boy crying."[16] Hearing him crying, she declares, "This must be one of the Hebrews' children." How does she know? Because he cries; if he cries, it is a sign that he is a Jew.

This crying does not express a personal tragedy, but a more fundamental tragedy – the tragedy of one who feels that he must become much more than he is, regardless of where he stands now. The Jew's soul weeps because the world weeps, and because he – the Jew – represents the world.

---

13. Genesis 1:7.
14. See *Sha'ar HaYiḥud VeHaEmuna*, ch. 10; *Likutei Torah, Bemidbar* 42b.
15. *Tikunei Zohar, tikun* 5, 19b; see *Likutei Torah, Derushim leRosh HaShana* 54d.
16. Exodus 2:6.

The Jew corresponds to the soul of the world, the conscious part within the world that bears within the world that which transcends the world. Hence, the Jew always feels that he must surpass and transcend himself. He feels this not as his personal and private problem, but as a limitation of the world that is merely the world, and of man who is merely man. He feels the pain, the inadequacy of all of existence, and because of this, he cries, regardless of whether his is wicked or righteous, whether he weeps for his own existence or for existence qua existence. The soul, which is the inwardness of all of creation, expresses its inner will to return from reality to the Source.

This explains our sages' statement that *teshuva* preceded the world.[17] If *Teshuva* preceded the creation of the world, it preceded everything that goes on in the world as well – including sin.[18] For *teshuva* is not intended only for transgressors; it is intended for every man, on every level, as long as he is merely man and as long as he aspires for more.

THREE LEVELS OF TESHUVA

Teshuva is not a one-step process, but a path on which there are levels and stages.[19] Essentially, *teshuva* is rectification of the soul; hence, the levels of *teshuva* parallel the three levels of the soul – *nefesh* (vital soul), *ruaḥ* (spirit), *neshama* (innermost soul).

On the first level of *teshuva*, a person rectifies the transgressions he committed by correcting his deeds. This is the initial, immediate, and most basic *teshuva*, analogous to emergency treatment administered to someone who is injured; an open wound is bandaged, a severed limb is

---

17. *Bereshit Raba* 1:4; *Pesaḥim* 54a.
18. *Likutei Torah, Derushim leRosh HaShana,* 61a: "This is [the meaning of] '*Teshuva* preceded the world.' The meaning is not that *teshuva* existed before the world's creation; for without a world, no sin is committed and there is no *teshuva*. Rather, the meaning [is] that *teshuva* with longing of the soul transcends time and space. For its aim is to cleave to Him, may He be exalted, to the light of *Ein Sof,* before Whom there is no differentiation of time. Contemplation of this leads to *teshuva* with longing of the soul…"
19. See *Likutei Torah, Bemidbar* 73a, s.v. *Ma tovu,* on the three levels of *teshuva* – "turn from evil," "do good," and "seek peace." There (74b), it also says that these three levels correspond to *nefesh, ruaḥ, neshama.*

reattached. This *teshuva*, too, is essentially rectification of the soul, but on this level, it relates to the sphere of action and to the first level of the soul, the level of *nefesh*.

THE SECOND LEVEL OF TESHUVA

The second level, higher than the level of correcting deeds, is that of rectifying thought. Even when a person has reached perfection from the standpoint of his deeds, even after he has done what needs to be done and refrained from doing what should not be done, the question remains: Where are his thoughts? Where is his personality? In what way is his human spirit truly a human spirit? These are the questions dealt with by *teshuva* on the second level – the level of *ruaḥ*. When a person rectifies his thoughts as well as their direction, when he restores his trends of thought to the proper place, he returns to the original human spirit.

Less is said about *teshuva* on this level, for people usually speak only about things they can point to. Sabbath observance or nonobservance can be easily discerned, but it is very difficult to tell someone that he is still far from the level of a human being. On the one hand, to be willing to listen to such criticism, one must be on a high level of innocence and readiness for introspection. On the other hand, this is something that is difficult, if not impossible, to define concerning others.

Yet, when a person is with himself and within himself, when external considerations such as what other people think of him, whether he is a good Jew, a good father, or a loyal husband are less important, he can concern himself also with questions such as "What kind of human being am I?"

The problem relates not to well-defined categories of mitzva and transgression, but to matters that are more inward and less-defined. Hence, their rectification must reach deeper, beyond deeds and into the depths of man's thoughts. Superficially, everything may seem to be okay, but deep down, in the inner experience, one reserves for himself the corruption, the distortion. It is not so difficult to renounce externals, outer forms and modes; when it comes to the innermost point, one must work much harder.

Teshuva must be in the nature of "Out of the depths I call You;"[20] it must spring from the depths of the soul itself.

THE THIRD LEVEL OF TESHUVA

From the foregoing level one can also reach the third and highest level of *teshuva*, rectification of the *neshama*. Here, we are not talking about the return to a former pattern, no matter how perfect, that existed before any distortion or corruption. Rather, this is a level that transcends everything that existed beforehand.

What, indeed, constitutes rectification of the *neshama*? The *nefesh* can sin and the *ruaḥ* can become impure, but the *neshama* always remains pure, a *neshama tehora*!

The level of *neshama* in man is a separate level, separate not only from man's physical being but also from his spiritual being, from the levels of the *nefesh* and the *ruaḥ*. According to the Jewish conception, the spiritual and the physical are not essentially distinct from each other. The spiritual is not essentially better and holier than the material; just as the material can be base and evil, so can the spiritual. In contrast to both the material and the spiritual stands the holy, which is separate and distinct in essence from every other reality.

At one time, scientific theory assumed a clear partition line between matter and energy. The assumption was that matter is of one nature, while energy is of another. In modern physics, however, matter and energy are conceived of as one combined essence, as different phases of the very same thing. The essential partition line of reality has moved beyond the physical world to the distinction between the material and the spiritual.

The Jewish conception rejects this division. It sees the difference between the material and the spiritual as a difference of form, not of essence. The essential division is between the holy, which is the distinct element, and the other modes of life, which can be material or spiritual. A person can be connected to the realm of the holy in a physical manner, and he can be far from holiness even when engaged entirely in spiritual

20. Psalms 130:1, the psalm added to the prayer service during the Ten Days of *Teshuva*.

matters. The Jew's *neshama*, however, the pure *neshama*, is a holy soul, and it belongs to the realm of the holy, which in essence is distinct.[21]

While the soul itself is pure, it may happen that the soul and the man are separated; the soul is found in one place and the man in another. In such a case, the *teshuva* of the *neshama* is its return to the man. The man (*adam*) – who on the one hand was created from the earth (*adama*), and on the other hand is epitomized by "I will be like (*edameh*) the Most High"[22] – attains, through the joining of body and soul, an overall perfection that surpasses the perfection of each one of his components alone.[23]

This level of *teshuva* is the level of man as envisaged in divine thought – not as he is and not as pure as he was (*tehora hi*), but as God wants to see him and as he fulfills the original aim. The preceding levels of *teshuva* merely prepared the groundwork so that the *neshama* can be returned to him.

The story is told that the Kotzker Rebbe asked his disciples, "Where does God reside?" They, of course, answered: "God resides everywhere." He responded, "Not so. God resides wherever man lets Him in." The same applies to the holy *neshama*. In order for it to reside in man, one must first make room for it.

In addition, one must find the *neshama* – and the *neshama* is to be found not outside, but inside. One who roams in all sorts of places so as to generate experiences will not find the *neshama* there. The *neshama* is found in the depths, when a person digs within his own being, searching for the true "I." After one divests himself of the external expressions and removes all the husks, a bond of near-identity is formed between the *neshama*, man's personal "I," and God.

The prophet Jeremiah asks God: "Why are You like a stranger in the land?"[24] Sometimes the state of the world is such that God, as it were, is a foreigner in it. It is man's job to nullify this foreignness;

21. *Tanya*, ch. 2: "The second soul of a Jew is truly a part of God from on high."
22. Isaiah 14:14.
23. See *Torah Or* 3d, s.v. *Lehavin hata'am shenishtaneh yetzirat guf ha'adam* etc., and the explanation given there.
24. Jeremiah 14:8.

moreover, he must nullify even the very possibility of saying that God does not belong here. Towards this end, man must search and discover within himself that God belongs, that He is present, that it is God who is his whole existence.

To find the *neshama*, man must transcend the external things; he must search for what truly matters to him, for the first, true, single kernel of life. That is where the *neshama* is, and that is thus where God is.

When man searches for God as he searches for the one he loves, indefatigably by day and by night, he will ultimately find Him in his innermost being. After his being is cleared of all the coverings and all the lies that obscure it – the lies that he tells others, and especially the lies that he tells himself – he will discover that "the rock of my heart and my portion forever is God."[25] When the essence of my heart is my holy *neshama*, God, too, is found there.

TO RAISE HEAVEN

One of the eternal and ever-recurring theological questions asks why the *neshama* descends to this world. After all, the *neshama* is pure even before its descent, and it is implausible to contend that after the descent, after investing the effort and taking such a risk, it should return to the same level of purity that it once possessed, even in the best case scenario!

In this regard, one *tzaddik* said: People think that man was created in order to rectify the soul. Not so! The purpose for which man was created is to uplift the heavens.[26] The *neshama* does not descend to this world merely to return just as it came. Rather, it descends so as to attain after the descent a level higher than it possessed before.

The question that a person must answer in this life is not whether he is meeting the quota of accomplishments required of him in his life, but whether he is exceeding it, surpassing what is required of him and even surpassing what he is capable of doing.

Restoring the *neshama* is the work of *teshuva* in its widest scope. A person descends and he must return, and the question is: Where? Should he return to the place where he was before, to correct what needs

25. Psalms 73:26.
26. R. Menaḥem Mendel of Kotzk (d. 1862).

correction and then continue from that point? Or should he perhaps go beyond that? Should he return to the past and fill in even what was missing in it, return and uplift the past itself higher than it ever was? The saying "to raise heaven" is connected with the highest level of *teshuva,* wherein a person rectifies not only the transgressions he committed, but also the mitzvot that he performed and, what is more, even the mitzvot that he did not perform.

The same question can be asked in a different way. The highest level of atonement is "I wipe away your transgressions like a cloud, your sins like mist."[27] The sky was cloudy, but the wind blew and scattered the clouds, leaving no sign that anything had been there before. This is perfect atonement, in which the sin disappears from existence in such a way that not even a trace of it remains. But aside from the cleansing of the sins and transgressions that a person committed, there remain the deeds that he failed to do, the moments that never existed. Is it possible to fill the vacuum of the past? Is it really possible to add on more than was there to begin with, to act against the laws of physics and to get more out of the system than is in it?

Obviously, in a finite and bounded world like our natural world, the answer to this question is negative. But within a certain relationship with the *Ein Sof* (the Infinite Being), wherein the boundaries of time, place, and the *neshama* are no longer relevant, one can do *teshuva* not only for what one did but also for what one did not do. This is the meaning of "before *HaShem* you will be purified" – to reach a level that precedes and transcends all of the world's definitions, to touch the existence of the *Ein Sof.* From there, one can complete everything, all that is missing and even more.

GREAT IS TESHUVA

Our sages tell us: "Great is *teshuva,* for because of it, willful sins are turned into merits."[28] The exalted conception of *teshuva* is that evil is turned into good; transgression is not only erased from the past, but is rewritten

27. Isaiah 44:22.
28. See *Yoma* 86b.

as mitzva. Turning darkness into light, nonexistence into existence, can be done only by going outside the system, beyond the bounds of reality.

Consider the following example from a non-spiritual sphere. In a two-dimensional system, it is impossible to turn left into right. Whichever direction one is facing, right remains right and left remains left. The only solution to the problem is to go outside the system, to another dimension from which it is possible to turn left into right.

Similarly, in order to transform transgression and past neglect, in order to change and add something to reality, something that was not there to begin with; one must transcend all the bounds of reality.

This requirement is quite a tall order, but it is not impossible, nor is it uncommon. As a matter of fact, it is found in the daily recitation of the *Shema*. "You shall love God your Lord *bekhol levavekha*, with all your heart"[29] represents the level of rectification of deeds and rectification of drives. "*Bekhol nafshekha*," "with all your soul," is the rectification of one's self, of one's direction, to the point of self-devotion. "*Bekhol me'odekha*," "with all your might," denotes that after you have done everything you can, do more; do what you are incapable of doing. *Bekhol me'odekha* means to transcend all your limits – and this, as we have stated, is also the highest level of *teshuva*.

When a person reaches his limit and then goes beyond it into the domain of what he cannot do, he thereby creates an *ein sof* in miniature within himself, and this *ein sof* touches the *Ein Sof* of the Holy One, blessed be He.

Once a person binds himself to the *Ein Sof*, not only is previous existence blotted out, but he can decide which new existence he wants. A different world is formed, a new heaven and a new earth, to the degree that a person is capable of asking and receiving.

This *teshuva* is the ultimate goal, and on a larger scale, it is the "macro-*teshuva*" of all of existence, the world's culmination and redemption.

It has been noted that the word *Shabbat* is an anagram of *teshuva*. There is a Sabbath before the world, and there is a Sabbath after the world. The Sabbath after everything, after all of the creation, descent, and hard

29. Deuteronomy 6:5.

work, is a *teshuva* to the primordial state, a return to the stage before the world existed, but on a higher level. Through the antithesis constituted by existence, by the world, we come to the synthesis of a new existence – an existence that is transcendent because it flowed within the reality of the world and elevated it, and thereby itself, to a more perfect level.

The Essence of the Day Atones[1]

AT LEAST NOT TO INTERFERE

"For on this day, atonement shall be made for you."[2] On this day, God grants atonement for all our sins.

An image of God's forgiveness and atonement is described by the prophets: "I wipe away your sins like a cloud, your transgressions like mist…"[3] When a human being wipes away dirt or erases writing, traces remain. When a wound in the skin heals, a scar remains in its place. God, however, wipes away sins as though wiping away a cloud. The skies are dark and gloomy, and suddenly "a wind passes by and it is no more;"[4] nothing remains, not a hint or a trace. The skies are clear, as though they had always been clear and always will be.

Changing the past reality and completely removing it from the world – from space, time, and existence – is not within the power of man, the created being, but only within the power of the Creator. Only God can determine retroactively that something did not happen, just

1. See Rambam, *Hilkhot Teshuva* 1:3.
2. Leviticus 16:30.
3. Isaiah 44:22.
4. Psalms 103:16.

as only He can determine that something will come into being and that something exists.

This is the essential nature of this unique day, the day that is outside the realms of time and place and on which gates are opened to the innermost place.

And what is man required to do on this day? At least not to interfere.

KOL NIDREI – DISCONNECTING FROM THE SHACKLES OF THE PAST

Before nightfall on the day before Yom Kippur, we recite *Kol Nidrei*. We declare that "*Kol nidrei ve'esarei… vekonamei vekinusei vekhinuyei…*," all the ties, designations, affiliations, labels, and definitions that I took, and perhaps also will take, upon myself, "*kulhon yehon sharan, beteilin umevutalin*," should all be dissolved, null and void. Henceforth, I release myself from all these, those of the past and those of the future, from this Yom Kippur to the next.

A person ascribes to himself all sorts of attributes – that he is an intellectual or not an intellectual; that he is a Ḥasid or not a Ḥasid; that he is emotional or rarely emotional. A person confines himself, assuming that he is incapable of certain things, that there are certain subjects about which he neither talks nor thinks, and that there are matters with which he has absolutely nothing to do. Thus, he tightly encloses himself in his shells, and the result is that nothing can influence him. For a person to be encased in shells, he need not necessarily be a respectable and slightly overweight adult with wrinkles; even a fourteen-year-old youth can enclose himself in an impenetrable shell.

We are afraid to part with "*kol nidrei ve'esarei vekinusei vekhinuyei*," not only because it is not convenient to do so and because it is difficult to give up habitual desires and old habits, but because holding on to these things constitutes our whole grip on reality. The "*kinuyei unedarei ve'esarei*" constitute my "I." The more "*esarei*" I add, the more vitality I receive; the more "*kinuyei*" that I add, the more powerful I become. These are the roots through which I am held to the ground and through which I draw my life.

For all these labels, affiliations, and so forth to be null and void, one must loosen for a moment this kind of grip on reality and let oneself go into the empty space. One must give oneself up, as in, "To You, O God, I lift up my soul."[5]

Yom Kippur is a long day. Again and again, we recite the confession. Sitting with oneself and with the congregation, one must remove one shell after another, as long as the gate is open.

Just before the holy day begins, each person declares – before the community notables, before the Torah scrolls which were removed from the ark, and before all who have come to pray together with the transgressors – that it is his will that *"kol nidrei ve'esarei vekinusei vekhinuyei"* should be null and void, not binding and powerless.

THE MIKVEH OF ISRAEL IS GOD

The Ten Days of *Teshuva* are a time of rectification, betterment, and perfection of deeds. They are the days most apt for this task, as they are days of closeness to our Father in heaven. About such days, the verse is expounded: "Seek God while He can be found, call to Him while He is near."[6]

Rosh HaShana and Yom Kippur are included in the Ten Days of *Teshuva,* but Yom Kippur is unique in that it is not only a day of *teshuva,* but also of forgiveness and atonement.

Teshuva and atonement are almost inversions of each other. *Teshuva* is an act of man. In *teshuva,* it is man who is active; he is the one who changes his behavior and returns to God. Conversely, atonement is an act of God, a supreme decree that descends from on high downward. Sins are pardoned, deeds are blotted out, and the past changes. Atonement has no necessary relation to man's actions.

What, then, is the reason for our great preoccupation on Yom Kippur with sins, confessions, and appealing for forgiveness?

Atonement is the cleansing of the soul, through which it reverts to its original state – *tehora hi.*[7] Hence, atonement is like immersion in

5. Psalms 25:1.
6. Isaiah 55:6.
7. As we say in the Morning Prayers: "The soul that You gave me *tehora hi* (is pure)."

a *mikveh*. God is willing to be Israel's *mikveh*, as our sages expound the verse, "The *mikveh* [lit., 'hope'] of Israel is God."[8]

To attain purity through a *mikveh*, one need only enter. The utensils immersed in a *mikveh* need not have any intention in mind; likewise, a ritually impure person who immerses need not meditate on the unity of God in order to be purified. There are only two requirements. First, one must immerse entirely; one must not leave one's hand or the tip of one's nose outside. Second, there must not be any dirt or interposition on one's body.

Similarly, on Yom Kippur, one must be entirely inside – within "the *mikveh* of Israel is God" – so that not even the smallest part of oneself remains attached to the sins one committed. No lust, habit, or conception may remain outside of the *mikveh*. Therefore, on Yom Kippur, one must make confession; t one must detach himself from all of his transgressions, gathering up his head or heart or other organs and bring them into "the *mikveh* of Israel is God." Second, one must make sure that not a trace of his transgressions remains stuck to his flesh, neither "deliberately" nor "inadvertently," neither "by bribery" nor "by folly of the mouth."[9]

Another law regarding the *mikveh* is that "if one immerses while holding a dead creeping thing in his hand, the immersion is of no avail to him."[10] He remains in his state of ritual impurity, despite the fact that he immersed in a *mikveh*.

Thus, before the immersion, one must cast off all the dead creeping things and rid himself of them; he must detach himself completely from transgressions he committed.

This does not only entail resolutions for the future, keeping far from sin from now on. After all, a person could turn aside from his evil way and resolve to follow the way of the good, but still fondly recall the

8. Based on Jeremiah 17:13, as in *Yoma* 85b: "R. Akiva said: Fortunate are you, Israel. Before whom do you become pure, who purifies you? Your Father in Heaven, as it says, 'I will throw pure water upon you, and you will be purified' (Ezekiel 36:25), and as it says, 'The *mikveh* of Israel is God.' Just as a *mikveh* purifies the impure, so God purifies Israel."
9. See the *Al Ḥet* confession.
10. Rambam, *Hilkhot Teshuva* 2:3.

transgressions he committed, take pleasure in them, and remember how good it was then. Hence, one must confess, review the sins one by one, and detach himself entirely from them. In a composed frame of mind, one must contemplate the matter and resolve to no longer have any connection to the sin, to separate from it forever. Only then can one immerse.

This explains why we make no confession for serious sins, such as violation of the Sabbath, whereas it is precisely for thoughts and inclinations of the heart, about which there is not even a single paragraph in the *Shulḥan Arukh*, that we confess in detail. The assumption is that on Yom Kippur, a Jew is no longer attached to his sins, at least not to the serious ones. But as for those points of inner attachment, which are less defined, there may still remain something – a fond memory, an inclination – that must be dissolved. The purpose of the confession, repeated over and over, is to resolve this question, to truly untie a person from his sins, even the most innermost ones, so that this day can indeed be in the nature of "the *mikveh* of Israel is God."

THE DAY PROGRESSES

We recite the confession twice in every prayer because Yom Kippur is a day that grows progressively more intense. The day that begins with *Kol Nidrei* progressively advances until it reaches its climax with the *Ne'ila* prayer, the culmination of the entire day. As the day progresses, we, too, must grow. Our Morning Prayer should not resemble our Evening Prayer, and our *Ne'ila* should not resemble our Musaf and Minḥa.

Thus, the confession that one made in the Minḥa Prayer before Yom Kippur is no longer sufficient for one who is offering the Evening Prayer of Yom Kippur a few hours later. He must make confession again, as it says, "My sin is ever before me."[11] It is possible that what was not a sin for the one who offered the Evening Prayer is a sin for which one must make confession when he offers the Morning Prayer. And it could be that the confession of the Morning Prayer is insufficient by the time of Minḥa, since the taint discovered now is deeper and more inward.

11. Psalms 51:5. In *Tanya*, ch. 29, it is explained that when a person ascends to a higher level of *teshuva*, he discovers more inward aspects of past transgressions, which he can now rectify.

WE HAVE SINNED BEFORE YOU IN WASTING TIME

The confession is long and detailed, but there nevertheless seems to be one *Al ḥet* that does not appear and that it would be worthwhile to add – the sin of wasting time.

God gave us the life of a year, and this period of time – from the previous Yom Kippur to this Yom Kippur – "we have robbed," "we have scorned," "we have corrupted," "we have abominated," and we have even killed.

We received this year on the condition that we return it, each day and each hour. Now that this Yom Kippur has arrived, what do we return to Him? He gave us these days so that we should improve them, so that ultimately we should return to Him more than what He gave us. At year's end, some people return a year with holes in it – here, a day is missing; there, an hour is gone. Some return only a few months out of the year, only a few days, and perhaps only a few hours.

For this sin, there might be no rectification; it is probably impossible to return the time that was lost. It is possible to return things or deeds or almost anything that exists in time. But it is impossible to return the time itself!

Nevertheless, we have it in our power to resolve that from now on – from this Yom Kippur to the next – we will endeavor to return twice as much.

NE'ILA – DO NOT HESITATE!

For an entire day, we have been in the "Day of Atonement" mode, in a different reality. We have been almost like angels, without eating and drinking. We are about to part, to say our final words – after all our *kavanot* (intentions) and confessions and reckonings – and those words must aptly summarize and conclude everything.

The King was with us and heard us. Now He is about to leave, and the King, as it were, says to us: "*Nu* – in one sentence, ask what you will, and I will grant it."

This is not the time to remain silent; this is not the time for thoughts. We should state briefly and succinctly, straight to the point, what it is that we truly want. There is no time now for elaborate meditations. One who searches now for meditations is likely to search for them until after the Evening Prayer, at which point there will be no one to talk to anymore…

This is the time to be bold – not to hesitate, not to be bashful, not to make a reckoning.

Over and over, we said in the course of the day, "We are brazen, but You are compassionate and gracious." That "we are brazen," we have shown You the entire year; now, You must show that You are "compassionate and gracious."

Sukkot

From Concealment to Revelation

THE JOY OF LIBERATION

From the Days of Awe, we go to the Festival of Sukkot. From the standpoint of law and justice, and of forgiveness and atonement, the Days of Awe exist in the realm of limits and bounds. On Sukkot, the limits are removed. Indeed, Sukkot is called "the season of our rejoicing;" in essence, it resembles the feeling of joy, which by its nature has no limits and whose theme is the breaking out and transcendence of limits and constraints.

An allusion to this is found in Jewish sources commenting on the verse, "His left hand under my head, His right arm embraces me."[1] "His left hand under my head," we are told, refers to the Days of Awe, Rosh HaShana and Yom Kippur; "His right arm embraces me" refers to the Festival of Sukkot. Whereas "His left hand" represents the dread of strict justice (as in Jewish mysticism, the left side represents justice and constriction), "His right arm" represents a softening of this system, emergence from it into an embrace, into the right arm (symbolizing

1. Song of Songs 2:6.

love and expansiveness). The "right arm," the Sukkot festival, draws near, caresses, and envelops.[2]

This aspect is reflected in the laws of the *sukka*. The Talmud teaches that the *sukka* must have at least two complete walls, plus the beginning of a third, which can be even a handbreadth long.[3] The shape of the walls, then, resembles the form of an embrace by the arm, the forearm, and the hand. In other words, the *sukka* itself is like a divine embrace.

The movement of the attribute of love is expansion from the center outward. In joy, there is this same outward movement – breaking out and emerging from a closed sphere and expansion and emergence into wide open space. Every day of the Sukkot festival, we recite the entire *Hallel* prayer, in which it says: "Out of the straits I called to God; God answered me with expansiveness."[4] "The straits" are the sphere of the attribute of justice, the sphere of bounded and restricting limits, whereas the "expansiveness" is the feeling of joy that follows from the very emergence from the straits.

The cycle of Rosh HaShana, Yom Kippur, and Sukkot is a process of entering limits and emerging from them. Rosh HaShana is the stern judgment by which the world must be measured and for which it must prepare. Yom Kippur is the day of transition; on the one hand, the essence of the day is purification, pardoning of sin, and beginning a new period, yet on the other hand, Yom Kippur itself is a serious day of introversion. In contrast, the Festival of Sukkot brings the joy of liberation. Sukkot is the culmination of the process, of the emergence from narrow straits to broad expanses, from the limits of judgment to the expanse of compassion and love. All that was veiled and concealed on Rosh HaShana and Yom Kippur – "*bakeseh*," "during the concealment" – is revealed before our very eyes "*leyom ḥagenu*," "on the day of our festival."[5]

The joy of the Sukkot festival also reaches a higher level: "You

2. See *Sha'ar HaKavanot*, introduction to the festival of Sukkot; see also *Likutei Torah*, *Devarim* 48c.
3. *Sukka* 6b.
4. Psalms 118:5.
5. See Psalms 81:4.

shall draw water *besasson* (joyfully) from the springs of salvation."[6] *Sasson* is inner joy, deeper than ordinary joy. On the Festival of Sukkot, this inner joy breaks out. It does not remain only in its deep and hidden place, or as an initial spark of thought; rather, it is revealed to all, like a burst of living water.

For this reason, the Sukkot festival is also "the *sukka* of Your peace."[7] Sukkot signifies the bursting of limits and the general union of existence, of the Jewish people, and of all the nations that come to the Temple on the Festival of Sukkot.[8] On Sukkot, we witness the union of the lower waters with the heavenly waters, as they, too, are offered upon the altar, and the joy and gladness of all of existence attaining liberation.

---

6. Isaiah 12:3.
7. The expression is from the *Siddur* in the blessing of *Hashkivenu*. See *Likutei Torah, Devarim* 31c.
8. As in Zechariah 14:16.

The Return to the Sukkot of the Wilderness

HISTORICAL MEMORY

Pesaḥ, Shavuot, and Sukkot are the three *regalim*, the major festivals on which a pilgrimage was made to Jerusalem. These three festivals have several common elements that join them into one system.

One of these elements is the dual meaning that informs each one of them. On the one hand, they are historical holidays serving as remembrances of key events in the history of the Jewish People in its early days. On the other hand, they are connected to the annual cycle of growth and agriculture. This dual meaning is expressed in the holidays' dual names: Pesaḥ – the Spring Festival; Shavuot – the Harvest Festival; Sukkot – the Festival of Ingathering. The two meanings of each festival complement each other, sometimes as like counterparts, and sometimes as opposites.

In the cases of Pesaḥ and Shavuot, the content of the historical remembrance is clear and unequivocal. These festivals mark turning points in Jewish history, the one-time, irreversible events of the Exodus and the Lawgiving. This is also how they are defined in the prayer book: "the season of our freedom" and "the season of the giving of our Torah."

In contrast, the point of the Festival of Sukkot is stated differently: "So that your future generations may know that I caused the people of

Israel to dwell in *sukkot* when I brought them out of the land of Egypt."[1] Apparently, the purpose of the Festival of Sukkot is to commemorate not a single specific event, but a period – not the heroic part of the Exodus, but the continuation, the time of wandering in the wilderness.

These *sukkot* were not a one-time event or an essential turning point. Nevertheless, not only is there a mitzva to remember them throughout the ages, but we are also commanded to build *sukkot* like those of our ancestors and to dwell in them as our ancestors did. In other words, we are commanded to carry out an act that is like a "performance," a repetition of what was done then, an act that is meaningful also for our real lives in the present.

FESTIVAL OF INGATHERING

Dwelling in *sukkot* in the wilderness epitomizes a life of uncertainty as to what will happen tomorrow. That uncertainty precludes building permanent structures; it allows only for temporary booths.

When the people of Israel entered the Land and settled in it, their lives changed dramatically from an unattached, up-in-the-air existence to a life of permanence and relative security. Such a life affords the possibility of planning for the future, establishing a permanent place of residence, and building permanent living quarters.

The nation's stable life in the Land of Israel was the people's dream when they were wayfarers in the wilderness. The Promised Land, "a good and spacious land,"[2] "where you will lack nothing,"[3] was their aspiration and goal ever since the exodus from Egypt. After this goal was realized, however, after life became stable, and permanent residence was achieved, the Torah's command was to recall the former period in the wilderness, the wandering and impermanence.

The combination of the Festival of Sukkot and the Festival of Ingathering is in itself a significant statement. The time of the ingathering is the end of the agricultural year, when people gather in and store away the fruit of their labor from the year that has passed, before the

1. Leviticus 23:43.
2. Exodus 3:8.
3. Deuteronomy 8:9.

beginning of the next season of labor. Such a time is usually a time of gratification and satisfaction, when people feel content about their present situation and experience the beautiful aspect of a set and established lifestyle. Precisely at this time, everyone is obligated to leave their home and dwell in a *sukka* – to return to the wilderness and to the transience of a nomadic life. This is not simply a commemoration, but an actual return!

A LIFE OF PERMANENCE

The uprooting of permanence, the commemoration and the symbolic act of return to the wilderness, raise the question: What is wrong with permanence? Is there virtue in exile and in wandering that obliges us to remind ourselves of this virtue and hold fast to it?

It appears that what requires examination and a different perspective is not the life of permanence itself, but rather various aspects of thought and feeling that accompany such a life.

After some time, a nation settled on its own land feels not only a bond with the land and ownership over it, but also confidence that things will continue as they are forever. Once a person builds a permanent residence, once he sows fields and plants vineyards, he begins to feel that his dwelling in this place is everlasting and that he cannot be uprooted from it.

Permanence, then, leads to complacency, smugness, and carefreeness. These qualities prevent a person from perceiving dangers and threats, whether external or internal.

By contrast, *sukka* dwellers in the wilderness know that their present residence is only temporary. Even if their dwelling in the *sukkot* is for an extended period, it is still uncertain and unstable. Their ability to forestall any danger is based precisely on the existence of doubt, on a certain measure of concern that the existing condition is not necessarily the everlasting one. Status quo can back up a claim or serve as evidence in any discussion, but it affords no certainty that the existing state will continue.

Another element resulting from a life of permanence is the transition from holding property to a sense of ownership, and from that sense to a feeling of absolute confidence in the justice of this ownership. After a certain period of permanent residence in a particular place (or, for that matter, of holding a particular office or job), one begins to sense that it is "mine" and, what is more, that "I deserve it." These claims need no rationalization or proof; the very fact that a certain reality has existed for a while becomes in itself justification for its existence.

The concern that people might justify a certain reality merely because of its ongoing existence appears in the Torah quite a few times. For example, "When God your Lord has thrust them [your enemies] from your path, do not say in your heart, 'Because of my virtue has God enabled me to possess this land.'"[4] The claim "I deserve it" is faulty not only because in itself it is not true, but primarily because it prevents one from beginning to search for the true justification and reason for his success.

DESENSITIZATION

There is one additional negative element of permanence. A life of permanence, especially in the midst of prosperity and success, affects a person in such a way that he is no longer capable of understanding the problems and needs of those who have not achieved financial security. The satiated do not understand the hungry, homeowners have difficulty understanding the homeless, permanent residents do not understand migrants, and the "haves" generally find it difficult to understand and empathize with the "have-nots."

This is true not only of those who have been wealthy and secure for generations. Surprisingly, even one whose parents experienced suffering, and even one who himself experienced hard times, quickly loses the ability to empathize with the sufferer. In human physiology, there is no faculty for remembering the sensation of pain; there is similarly a psychological mechanism that represses the recollection of suffering. One who becomes wealthy not only does not want to be reminded of the time in which he was poor, but often loses all perception of and sensitivity to poverty.

The destitute nomads who came in from the wilderness feel, after leading a settled and established life for a short while, that their stability

4. Deuteronomy 9:4.

and security have existed from time immemorial. Consequently, they harbor hostility toward the stranger and the homeless.

The mechanisms of forgetfulness and repression, and the consequent desensitization, are so powerful that it is apparently impossible not to be affected by them. Not only do base and degenerate people who rise in rank behave callously toward those who used to be their equals, but even refined and sensitive people cannot completely avoid this.

On the other hand, forgetfulness is an important defense mechanism, not only a defect in one's mental capacity. If a person were to remember everything, if he were to constantly recall all the pain, suffering, and humiliation he ever experienced, he would be unable to carry on with his life. Only because man is able to forget and repress many memories can he move on and go forward.

Thus, the inner change that takes place with the transition to a life of permanence – with both the good and the bad that it entails – cannot be entirely nullified. However, one must make sure that it does not deteriorate into total forgetfulness and callousness. "Jeshurun thus became fat and rebelled. You grew fat, thick and gross ... You forgot the God who bore you"[5] is one of the possible by-products of success and security.

KNOW FROM WHENCE YOU CAME

Although it is impossible to entirely avoid forgetfulness and desensitization, it is certainly possible to fight these phenomena.

Toward this end, it is necessary to continually remind oneself and to be reminded of one's past, of suffering, of wandering, of insecurity. Memory has the effect that although the spontaneous feeling of relationship to the sufferer and the needy no longer exists, at least in one's consciousness one knows otherwise.

When a person always remembers that he or his ancestors were at one point homeless wanderers, he prevents the growth of the feeling that there is a clear difference between "us" – the successful, secure and strong ones – and "them" – the insecure and helpless ones. He avoids the conclusion that "they deserve" to remain as they are. One

5. Deuteronomy 32:15–18.

who remembers that he, too, was born in exile cannot regard himself as integrally rooted in his new country.

Conversely, when one tries to forget and repress the past, a fictitious feeling of deep-rootedness automatically crops up, without any cultivation. As a result, he can at most tolerate the stranger, without regarding him as a brother.

For this reason, it is precisely in the book of *Deuteronomy*, which is the preparation for the entry into the Land of Israel, that Scripture reiterates: "Remember that you were a slave in the land of Egypt."[6] The people of Israel who are no longer in Egypt and who are about to enter and settle permanently in the new land are liable to quickly forget, upon attaining permanent residence, that neither the condition in which they find themselves nor the justification for it is to be taken for granted.

Recalling the fact that we were slaves in Egypt, and the duty to keep on recalling it, serve to prevent the desensitization and indifference that tend to result from a life of permanence.

If indifference is the tendency in ordinary times, then all the more so is it the tendency in times of rejoicing and rest. A person who is enjoying the company of his family while rejoicing in the feasts of the festival is likely to develop a bad case of indifference toward those who are in need. That is why, when we are told, "You shall rejoice before God…you, your son, and your daughter," Scripture adds, "and the Levite who is within your gates, and the stranger, the orphan, and the widow in your midst."[7] When it says, "You shall rejoice…in all that is at your disposal," we are commanded to include those who did not receive an inheritance and remained wanderers with no base in the land: "Be sure not to forsake the Levite as long as you live in your land."[8]

FACE TO FACE

Deeper and broader significance to going out to the *sukka* can be discovered through a basic understanding of the period of wandering in the wilderness.

---

6. Ibid. 5:15 et al.
7. Ibid. 16:11.
8. Ibid. 12:18–19.

The Jewish People's condition in the wilderness was, in the religious sense, incomparably better in many ways than any subsequent condition in which it found itself. The people had a special relationship with God; in every moment of its life, the entire people was concentrated around God's Tabernacle, and all wings of government were in the hands of God's prophet.

In addition, the nomadic life in the wilderness – and to an even greater degree the livelihood provided by the manna, which brought freedom from all subordination to the means of subsistence – created a situation in which the divine rule and presence were quite tangible:

> He subjected you to the hardship of hunger and then gave you manna to eat, which neither you nor your ancestors had ever experienced, in order to teach you that man does not live on bread alone, but that man may live on anything that God decrees.[9]

In other words, the Jewish people's condition in the wilderness is the proof that a people can survive even if it is beholden to God alone, without devoting itself at all to material means, but only to the divine purpose.

Thus, Israel's life in the wilderness reflects the ideal. It is a period if not to return to, then at least to yearn for and to recall, a period whose ideals we should draw from.

In the Prophets, the wilderness period appears as one that we long for as the setting of our people's youthful love and bridal devotion, to which we wish to return.

The prophet Ezekiel says, "I will bring you into the wilderness of the peoples, and enter into judgment with you there, face to face."[10] He prophesies that the beginning of the future redemption will once again be a going out to the wilderness, as in the first instance.

The prophet Hosea portrays the return to the wilderness in warmer terms, as a return to a more perfect and ideal state: "Therefore, I will speak coaxingly to her and lead her into the wilderness and speak to her tenderly. I will give her her vineyards from there, and the Valley

9. Ibid. 8:3.
10. Ezekiel 20:35.

of Akhor as a door of hope. There she will respond as in the days of her youth, and as in the day when she came up from the land of Egypt."[11]

The connection to the future redemption appears most prominently elsewhere in Hosea: "I am God your Lord from the land of Egypt; I will yet again settle you in tents, as in *yemei moed*."[12] "*Yemei moed*" are, on the one hand, the early days, the days of our original innocence in the wilderness, which God will restore us to at the time of the future redemption. On the other hand, an additional meaning lies hidden here: "*Yemei moed*" are the festive days of the Sukkot festival. In other words, at the future redemption, God will settle us permanently in the same condition to which we go out temporarily on "*yemei moed*" – the days of the Sukkot festival.

RETURN TO THE WILDERNESS

The Festival of Sukkot as the time of the ingathering is a festival of thanksgiving and rejoicing – thanksgiving of the farmer for his prosperity and thanksgiving of the land for Israel's settlement in its midst.

Hence, in contrast to the agricultural attachment, we are to stress the other side of our existence. We are to stress our non-dependence on the land, which we subordinate to a greater and higher purpose.

On the Festival of Sukkot, a time of rest and contentment, mere commemoration is not sufficient. In order to deepen the rational knowledge, the factual commemoration, it is necessary to do things that will add an emotional dimension and real experience to this memory. On Sukkot, it is not sufficient to be reminded "that I caused the people of Israel to dwell in *sukkot* when I brought them out of the land of Egypt." Rather, "all citizens in Israel shall dwell in *sukkot*."[13]

This explains the unusual use of the term "citizens." Precisely the citizen – one who feels that he has struck roots in the land, that he has a connection with the place and the soil, that he is a permanent resident of the country – needs to go out and live in a *sukka* again, even if only for a few days. He specifically must be reminded of the wanderers coming

11. Hosea 2:16–17.
12. Ibid. 12:10.
13. Leviticus 23:42–3.

from the wilderness; he must nullify the feeling that "we" are different and have more privileges, and he must re-experience the sense of the common destiny of all of us.

We go out to the *sukka* for the sake of a more exalted existence, in which we return to our original independent lives. We return again to the original state of the Jewish People and relive the youthful devotion and bridal love.

The Season of Our Rejoicing

YOU SHALL REJOICE IN YOUR FESTIVAL

In the Jewish tradition, the Festival of Sukkot is designated by a number of names, but the epithet used in the prayerbook is the "Season of our Rejoicing."

Indeed, the Festival of Sukkot is marked by a special emphasis on joy – from the *Simḥat Beit HaShoeva*[1] during the festival to Simḥat Torah, on which the joy is expressed even more intensely. The "Season of our Rejoicing" is thus an essential and basic component of the festival.

This title, however, which fixes a time devoted to rejoicing, raises some fundamental questions and even a degree of natural resistance: How is it possible to rejoice by the calendar? How can one order one's heart to rejoice on a predetermined date?

Of course, this question does not pertain only to the Festival of Sukkot. The "Season of our Rejoicing" is but one link in an elaborate chain of experiences on fixed dates of the Jewish calendar. Just as there are times designated for rejoicing, there are also days designated for serious contemplation, for sadness, and for mourning. The two extremes are, in fact, interconnected: only those who can mourn on Tisha B'Av, we

1. See the essay entitled "*Simḥat Beit HaShoeva*" below.

say, are capable of rejoicing on Simḥat Torah. In spite of the emotional distance between the two poles, there is a profound bond between them, for both draw on the same inner strength.

INNER DISCIPLINE

The ability to rejoice, to contemplate, or to mourn by the calendar derives from inner discipline, which is an integral part of religious life and one of the decisive elements in the very constitution of a religious person.

Even the most superficial observance of mitzvot requires a high degree of internalization, appreciation, and acceptance. External pressure to conform is insufficient. One needs inner strength to perform mitzvot in general, as well as to keep them regularly, in various situations and states of mind. The observant Jew derives such strength from an inner commitment to certain values, which is termed the "yoke of God's kingship" or "the yoke of the mitzvot." Only by virtue of this commitment can he act the way he does.

Obviously, the depth of this value-oriented attitude differs from one person to the next. However, even when an individual's religiosity is a religion of rote, he possesses the capacity to live according to his inner consciousness, no matter how weak and undeveloped it may be. Such individuals may well be the product of an indoctrinating education, of ignorance, or of spiritual cowardice; they may have no understanding whatsoever of the significance of what they affirm and practice. Nevertheless, the very fact that they are "religious" – namely, people who observe the commandments – attests to the fact that they do have an inner life, a life determined by values.

All this may seem self-evident, and the emphasis upon it therefore unnecessary. In today's world, however, because of many historical and cultural factors, the religious individual is not perceived as religious in the full sense of the term. Rather, he is perceived largely as a creature of habit, as a personality fashioned by affiliation with a certain sector of the community. Precisely for this reason, it is important to note that there must be a spiritual, inner component that allows for the existence of such a life.

THE HEAVENLY YOKE

Accepting the "heavenly yoke" is a personal decision that an individual consciously makes of his own free will. Nonetheless, it entails real subordination and discipline. Even the religious philosopher or mystic who has had the most profound, authentic spiritual experiences cannot constantly identify completely with every mitzva performance. Although he may understand and feel their significance and be able to perform them without reservation, it is simply not possible for him to do so with spontaneous and natural willingness at every given moment. It has been noted by many philosophers that spontaneously performed human activities are generally associated with specific physiological functions and their attendant mental aspects. On the higher level of our existence, and surely in the realm of our relationship with the divine and with the commandments, there can be no such reflex performance, certainly not of all the mitzvot at all times (except in the case of rare individuals). Accepting the heavenly yoke is an inner commitment, and precisely for this reason it is more serious, constant, and not subject to change.

In a certain sense, the need for the decision to accept the heavenly yoke stems from the very idea of a mitzva – the performance of a higher law that man cannot totally identify with or comprehend. By definition, if the commandments are completely divine, they cannot possibly be also completely human. The believer cannot expect performance of mitzvot to flow only from within, for he himself believes that their source is above and beyond him. Accordingly, the religious person cannot rely on his inner strengths and drives; he must construct and develop a unique orientation toward his religious life to prepare himself for the performance of certain acts. It is necessary for him to bring himself to the performance of the commandments at the right time and place; he must arouse within himself empathy with the observance of the mitzvot, both as a totality and as individual acts on each particular occasion.

INNER EXPERIENCE

A large body of Jewish contemplative literature addresses man's need to bring himself not only to the performance of an act, but also to an experience – discussing the question of proper intention and preparation of the heart (*kavana*).

A high religious level is expressed not only through the punctilious performance of mitzvot, but primarily by preparing the inner self for a more intimate identification with those mitzvot. There is a widespread notion that such preparation is not a Jewish idea, but this is not so; this preparation, focused intention, or meditation is an essential part of the religious person's world. In Judaism, it is demanded before and during the performance of mitzvot.

These contemplative procedures (*kavanot*) exist in a number of forms. For those who are so inclined, there is a detailed system of mystical exercises; for others, there are intellectual contemplative procedures. Everyone, irrespective of his spiritual state, is enjoined at the very least to recite a blessing before performing a mitzva. In addition, there are many intermediate acts and spiritual preparations whose performance is not fixed in time and whose purpose is to bring the individual to a state of readiness for the momentous event – the mitzva.

The deed itself is, of course, indispensable. Without it, of course, there is no point to the various *kavanot*. The physical performance itself always entails a certain inner experience; ceremonies, words, and formulas are always aids to spiritual intention. But the principal element of the intention is the preparation of the soul for the performance of the mitzva and for the experience.

Some view this approach as relinquishing the authentic experience, a loss of spiritual and emotional spontaneity. According to this romantic worldview, one should cultivate spontaneity of feeling and reject all clearly-defined preparation for experiences and emotions.

This attitude is not restricted to the religious life; it applies to other realms of feeling as well, such as romantic emotion and artistic creativity. It informs such concepts as "love at first sight" and "artistic inspiration." Yet it is precisely in these other realms that one can see the flimsiness of this approach, how illusory and imaginary it is. Spontaneity cannot bring about true creativity or real emotions. Spontaneous inspiration hardly ever exists, and even if it does, it cannot serve as a source of significant creativity on its own. Human beings have created many valuable things in a wide range of realms – from philosophical and scientific thinking to literature and art and poetry – but these accomplishments are thanks to a combination of many factors that have nothing to do with spontaneity, such as extended preparation and hard work, sometimes combined with external pressures and material demands. The same applies to other areas of personal development, even to the highest levels of experiences: love, identification, and self-devotion.

PRACTICE, LEARNING AND TRAINING

Closer analysis reveals that, to a certain extent, the whole uniqueness of man rests on achieving distance from the pressures of physiological spontaneity, and on replacing it with preparation and awareness.

The lower the level of a living creature, the more it is subject to instinctual pressure, to the pressure of natural spontaneity. Each higher level of development demands a further release from these pressures and their replacement by processes of practice, learning, and training. In human beings, even a hereditary skill such as the ability to walk requires a long period of practicing and learning. If this is true for a simple physical activity, then spiritual activities, which are more complex and subtle, clearly require even more complex training and conditioning!

Several Jewish sages have noted that the terms *emuna* (faith) and *imun* (training) stem from the same root,[2] indicating the need for inner training and habituation in order to develop faith and to be capable of attaining meaningful religious experience. This need for training, however, does not imply that there is no place for spontaneous religious experience, but rather that such spontaneous experience by itself cannot serve as the basis of religious life. Only by cultivating awareness and understanding through conscious and ongoing preparation can one draw the capacity for meaningful and profound experience from the inner resources in his soul, and only then can he act upon it. Although such religious experiences are not built out of complete spontaneity, they are no less authentic. They are simply more human by virtue of being guided and directed.

If a person can prepare himself for the inward life through voluntary inner discipline, he can also bring himself to genuine experiences, even if they are not activated by external stimuli. Thus, although

2. See *Tanya*, ch. 42.

the question of how one can be happy according to the calendar is not completely resolved, we can at least comprehend the possibility.

JOY OVER WHAT?

What is the nature of the inner preparation required in order to attain a true feeling of joy, and why is the theme of joy connected specifically with the Festival of Sukkot?

The experience of joy on a festival would be more understandable in the context of days of commemoration, days on which specific events occurred and whose anniversaries evoke memories of joy. Even if these memories themselves do not constitute external stimuli, they are references to the existence of a certain feeling and might thus generate the emotional experience. The Festival of Sukkot, however, the "Season of our Rejoicing," is not a commemoration of any specific historical event. These seem to be days designated for joy without any inner justification.

In order to understand this, we must first consider the nature of the emotion that is the antithesis of joy – namely, despondency.

The inner basis of despondency is pride, and it is pride that sustains and feeds the emotion. For at its root, despondency is nothing more than a prolonged expression of one question – "Why do I deserve this?" – whose underlying assumption is, "I deserve better." Whether there is any objective basis to this assumption is totally irrelevant, for the essence of this feeling is always internal and subjective. Since "I deserve better," why was I deprived? If it is mine and deservedly so, I simply must have it!

The greater and more intense a person's belief in his deservedness and merit is, the stronger his feeling of humiliation, deprivation, and injustice when he is "robbed" of the thing. As this feeling intensifies, so does his self-preoccupation and his anger toward God, the world, society, or the incident – toward whoever is not "me."

There is only one solution for such despondency. When a person (or an entire society) lowers the level of what he "deserves" to a minimum, then everything that he has will always seem like a gift over which to rejoice.

This is not to say that one need not struggle to attain the things that are important to him. The point is that these efforts should never bring him to a state of despondency and depression, but rather to a positive feeling of activity and creativity.

THE RECIPE FOR JOY

One of the simple explanations for the commandment to dwell in a *sukka* on the Festival of Sukkot lies in the dual feeling that the experience creates. On the one hand, there is the sense of exile, of leaving one's house to dwell in a temporary structure, but there is also a feeling of recollection as we remember the exodus from Egypt. In dwelling in the temporary structure of the *sukka*, we give up all our bounty and abundance; we return to the nation's original condition, to the experience of wandering and deficiency, wherein there is only faith and hope for the future, but nothing substantial in the present.

Indeed, if one can live temporarily in the wilderness and once again be a wandering, dispossessed exile, he can view his life in a different – joyful – way.

The time of the ingathering is a source of joy for some, who celebrate their success, and a source of frustration and despondency for others. On Sukkot, the Festival of the Ingathering, we are commanded to dwell in the *sukka* – the primordial state, in which one sees life's simple and basic graces, and one rejoices in what he has instead of making demands and recalling nonexistent rights.

This return to the primordial point, to the place from which things begin, is what enables one to attain joy. The days of Sukkot, then, are like a recipe for joy. Through the humility of putting oneself where he belongs, a person learns to appreciate life's gifts – the blessings that exist. The less he believes in "I deserve better," and the more he experiences the original condition of deficiency and the exile, the more he will appreciate all the bounty, and attain happiness from it.

This joy is perhaps not ecstatic, but it is true joy that will grow from day to day – from the joy of the festival to *Simḥat Beit HaShoeva* and to Simḥat Torah.

Seven Shepherds and Eight Princes of Men

THE USHPIZIN

There is a custom to invite one of the historic leaders of the Jewish people on each of the seven days of Sukkot – namely, Abraham, Isaac, Jacob, Moses, Aaron, Joseph, and David. The prophet refers to these seven *ushpizin* (guests): "We shall raise against him seven shepherds and eight princes of men."[1] They are called the "seven shepherds," for they shepherd Israel as a shepherd leads his flock.[2] What is the connection between these figures and the Sukkot festival in particular?

The seven "shepherds," seven eminent historical leaders of Israel, are distinguished from the other leaders of Israel in that they do not belong to history alone (although they certainly influenced history). These leaders are above history in that they have continued to lead the Jewish People throughout the generations, even in our own times. We

1. Micah 5:4.
2. Some of the "shepherds" were, at an early stage in their lives, actually herdsmen. As our sages say of Moses, and similarly of King David: "God said, 'Let the one who is skilled as a shepherd of the flock … come and shepherd My people.;" (See *Shemot Raba* 2:2, 4).

sense that they are present among us not as memories from the past, but as direct influences on each of our souls.

The shepherds are our forefathers, the forbearers of all the souls of Israel. Regardless of whether they are our biological forefathers, like the three Patriarchs, or our spiritual forefathers, as in the case of Joseph and David, we bear a part of their essence within ourselves. They are not external figures, but rather form our inner essence.

On the "Festival of the Ingathering," we gather together all the separate parts of existence. It is a festival of reconciliation, peace, and culmination, in which everything is put in its place – the reunification of existence.

When we sit in the shade of the *sukka*, "in the shelter of the Most High,"[3] we invite ourselves to receive the *ushpizin*, who are a part of ourselves. For the sake of this invitation, we must go out to a place that is outside of civilization, outside the usual order of life. There, we build ourselves a temporary structure and cover it in shade, under the lofty hand of God, which protects and shelters us: "I have sheltered you with My hand."[4] There, we meet ourselves – not as we are throughout the year, but as we are together with our forefathers, in the ideal form of what we are in essence.

On this festival, as the *ushpizin* assemble, we should be willing to receive them, to integrate within ourselves all these parts of our being. We open the door and invite them, one by one, to enter and give all that they have to give. We invite them to the *sukka*, to enter together with us into the source, into the place that includes us all.[5]

THE PEOPLE OF ISRAEL PROVIDE SUSTENANCE FOR THEIR FATHER IN HEAVEN

The "seven shepherds" are so called because they provide guidance and sustenance, just as a shepherd guides and provides sustenance for his flock. On a simple level, the "flock" that they shepherd consists of the souls of Israel; the "seven shepherds" guide and nourish the souls' spiri-

3. See Psalms 91:1.
4. Isaiah 51:16.
5. Or as it says in *Sukka* 27b, "All of Israel are able to sit in one *sukka*."

tual faculties. The "seven shepherds" are leaders of the Jewish People who guide the people and show them the way they are to go; they nourish the souls of Israel with Torah and mitzvot[6] and with insight into divinity.

However, the "shepherds" have additional significance as well. God refers to the community of Israel as "My brothers and friends (*rei'ay*)"[7] and as "My sister, My love (*ra'ayati*)."[8] The people of Israel are God's *rei'a*, God's "friend," in the sense that they are His *ro'eh*, His shepherd. The community of Israel shepherds and nourishes God, as it were. As our sages put it, "The people of Israel provide sustenance for their Father in Heaven."[9]

In order to understand to this astounding statement, one must conceive of "sustenance" in the broadest sense. Sustenance means nourishment, to feed in order to keep body and soul together. When a person does not eat, the soul is gradually separated from the body – first, there is impairment of the soul's ability to think, walk, and act, until finally there is complete separation – death. Conversely, when a person eats, he strengthens the connection between his body and soul; when a person nourishes and provides sustenance to someone else, he keeps that person's soul in his body.

This is true in the macrocosm as well. The universe is like a body, and God is like its soul.[10] Thus, building and strengthening the connection between God and the world is conceived of as sustenance, and those who serve God and reveal His presence in the world "shepherd" and "nourish" Him, as it were. This does not mean that without our service, God would cease to exist; rather, it means that without our service, He cannot be expressed. His presence would not be felt in the world.

6. As explained in a number of sources, the Torah is the soul's nourishment and the mitzvot are the soul's garments.
7. Psalms 122:8.
8. Song of Songs 5:2.
9. *Zohar* III, 7b.
10. "As God fills the whole world, so the soul fills the whole world. As God sees but is not seen, so the soul sees but is not seen. As God nourishes the whole world, so the soul nourishes the entire body. As God is pure, so the soul is pure. As God dwells in the innermost recesses of the universe, so the soul dwells in the innermost recesses of the body" (*Berakhot* 10a).

This hyperbolic conception appears in a different manner in an interpretation by our sages, commenting on the verse, "You are My witnesses... and I am God:"[11] As long as you are My witnesses, I am God, but if you do not attest to Me, then I, as it were, am not God.[12]

By definition, a witness is not simply someone who saw something, but someone who can also recount it, someone who by virtue of his testimony has attained a new awareness and is able to express it. Our task as shepherds, as witnesses, is to maintain God's presence in the world. Without our worship, without our efforts and self-devotion, God is, as it were, not present in the world.

The two aspects of shepherds – shepherding the souls of Israel and sustaining God – are interrelated.[13] The seven shepherds nourish the people of Israel with spiritual faculties through which "the people of Israel provide sustenance for their Father in Heaven;" Abraham nourishes them with love, Isaac with awe, Moses with knowledge, and so forth.[14] In other words, the shepherds, as it were, shepherd God through the souls of Israel – by means of the seven spiritual faculties that they cultivate in Israel and through with which the people of Israel serve God.

PRINCES OF MEN

In addition to the "seven shepherds," the prophet also refers to the "eight princes of men" – Jesse, Saul, Samuel, Amos, Zephaniah, Zedekiah, the Messiah, and Elijah.[15] Although they too influence the souls of Israel in every generation, these leaders are not shepherds; their relationship

11. Isaiah 43:12.
12. *Midrash on* Psalms 123.
13. *Torah Or* 33c: "The explanation of the matter is as follows. *Ro'eh* has two meanings: (a) one who sustains others, as in 'nourish us (*re'einu*), feed us'; (b) one who nourishes himself, as in 'the she-asses were grazing (*ro'ot*) alongside them'... So, too, in the case of the seven shepherds (*ro'im*), both these elements are present, for they nourish the community of Israel."
14. See *Likkutei Torah, Bemidbar* 29c: "As it is written, 'The soul of man is the lamp of God.' The community of Israel's souls is called 'menorah.' [This menorah] bears seven lamps, corresponding to seven levels in divine service... Now, it is Aaron who kindles these lamps, for he is one of the seven shepherds who cause vitality and godliness to flow to the community of Israel's souls..."
15. *Sukka* 52b.

to the community of Israel is of a different nature. The shepherds' guidance penetrates and becomes an intrinsic part of the souls of Israel. The one who leads and the one who is led are thus no longer two different figures; rather, they are unified and become, in essence, one. By contrast, the influence of the princes does not penetrate the soul's faculties; it surrounds and envelops the soul.

The first of these two types of influence becomes, consciously or unconsciously, part of one's inner being, part of one's consciousness and emotional life. The second type of influence, that of the princes, always operates from without. It changes not one's inner being, but the general climate, the surrounding atmosphere.

All of the "princes" were prophets sent my God to direct Israel, with the exception of one. Jesse, the father of David, acted on his own, without holding any public office of any kind. Officially, his words and actions had no binding force on other people. Nevertheless, he and the other "princes of men" influence the world by their very existence. Because they exist, the world in which they live is no longer the same. Perhaps nothing specific has changed, but the world as whole is a different world.

A person may be a teacher and leader, and thereby influences the world; but there are others who influences the world not by what they say or do, but by the fact that they exist. This is "surrounding," indirect influence.[16]

By way of analogy, these two types of influence can be compared to the effects of electromagnetic forces and the force of gravity. While

16. See *Torah Or* 34a: "The distinction between the shepherds and the princes of men can be better understood in light of the following. R. Yoḥanan b. Zakkai was the great master of Torah, the Torah teacher of the entire nation, and yet he said to R. Ḥanina b. Dosa, 'Ask for mercy on my behalf,' for [the power of] R. Ḥanina's prayer exceeded his own... Now, we do not find that R. Ḥanina b. Dosa approached the stature of R. Yoḥanan b. Zakkai as a teacher of Torah, nor do we find laws attributed to him in the Mishna. The explanation of this matter lies in the difference between the shepherds and the princes of men... For R. Yoḥanan b. Zakkai shepherded and sustained Israel, like Moses, whereas R. Ḥanina b. Dosa lacked this dimension, but he was a perfect *tzaddik*, unblemished, so that our sages said that the world to come was created solely for his sake, and from him the souls of Israel received the ways of [divine] service and piety..."

heat and electricity create effects by sending waves out to an object, gravity affects the object simply because of its very existence. Because gravity exists, it has an effect; nothing can escape it.

Thus, we find the Messiah among the "eight princes of men." Even though the Messiah never existed in the world and never acted in it, the very belief in the coming of the Messiah is a motivating force; our world looks different because we expect him. Hence, the Messiah is not a prince of the present, but a prince of the future.

FESTIVAL OF JOININGS

The dual influence, surrounding and inner, characterizes everything connected with the Festival of Sukkot. The seven shepherds relate to the eight princes of men in the same way as the seven days of Sukkot ("You shall dwell in *sukkot* seven days") are connected to the eighth day of Shemini Atzeret. In fact, the same relationship exists between the mitzva of dwelling in the *sukka* and the mitzva of taking the *lulav*.

We take the *lulav* and *etrog* in our hands and shake them; we form a direct, inner relationship with them. In contrast, we need not form any relationship with the *sukka*; we exist inside it, and as a result of our very presence, it influences us by its existence around us. When we take the *lulav* in the *sukka*, we join the surrounding influence with the inner influence.[17]

Similarly, when we invite the seven shepherds into the *sukka* in which we are enveloped during the Festival of Sukkot, we join their inner influence with the surrounding influence of the Clouds of Glory.

17. *Siddur Admor HaZaken, sha'ar halulav,* 265a: "This would also explain why the *lulav* should be taken precisely in the *sukka*. For the root meaning of the *mitzva* of the *sukka* roof and of the *mitzva* of taking the *lulav* is the same, only that via the roof the light is drawn as surrounding light, whereas via the *lulav* it is drawn as inner light, corresponding to *da'at*..."

Simḥat Beit Hashoeva: The Rejoicing of the Water-Drawing Place

TRUE JOY

Each one of the three pilgrimage festivals expresses a particular theme, an intrinsic quality that is the focus of the holiday.

Pesaḥ, the "Season of our Freedom," is the festival of redemption. Indeed, our future redemption is intrinsically connected to the first redemption, as our sages say: "In [the month of] Nisan they were redeemed, and in Nisan they are destined to be redeemed."[1]

On Shavuot, the "Season of the Giving of our Torah," we received the Torah. On this day, we emphasize the giving of the Torah in each generation and to each individual.

On Sukkot, the "Season of our Rejoicing," we draw forth not redemption or Torah, but joy for the entire year. Indeed, the message of joy is of no less importance than that of redemption and the receiving of the Torah!

There are various degrees and modes of happiness. There is the joy that results from ingathering, which is certainly experienced on Sukkot.

1. *Rosh HaShana* 11a.

When the barns are full of grain, one will certainly be in a good mood, but this is "joy that depends on something." Just as "love that depends on something – when the thing ceases to exist, love ceases to exist,"[2] the same applies to joy. Joy that results from something is not joy in essence, but joy that is dependent on that thing. The lack of that thing mars the joy.

Real joy, on the other hand, is not attached to things, but is rather joy of the essence. When we rejoice in this manner, the joy cannot be taken from us. This joy is not dependent on anything; anywhere and always, in good times and in bad, during ups and during downs, we can always receive and draw sustenance from the "Season of our Rejoicing."

THE JOY OF THE LOWER WORLDS

The nature of this joy can be learned from the *Simḥat Beit HaShoeva* ceremony, the celebration of the water-drawing that took place in the Temple. Throughout the entire year, a libation of wine was poured on the altar. On the seven days of the Festival of Sukkot, a libation of water was poured in addition to the libation of wine. The water for this libation was drawn from the Shiloaḥ spring, to the accompaniment of especially joyous rites.

On the second day of Creation, God divided the world into two, separating "the waters below the firmament from the waters above the firmament,"[3] the upper waters from the lower waters. This division is the fundamental division between upper creatures and lower creatures, between those that are "close" to God and those that are not.

The *Tikunei Zohar* writes that ever since the division, the lower waters have been weeping, "We, too, wish to be before the King!"[4] This represents the weeping of the entire world, which weeps because it is below. It bitterly complains because it wants – but is unable – to be above. This weeping stems from the sorrow of separation, from the suffering of detachment.

After time, of course, there are some waters that no longer wish to ascend, but from among the waves, one sound is heard – the sound

2. *Avot* 5:16.
3. Genesis 1:7.
4. *Tikuna Arba'in*, 80a.

of the waters themselves. The sound of their inner nature transcends any descent; it is the sound of the lower waters yearning to ascend.

Despite the fact that there was a water duct that brought water into the Temple throughout the year and provided all the water that was needed, the water for the water libation on Sukkot was drawn from the Shiloaḥ spring itself. The joy of the *Simḥat Beit HaShoeva* is the joy of the lower waters, which, despite their state of separation, succeed in ascending and in being taken up to the Temple Mount, to the heights of the Sanctuary, to the point of their ascent to the altar, to stand again "before the King." Hence, on every step, we sing, blow trumpets, and dance. In order to reach the "springs of salvation," the wellspring of joy, one must draw water from the lowest place, from a spring that flows up from below. The *Simḥat Beit HaShoeva*, the most jubilant rejoicing in the Temple, therefore begins with a descent to a low place, and it is precisely from there that the great rejoicing breaks out.

The water of the Shiloaḥ is not fast-flowing river water, nor is it the open mass of ocean water; it is water that issues in a slow trickle from the earth. Each drop must struggle through clods of earth and seep through cracks in rocks in order to become refined and burst forth as water. When these drops succeed in climbing, breaking through all the subterranean shells and issuing forth in a small stream, what results is "the spring of salvation." This spring symbolizes all of the lower waters, in their distress and in their salvation.

"YOU SHALL DRAW WATER BESASSON"

What results from our efforts, from our drawing of water, is *sasson*: "You shall draw water *besasson* (joyfully) from the springs of salvation." There is a difference between *sasson* and *simḥa*. Although they are usually understood as synonymous terms for joy, *simḥa* can be quiet and tranquil; *sasson* erupts in excitement, rising and uplifting from the depths of the earth. On the way up from below, there are obstructive shells, rings of iron that throttle progress. But when the essential basis of all of lower reality is uncovered, when the yearning of the lower waters is roused and declares that "we, too, wish to be before the King," there is nothing that can stop the *sasson* from bursting forth higher and higher.

In our time, the *Simḥat Beit HaShoeva* is celebrated primarily through dancing, as the Mishna teaches: "Men of piety and good works used to dance before them."[5] What is dance? In a dance, the people who dance join together, and no one is left by himself. The melody, manifest or obscure, envelops and unifies everyone. The dancers kicks the earth so as to ascend heavenward. Again and again, the dancer strikes at the lowest part of the world, because he does not want to be there; he wants to elevate himself above the surface of the ground. It is as though he declares, "I do not agree to remain with the lower waters that do not wish to ascend. I still wish to ascend!"

The desire for ascent, for transcendence, makes revelation possible. In the Jerusalem Talmud, our sages explain that this rejoicing is called the "*Simḥat Beit HaShoeva*" (literally, the rejoicing of the drawing place) because it is from there that they would draw *Ruaḥ HaKodesh* (the holy spirit). Indeed, the prophet Jonah received *Ruaḥ HaKodesh* at a *Simḥat Beit HaShoeva*.[6]

The joy of the "Season of our Rejoicing" results from the knowledge that ascent is possible no matter what happens, good or bad. To achieve this goal, we extend our hands to one another and kick the lower world. To be sure, the ascent and the climb are difficult; it may be impossible to reach the firmament. We may rise and fall, but this dance – the will to ascend and the possibility of doing so – cannot be taken from us dwellers down below. Through this dance, it is possible to connect with the Heavenly and to draw from there *Ruaḥ HaKodesh*.

5. *Sukka* 5:4.
6. Jerusalem Talmud, *Sukka* 5:1.

The Month of Ḥeshvan

Ordinary Days

We naturally live between and on special dates; our lives pass from one event to another. However, during the year there are also quite a few ordinary days and periods, which have no unique positive or negative qualities.

The Talmud cites the *Book of Ben Sira* as teaching that "All the days of the poor are evil." The Talmud asks, "But are there not Sabbaths and festivals?" and then answers, "A change of routine is the beginning of bowel trouble."[1] The poor man is always miserable. During the week, he eats and drinks very little. When the Sabbath arrives, he presumably has a better meal, but then he gets bowel trouble because he changed his routine.

What are the sages trying to teach us here? It is well known that "true poverty is the lack of knowledge;"[2] one who lacks knowledge has the same problem as the poor man who overeats on the Sabbath. For him, there are plain days, days without any spiritual exaltation. One would think that the arrival of Sabbaths and holidays, on which there

1. *Ketubot* 110b.
2. *Nedarim* 41a.

is a certain elevation of the soul, would affect some kind of change for the better. Yet, "a change of routine is the beginning of bowel trouble;" often, a person is left only with heartache, as the holidays merely accentuate the emptiness of his other, ordinary days.

A DIFFERENT PERSPECTIVE

People can bear suffering, illness, pain, depression, and all such burdens – on condition that they are more or less regular. It is far more difficult to endure sudden shocks, departure from the ordinary course of things. The human body has regulatory systems that enable it to shift from one pace to another, but the soul has far fewer tools for this. Hence, many people can live with the tension of the month of Tishrei, for that is the "routine" of this month; one runs from mitzva to mitzva, from *Seliḥot* to *Ne'ila* to Simḥat Torah.

In contrast, it is known that the fewer the days of vacation, the better one works and studies, because days are lost both before and after each day of vacation. One would think that a person who rests for several days would then be full of energy, but as a rule he is actually more tired than he was before his vacation. The change of pace is debilitating.

In this respect, completely ordinary days would seem to be better days. On such days, a person can develop a routine that brings about gradual progress, step by step. Their drawback, however, is that they offer the person no way of arriving at a critique of his habitual patterns of behavior. The monotonous repetition of day after day after day prevents one from attaining the kind of awareness that the Sabbath brings to the week or that the festivals bring to the year. In other words, festivals and Sabbaths are not just times of uplift; rather, they meet the need to break up the course of time so as to understand and to feel what it is that we are actually lacking.

"If a person commits a sin and repeats it, it becomes to him as though it were permissible."[3] Even if a person knows that he commits a sin, when he repeats the same sin several times, it becomes part of his routine; he no longer pays attention to it as something requiring correction. Conversely, a person can perform a mitzva so many times that

3. *Yoma* 86b.

it becomes to him not only like something permissible, but like something entirely ordinary, something that is simply done.

This may be the meaning of the verse, "And the people of Israel walked on dry ground in the midst of the sea."[4] While the fact that the people of Israel walked in the midst of the sea is certainly extraordinary, why do we emphasize that they walked "*on dry ground* in the midst of the sea"? When a person walks every day on dry ground, he stops feeling the wonder of it; he only recognizes the wonder and the miracle when he walks "on dry ground in the midst of the sea." The moment a person sees things from a new perspective, even the routine ceases to be banal and ordinary.

That is why we have Sabbaths and festivals – so that we can discern the other aspects of all the things that are already known to us and so that we do not sink into the rut of a life that has nothing special about it.

THE ROUTINE OF THE SPECIAL

However, even the special and unique can become routine. The Sabbath is liable to turn into just another day, like all the others – except for the fact that it is Sabbath. The festivals, too, can be perceived simply as occasions that recur annually.

This, in fact, is what happened with the manna in the wilderness. On the first day, the people of Israel were surely astounded, and on the third day they were still slightly amazed. But after a few days, they already knew that the manna was supposed to fall, and that it would fall precisely according the ration of one *omer* for each person. In the first years of the State of Israel, there were ration cards on which was written, "This is a family of so-and-so many souls," and one would go the store and receive rations accordingly, without there being anything wondrous or exciting about it. This is also what happened with the manna that fell from heaven; in our eyes, a recurring wonder ceases to be considered a wonder.

In the same way, the body senses only drastic changes. In an experiment, a frog was put inside a container of water, and the temperature of the water was gradually raised. The frog did not leave the

4. Exodus 15:19.

water even when the water reached a boiling point; it was cooked in the water because the change was so gradual that the frog did not sense it! In many respects, we are the same way. We adjust to small changes – in the weather, in events – and after we get used to them, nothing moves us.

In this way, we tend to grow accustomed to the annual cycle and even the truly extraordinary. We become like the legendary tourist who visited the Western Wall. When asked, "How was it?" he replied, "It is a western wall like all other western walls."

BREAKING THE ROUTINE

The Talmud cites the verse, "Then you will come to see the difference between he who serves God and he who does not serve Him"[5] and asks what the point of difference is between one who serves God and one who does not. Our sages explain that one who does not serve God repeats his study of the same chapter a hundred times, whereas one who serves God repeats his study of the chapter a hundred and one times. Can it be that a difference of one time turns a person from one who does not serve God into one who serves Him? To answer this question, the Talmud cites Hillel the Elder: "Go and learn from the mule-drivers' market." It costs one *zuz* to rent a mule for a distance of ten parasangs, but a distance of eleven parasangs costs twice as much. Why? Because the eleventh parasang exceeds the distance the mule is used to traveling.[6]

Of course, not many people review their studies a hundred times, and that itself is certainly a high level. Yet one who reviews something a hundred times remains within a certain limit; this suffices him, and he gets into a certain routine. By contrast, one who reviews his chapter a hundred and one times breaks this limit. The hundred-and-first time is important not because it is one more time, but because it indicates that the person does not allow himself to fall into a routine, a habit of study.

In other words, the central point is that of breaking the routine. This is also expressed by our sages elsewhere when they teach that "According to the labor is the reward."[7] The reward is not according to

5. Malachi 3:18.
6. *Ḥagiga* 9b.
7. *Avot* 5:23.

the deed, but according to the effort. In the middle of one's daily routine, he suddenly remembers that he must pray the Minḥa Prayer. He pulls himself up, drops what he is working on, disengages from all the things that are occupying him, and goes off to pray. Such a person is capable of experiencing a sudden awakening. The point of change is of great significance. The Ba'al Shem Tov used to say that when a person who is preoccupied with his activities passes a synagogue, hears the "*Kedusha*" prayer being recited, and is startled, for he remembers that he has not yet prayed, the heavens and highest heavens quiver along with him.

The foregoing applies to one who passes outside the *beit midrash* (study hall) and experiences a sense of shock, but one who sits continually inside the *beit midrash* may not have such an experience. He has a time for the Morning Prayer, a time for the Minḥa Prayer, and a time for the Evening Prayer, and he is liable to fall into a routine in which nothing can awaken him. Of this predicament, our sages say, "Better is one self-reproach in a man's heart than many lashes."[8] The essential thing is not that the person strikes his heart when pronouncing the confession or the *Al ḥet*, but that his heart strikes him from within for each and every transgression.

A person can sit in a protected environment and be convinced that he has attained perfection, but his essence is revealed when he goes out into the world. The Rebbe of Kobrin would sing: "Angel, Angel – you have no wife and children. You have no worries about making a living, you have no troubles – that is why you are an angel. Come down to us, to this world! Take a wife, father children; you'll have troubles, and we'll see whether you remain an angel!"

A person must build himself from within, not from without, in order to be able to make a change even during the plain and ordinary weekdays, when nothing breaks up the regular pace of things. If one lives his life mechanically, like a machine, the flashes of inspiration and uplift cannot be expressed at all.

8. *Berakhot* 7a.

SHAME VS. GUILT

Anthropologists distinguish between cultures of shame and cultures of guilt. In cultures of shame, the essence of a person's life lies in his ability to look others in the face. In such a culture, a person who commits an indecent act known to others will commit suicide. In Near and Far Eastern cultures, people are capable of feeling slight remorse, but they cannot bear losing face and are even willing to die to restore their dignity.

By contrast, in cultures of guilt, the emphasis is placed not on what is more dignified, but rather on how the person himself feels about what happened. In Jewish culture, although what others say is also important, the essence must spring from one's inner being. Everything that a person builds externally is a delusion.

The Talmud asks: Who "acts charitably at all times"?[9] This refers to someone who supports his sons and daughters while they are minors. Since a father is not legally liable for the maintenance of his minor children, the support he provides for them is regarded as *tzedaka*, charity, and since children are constantly in need of financial support, a father who supports his children fulfills the mitzva of *tzedaka* at all times. But the sages add a caveat, for we are told, "he shall not come at all times into the holy place."[10] In other words, this type of "acting charitably at all times" will not enable one to enter the holy place. One may indeed fulfill his minimum obligation to act charitably, but in order to enter the holy place, one must do more.

To be sure, one who fulfills his obligations not only does no harm but is considered a decent person, which in itself is often a great credit. But to enter the holy place, it is not sufficient that one makes no trouble. There are other requirements, requirements that cannot be constructed from without; for if they come from without, they will be forgotten. The routine overwhelms everything except what a person, in his inner being, works to attain. Only what one works on through his inner life endures for long.

---

9. As it says, "Happy are they who keep justice and act charitably at all times" (Psalms 106:3).
10. Leviticus 16:2.

THE UNIQUENESS OF THE ROUTINE

While the holidays give us opportunities of change and uplift, it is good that there are also time periods that are more or less "flat." These ordinary periods are, in fact, the time of the trial: Did the person, on his own, truly accomplish something within his own being? Or perhaps everything that happens to him comes from without? A person may be artificially placed into an atmosphere of burning enthusiasm and exaltation, but this cannot last for long. A candle may be lit once, twice, or three times, but if it contains no fuel, it will not burn, even if one stands constantly beside it with a match.

In an experiment performed on human beings – and which is also used sometimes as a method of torture – a person is put into a place where there are no external stimuli whatsoever: soundless, sightless confinement. After some time, many people start yelling, "Let me out of here!" They cannot bear it, and some even lose their sanity. But there are also people for whom such an experience becomes a turning point; precisely the absence of external stimuli causes them to bolster their inner essence.

This is exactly what God does with us in the ordinary periods of the annual cycle. He gives us a time period in which there are no special occasions, as though calling to us: "Let's see what you are when you're alone!"

Sometimes, even a decent man does not wake from his slumber, but rather continues to exist as though he were merely a copy of something or someone – until he is shaken up. Only then does he wake up, change, and take on the form of a human being. That is why sometimes the request is made in heaven that something should happen to a certain person – so that he should awaken and begin to move. We, however, wish to not experience trouble or misfortune.

Here, our human power enters the picture, the power we have by virtue of our being human – our ability to accomplish through inner effort. In other words, the only remedy for ordinary days and ordinary life is avoidance of living life haphazardly; rather, we should build our lives consciously, with premeditation.

Yod-Tet (19th) Kislev

Yod-Tet (19th) Kislev

ROSH HASHANA FOR HASIDISM

Yod-tet Kislev, the nineteenth day of the month of Kislev, has been established among Chabad Hasidim as a day of rejoicing, ever since the release of our Master and Teacher, R. Schneur Zalman of Liadi, the author of the *Tanya,* from his imprisonment. New insight and great enthusiasm have characterized the celebration of this day ever since R. Shalom Dov Baer of Lubavitch wrote his famous letter about the importance of this day and the ways in which it should be celebrated.

Besides the designation of the date, "*Yod-tet* Kislev," this special day is also referred to as the "Festival of Redemption" and as "Rosh HaShana for Hasidism." Such special reference rouses our interest to discover why this day has merited to be crowned with such wreaths of honor, in particular since they do not seem to be directly related to the significance of the event being celebrated.

On the simplest level, we can explain that the date on which our Master and Teacher was exonerated from the accusation that imperiled his life and the lives of all Hasidim deserves to be remembered as a day of salvation for a Jewish leader and all his followers. The Halakha teaches that when a person is saved by a miracle, his descendants and disciples are obligated to recite a blessing – with God's name and kingship – over the memory of the miracle. When a miracle saves an individual who is singular in his generation – certainly when it is a miracle that involves the sanctification of God's name – not only his disciples, but all Jews are obligated to give thanks for this miracle. Indeed, we find that our great religious authorities established festive days in commemoration of miracles that occurred to communities and individuals, days which they took upon themselves and their posterity to observe.

The release of our Master and Teacher, with all the miraculous events connected with it and the aspect of redemption and salvation that it bore, is certainly deserving of blessing and thanksgiving on the part of all his disciples. All Hasidim throughout the generations are his disciples and learned Torah from him, and the obligation of thanksgiving and blessing certainly applies to them. This is true all the more so since his release entailed the sanctification of God's name; thus, not only his disciples but all Jews share in this obligation.

THE TRIAL OF HASIDISM

The foregoing, however, is but the outer cover of the matter; its inner content is more profound. To appreciate the day's historical importance, let us recall the period in which the events occurred.

In the days of R. Schneur Zalman of Liadi, the Hasidic movement was gaining strength, but opposition to the movement was also growing. After the death of the Vilna Gaon, the main opponent of Hasidism, this opposition not only did not weaken, but grew stronger, assuming a sharper and harsher tone from day to day. The pressure that community leaders exerted on the Hasidim through bans and other means caused much animosity. Although the false accusations against our Master and Teacher were acts of individuals, they expressed the prevailing spirit of hatred and the exacerbation of the spiritual struggle that was capable of reaching even such levels of conflict.

The imprisonment and trial of our Master and Teacher were a testing ground for action to be taken on a larger scale. Had he been found guilty, the Czarist government would have brutally suppressed the entire Hasidic movement. Since the opponents of Hasidism were collaborating with the authorities and intended to treat the Hasidim like a deviant sect, the result would have been the end of Hasidism. The trial of our Master and Teacher was the trial of Hasidism in general, and his exoneration entailed the exoneration of the entire movement, the refutation of the charges against it, and its release from the pressure brought upon it by foes from within and from without.

The release of our Master and Teacher from imprisonment on *yod-tet* Kislev (despite his later imprisonment on the same charges) can therefore be viewed as the end of the great conflict waged against Hasidism. Of course, Hasidism still had many opponents, and there were great Jewish leaders who still had reservations about it, but the active conflict and the attempt to exclude the Hasidim from the community of Israel practically ceased thereafter.

From a historical perspective, the day of redemption is the day the way was opened wide to Hasidism, which from then on grew stronger and spread prodigiously. This day is indeed "Rosh HaShana for Hasidism," the day that marks the commencement of a period in which Hasidism grew stronger and expanded, including in its ranks tens of thousands of new adherents. It marks the beginning of a new period, when the animosity and active conflict died out, so that even those outside its ranks no longer oppose (*mitnaged*) it, but, rather, respect it as one of the groups that comprise the Jewish People and bring it honor.

THE TRIAL IN THE HEAVENLY COURT

Despite the importance of *yod-tet* Kislev as "Rosh HaShana for Hasidism," that conception likewise does not entirely express the essence of the day.

All the events of history are directed by supernatural forces, even the smallest matters and minor incidents; "one does not bruise his finger below unless it is decreed on high."[1] This is all the more true regarding events of decisive historical importance, which are surely directed by Providence and whose every turn is interconnected with the divine. Our sages teach that the wars in our world result from the wars between the celestial princes of the nations in a world higher than our own.[2] Indeed, it is true in general that external conflict arises out of a cause more

1. *Ḥullin* 7b.
2. See the commentators on Daniel 10:20–21.

fundamental than its outward manifestations; conflicting views are deeper than those that are visible and apparent to the eye.

The inner basis of the conflict between the Hasidim and their opponents was to what extent it is permissible or desirable to reveal the concepts of Hasidism to all Jews. The great concern was that the spread of the Ba'al Shem Tov's approach among the masses – the simple and even ignorant – might lead to a decline instead of to an uplift. It was feared that the Ba'al Shem Tov's views about the manifestation of Godliness in all things and about the eminence of every Jew qua Jew might lead to a lack of restraint, decline in Torah study, and disrespect toward Heaven if preached to those not qualified to comprehend matters on the requisite intellectual level.

This indictment of the revealing of Hasidism is not just a concern voiced by the Jewish leaders of that generation. It is, in fact, a fundamental question that warrants judgment. Are we truly fit to receive these conceptualizations? Was the disclosure of the Hasidic approach the means to ascent and uplift, or was it unsuitable for that end? Is it possible that the disclosure, which was not made at the right time and place, did more damage than good?

This is the question to which Hasidism was subjected, and this is the indictment to which it was compelled to respond.

It is no wonder that the person on whom it fell to be the Hasidim's representative in this judgment was our Master and Teacher, in whose teachings the revelation of the Hasidic approach plays a greater and more pronounced role than in any other branch of Hasidism.

Heavenly judgments do not remain exclusively in the upper worlds; they are also manifested below, in this world. Like other manifestations of divine emanation, these judgments descend, unfolding from level to level and from world to world until eventually reaching its lowest level in our world.

The subtle spiritual indictment of Hasidism, the abstract concern that perhaps the time had not yet come for the disclosures of Hasidism, and the trial as to whether the Hasidim indeed attained uplift through the approach they preached – all this descended from level to level, until reaching the crudest form. The heavenly indictment was expressed in this world in the form of rude slander, and the trial was held by the Russian government, yet, in its inner essence, this trial was the heavenly trial about Hasidism, and the verdict, in which our Master and Teach was exonerated, was an echo and shadow of the heavenly verdict. Hasidism was vindicated in the upper chamber; the earthly government merely expressed the verdict of the heavenly court in worldly form.

In this respect, the day of *yod-tet* Kislev – the day of judgment for Hasidism and the day of its exoneration in the Heavenly court – is "Rosh HaShana for Hasidism," for the movement was put on trial and merited to be vindicated. Not only were its main ideas deemed acceptable, its outward manifestation and expression in the lives of Hasidim everywhere and in every age were as well.

In the Ba'al Shem Tov's vision in the chamber of the Messiah,[3] he was told that the coming of the Messiah depends on "when your [the Ba'al Shem Tov's] springs overflow abroad." Thus, spreading Hasidism in the world and its disclosure among the masses is the key to bringing near the redemption.

The heavenly trial, then, was a trial about the ways in which God's light should be revealed in the world and about bringing near the redemption. The verdict below, which delivered Hasidism from its physical straits, was also the heavenly verdict that Hasidism should be revealed in the world and, moreover, that through Hasidism there would be a revelation of divine light and the bringing near of the universal redemption.

Hence, this is the "Festival of Redemption" on many levels; indeed, it is a festival of universal redemption, representing the entire world's deliverance from its straits and limitations.

3. Cited in *Ben Porat Yosef*, p. 127, *Keter Shem Tov* p. 1.

Ḥanukka

A Stiff-Necked People

WHAT IS ḤANUKKA?

In the *"Al HaNisim"* prayer recited in the *Amida* and Grace after Meals prayers of the Ḥanukka festival, a detailed description is given of the Hasmonean wars, beginning with the religious persecutions and followed by the battles, the victory over the Greeks, the purification of the Sanctuary, and its eventual consecration.

Judging from this prayer, this war appears to be the main point of the festival, certainly more important than the miracle of the flask of oil mentioned in the Talmud.[1] The war is the reason for the institution of the festival; hence, each year upon the advent of Ḥanukka, this war resurfaces in our memory.

What is the meaning of the war that was waged in those days, and what is the nature of the victory that was won, which we are to celebrate in our own time?

In order to gain a deep understanding of what happened in the days of Mattathias, the High Priest, one need only look around at the present situation in our generation. Today – more than in any previous generation – we can understand the atmosphere that prevailed in that

1. *Shabbat* 21b.

time, as the culture that surrounds us penetrates our midst. Now more than ever, we can understand the meaning of this war and the issues that were the focus of the struggle.

WORLD-WIDE CULTURE

In order to consolidate the power of their empire, the Greeks transformed the lower expressions of Hellenistic culture – language, lifestyle, gods – into universal culture. They destroyed temples of other gods and fought against other belief systems, but not for religious reasons; rather, their goal was to combine the Greek culture and cult with the local forms of the same.

Hellenistic culture was indeed successful in blending into the local culture of the Sidonians, the Philistines, and many other nations throughout the empire, from India to Egypt. The enlightened among the nations of the world had in any case ceased believing in their own gods, whose cults they regarded as mere popular folklore. In their eyes, remaining faithful to a certain god was not an issue; on the contrary, there was an attitude of openness to other cultures, to additional gods and cults. To be sure, there were differences between the gods and rites of the various nations, but since they were all equally devoid of truth and meaning, there was no contradiction between them. The blending of cultures was therefore possible, and even deemed desirable for the sake of international relations.

The general attitude toward the Hellenistic orientation is witnessed today, when the universal culture radiates tolerance and enlightenment. For most people today, one's way of life is not a matter of much significance; when someone does not truly believe in the path he follows, and his fellow man likewise does not believe in his own divergent path, the two of them have no trouble living in peace with each other. Tolerance toward everything does not indicate respect for others' principles, but rather a general devaluation of principles, which makes possible the acceptance of foreign and even opposing ideas.

WHAT IS A JEW?

Although the war against the Greeks brought the Jews political independence, the background for the outbreak of the rebellion was not national or political. For hundreds of years, the Jews had lived in the Land of Israel under foreign rule, and concepts of liberation and independence had not constituted cause for war. Nor was the war waged against the Greek language or against Greek culture as a whole. The bone of contention was much more a matter of principle; there was something about the nature of the Greek attitude that did not allow the Jews to continue living under their rule.

Tolerance and mutual acceptance were the guiding principles of Hellenistic culture. The Greeks demanded that the Jews be open toward their gods and their views, just as they themselves were prepared to be tolerant toward the Jewish cult. The Greek religious persecutions were not ideologically motivated. On the contrary, the Greeks tried to force our ancestors to apostasy as a result of a world view that does not regard principles and ideology as sacrosanct. The Greeks thought that the Jews' opposition to pig meat and to Zeus was no more than obstinacy on the part of uneducated people. Hence, they tried to compel them to give up their foolishness and behave properly.

The Jewish way, however, is in its essence intolerant. The Jew denies the very existence of other gods, and certainly cannot accept any kind of combination with them. The *Midrash Raba* expounds the name of Mordekhai *HaYehudi* (the Jew): "Why was he called '*Yehudi*'? Because he repudiated the worship of other gods."[2] It appears that the basis of this midrash is the interchangeability of the letters ה and ח; the definition of יהודי (*Yehudi*, Jew) is thus יחידי (*yeḥidi*, singular). In Judaism, there is singularity, because by its very definition it excludes any other faith.

The same point is illustrated in the halakha's requirements regarding "sanctification of the divine name." According to the halakha, a Jew may transgress any of the mitzvot of the Torah in order to save his life, with the exception of the three most serious transgressions: worship of other gods, forbidden sexual relations, and murder. However, at a time of religious persecution, one must give up his life even if demanded only to deviate from a Jewish custom. Even though it is not a mitzva

2. *Esther Raba* 6:2.

but only a custom, one must give up one's life rather than change one's shoelace to a different color![3]

When there is an attempt to strike at matters of principle, the Jew cannot compromise. At a time of religious persecution, our adherence to principle is on trial, and at such a time we must stress that our whole essence lies in the fact that we cannot be flexible one iota.

It appears that there can be no compromise between the Jewish conception, which cannot yield its exclusiveness and has no option of negotiation, and that of the Greeks, to whom no value is sacred except for the ability to tolerate all values.

SENSIBLE JUDAISM

The first Jewish Hellenists were not public transgressors or troublemakers, but rather people who were prepared to be flexible about their Judaism. The Hellenists essentially "abandoned God and His anointed," but they had not yet given up their Jewish way of life. They assumed a flexible scale of values, and their attitude was, "This is the path I follow and in which I am comfortable, but it has its limits."

To them, Judaism is a world in which it is possible to live as long as it is bounded by limits, boundaries that each person sets for himself. If there is something in Judaism that is incompatible with their world view, out of step with current thinking, or – forefend – intolerant, that part of Judaism must be set aside.

Nowadays, such people would be called the "sensible religious." They retain certain habits from the parental home for which society is willing to forgive them, since everyone knows that they do not take these habits seriously. Everyone knows that, when push comes to shove, these Jews will not stand by their Judaism to the very end.

In the eyes of these Jews, Judaism is just another habit among many others. Some people are accustomed to wearing clothing of a certain color or shape, but other than habit, there is no real reason for their doing so. Needless to say, if one day they are requested to dress differently, they will meet the request and not stubbornly resist. Judaism is liable to be viewed in the same way – as a collection of customs

3. *Sanhedrin* 74b.

that are of no real importance and of only sentimental value. Even if a person and the members of his household wish to follow these customs, that commitment is only up to a certain point; he certainly will not be willing to give up his life for them.

Even before they became infidels, the Hellenists did something much more basic – they abandoned Judaism's uncompromising exclusiveness.

In our day, if someone were to rise up and act as Mattathias did, an advertisement condemning the act would presumably appear in the newspapers in the name of all sensible religious Jews. Such an advertisement may have appeared in the Hasmonean period as well, signed by the High Priest and other personages: "The Jewish leadership strongly condemns this act, which to our minds brings dishonor to Judaism. This is the act of a few fanatics, who are neither to be emulated nor supported."

In fact, at the outset, the Hasmonean revolt was not supported by the majority of Jews in the Land of Israel; the rebels comprised approximately ten percent of the Jewish population. Yet their willingness to give up their lives for the mitzvot of the Torah and their rejection of compromise under any circumstances led them into a war against the Greek empire.

AT THIS TIME

On the festival of Ḥanukka, we celebrate the Hasmonean victory over the Greeks and the Hellenism that spread among the Jewish People. Each year during this festival, we are reminded that we must continue the struggle to maintain our singularity – particularly in our time, when we are faced with the very same issue. Ḥanukka marks the encounter between a stiff-necked, intolerant Jewish people and an open, tolerant world.

The Hellenistic world was very much like our own. Neither world has major values of significance; hence, neither is marked by the clash of opposing values. There is no conflict between beauty and truth, between science and Torah, or between technological progress and preservation of the existing order. The conflict with Hellenism was much simpler, like our conflict with the world in which we live today.

In our day, most people do not accept world culture out of belief in and recognition of the truths of its philosophy, but because of widely accepted norms; similarly, in those days, most Hellenists did not accept Greek culture out of faith. A certain percentage of the population accepts this outlook of flexibility as a principle; others see that society behaves this way, and they are influenced by its approach. Finally, this outlook penetrates even people who are basically believers. Gradually, they are convinced that the correct attitude toward principles is: "I respect your way; now you, too, respect mine."

In the world today, everything is negotiable; a compromise can be reached about every issue, because values are relative and of no real importance. All values are equivalent to one another, because there is a limit to the degree of one's investment in them.

Conversely, the celebration of Ḥanukka is built on the assumption that there is such a thing as a Jew and that the Jewish essence cannot be compromised. Moreover, it is rooted in the principle that I must agree that the essence of a Jew is found within me as well.

In commemoration of the Jewish victory over Hellenism, we celebrate Ḥanukka as the festival of those people who are still moved by zeal for their Judaism. Ḥanukka is perceived by the public as a pleasant holiday, for it entails many delights and hardly any duties, but in essence, it is a religious-zealous holiday!

The direct result of the war that we recall and celebrate on Ḥanukka was Judaism's survival. Had the Hasmoneans not undertaken the struggle, or had they lost it, it is reasonable to assume that our fate would have been like that of the other peoples of the region – the Philistines, Ammonites, and Moabites – who assimilated to the point of the loss of their ethnic identity and their disappearance from the stage of history. The war was over the preservation of Jewish selfhood; miraculously, we have thus far prevailed in this aim.

Wars, victories, and defeats are historical events, and just as they unfold before our eyes, so do they vanish from historical memory. Jewish statehood was lost at least twice, and the Jews wandered countless times from place to place, yet we remained alive. If, however, the people's distinctiveness is lost – even if only once – then it no longer matters whether we have territory or a flag. Without the people, we have nothing.

On Ḥanukka, then as now, we struggle not for our independence, but for our selfhood. Our victory in war more than two thousand years ago entailed more than our survival. We are not just a race that survives, but a complete spiritual entity called "Judaism," which continues to pulsate with life.

Tu BiShevat

Man – The Tree of the Field

THE NEW YEAR FOR TREES

The *Tikunei Zohar* teaches:

> You created heaven and earth, trees and grasses and human beings, so that the higher worlds could be known through them ... and so the higher worlds could be known through the lower worlds.[1]

The Holy One, blessed be He, created all the various elements of this world so that by contemplating them we could recognize the higher worlds, for all the lower worlds, to the very last detail, are a descent and downward gradation from the higher ones. The entire universe is designed like a map, but its meaning remains concealed; God did not clearly explain how and what we may learn from each thing. We therefore must study and investigate on our own what it is that the creations of this world teach us.

Many verses indicate that there is a connection between the tree and man, often comparing them to one another: "For the [existence of]

1. *Tikunei Zohar*, Introduction, *"Pataḥ Eliyahu,"* 17a.

man is the tree of the field;"[2] "He is like a tree planted beside streams of water;"[3] "He will be like a lone tree in the desert."[4] It appears, then, that much can be learned about man, his soul, and his manner of worship by observing trees and their growth. *Tu BiShevat*, the New Year for the trees, when we focus on our bond with the Land of Israel and our love for it and its plant life, is an opportunity to focus on learning from the trees.

"LIKE A TREE PLANTED"

One element of comparison between trees and man relates to the tree's connection to the earth. Just as the tree grows in the earth and is like one of its creations, man similarly has "soil" from which he draws sustenance. And just as a tree that is detached from the earth will surely die, so, too, man – the individual as well as the community – cannot survive in detachment, as a self-contained creature.

One of the basic sources of modern man's suffering is his lack of social belonging. The personal loneliness that many feel and the general sense of alienation that people experience nowadays are expressions of the fact that man has ceased to be "planted in the earth."

Today, most social affiliation is based on practical need, not meaningful values. People join groups to protect their common interests, but this is almost like professional affiliation; they do not feel that this is their home, that there is a place in which they are planted. The social unit comes together as a contingency to build mutual defensive and offensive mechanisms, but no more than that. Many people are like nomads who incidentally arrive at a certain place, but there is no meaningful tie that binds them to it. They feel no special relationship with their place, and are therefore easily uprooted. In a certain sense, modern people are like plastic decorative plants, which are lifeless and therefore can "flower" without any need of the earth.

This reality results from the aspiration to the ideal of personal freedom; the individual wishes to detach himself from any social bond and endeavors to turn himself into the essence and foundation of all

2. Deuteronomy 20:19; see *Sifrei* and Ibn Ezra loc. cit.
3. Psalms 1:3.
4. Jeremiah 17:6.

existence. The insistence on the right to be an independent individualist allows one to adapt everywhere equally, because in any case one does not truly belong anywhere.

Verses in Psalms describe the *tzaddik* as a tree planted in excellent soil, a comely tree that bears good fruit: "The righteous bloom like a date-palm, they thrive like a cedar in Lebanon. Planted in the House of God, they flourish in the courts of our Lord;"[5] "He is like a tree planted beside streams of water."[6] A person who is connected to a place and has a positive relationship and a commitment to his surroundings has a chance to develop, blossom, and be fruitful.

By contrast, the wicked person is cursed that he will be "like tumbleweed, like straw before the wind."[7] He will be like a dry shrub that is uprooted and driven by the wind from place to place. One whose life is not built upon a lasting root feels that relationships and commitments shackle, imprison, and suffocate him. Such a person chooses to live like a hewn tree – a life that draws no nourishment from any source, does not develop in any direction, and cannot truly be termed life at all.

The same phenomenon is discernible on a larger historical plane as well, in particular in the great rebellions within Jewish society during the last few generations. Part of the social essence of the Jewish People was always the sense that a Jew is planted in ground from which he draws sustenance and on which he tries to build. Even when a process of renewal unfolds, there is never transformation into a completely new creature; a part of the past is always preserved. An analogy to this may be drawn from the rings on a tree trunk, which attest that despite all the renewal and growth of new branches and leaves, the tree has not replaced its essential self of old, but has only added new layers to it.

During the last few generations, the Jewish People has undergone a revolution of detachment based on the conception that the past is repulsive and shameful. For ideological and practical reasons, people severed all connection with their past; as a result, their children had no ability to get to know their larger family and identify with their roots.

5. Psalms 92:13.
6. Ibid. 1:3
7. Ibid. 83:14.

Some intentionally cut off their connection with the past, while others were subjected to this process without their knowledge, at times even under duress or by deceit.

Thus was created a disengaged and rootless reality, and this is the reason many today have a sense of displacement from their past. This is a major reason for the inability of many people to identify with their own Judaism.

In order to fill the void created as a result of this great detachment, one must make a personal effort to find soil from which to draw sustenance – a kind of home and homeland. There is no choice but to search for, or at least reconstruct, a place and an atmosphere from which one can draw nourishment and thereby grow.

UNTO OLD AGE

Another aspect of analogy between man and tree lies in the verse, "The days of My people shall be [as long] as the days of a tree."[8]

A healthy, un-grafted tree may live for more than two thousand years. In fact, there are trees known to be four thousand years old! It is actually not clear what causes the death of a tree at all; as long as the tree's life is not ended by an accident or some other external event, it has the potential to continue living for a great many years.

Not only can a tree reach an extremely old age, but it can even bear fruit at such an age. Even very old trees continue to be fruitful, and the quality and quantity of their fruit does not seem to be impaired by their age.

The normal course of a human being's life, on the other hand, is slightly different. A person's development starts with a process of growth, but even before he reaches full maturity, a process of aging and deterioration sets in. Unlike trees, we do not grow all our lives. At a relatively early stage, a decline begins, and the period of maturity and fertility is usually quite limited.

The "days of My people" – and no other nation – are compared to the days of the ever-growing tree, which continues to bear fruit even after reaching the age of four thousand years. Other nations grow, peak,

8. Isaiah 65:22.

decline, and die, but the days of the Jewish People are days of continual growth.

This is true for the Jewish People, and it is true for the individual. The individual Jew never "retires," neither as a human being nor as a Jew. As long as he lives, he should continue to blossom, grow, develop, and, above all, bear fruit. A person who is healthy and not beset with special impairments is expected to continue being fruitful until the Angel of Death cuts him down; this is the essence of "the days of a tree."

Every person has a period of growth and development, followed by a period in which he is fruitful – provided we are dealing with a living tree and not a block of wood. In this regard, one must remember that the first fruits of every tree are forbidden as "*orla*."[9] Similarly, the first things that a person accomplishes at a young age may be "*orla*;" they have not developed to the degree necessary. As he continues to grow, however, there comes a time when his fruits have properly ripened.

THEY ARE OUR LIFE

On the surface, it seems as though a tree draws sustenance for its growth from the earth, using the water it drinks to circulate the nutrients. In reality, however, we know that trees draw their nourishment mainly from the air and sunlight. Trees need water, of course, and they must be planted in soil, but they do not "eat" soil or compost. Even the largest of trees builds nutrients primarily from air and sun, using the products to form leaves, branches and its trunk.

In other words, we may say that the tree lives basically from above – via the leaves that absorb the oxygen and the sunlight – and not from below – via the roots, which fulfill the secondary role of conveying water.

The fruits that we eat were formed from sun and air, although our consumption of them is tangible, physical. The entire world is nourished by plant products, whose source of life and growth is the intangible.

"Man is the tree of the field:" Man, too, lives mainly from above, not from below, from this world. The basis of our existence, like that of the tree, is intangible. Essentially, our life is made up of higher things,

9. See Leviticus 19:23.

not of those things that seem to be its basic elements. The latter are merely instruments.

This is an important distinction: "For they are our life and the length of our days;"[10] "It is your life."[11] The physical things that seem to us to be the basis of our lives are not the main elements; their whole purpose is only to prepare, to assist, to help us do the important things.

A person must know where his life truly lies, what is primary and what is secondary. People generally see themselves from the neck down, whereas what is above the neck is not of primary importance to them. In reality, our lives as human beings are based and depend on the part above the neck; that is the part where life takes place.

This is not a simple distinction, because the other parts of our lives take up more space. Nevertheless, we must remember that beyond all those elements, there is another, higher center, on which everything depends.

BRANCHES AND ROOTS

Another quality common to all trees is the relation and proportion between roots and branches. This relation and its human parallel is noted in *Pirkei Avot*: "Everyone whose wisdom is greater than his deeds, to what may he be compared? To a tree that has many branches and few roots. The wind comes, uproots it, and overturns it."[12]

A tree that develops many branches without developing roots must be pruned in order to preserve a proper ratio between them. Since a person has no gardener to prune him, he has no choice but to develop roots. When he reaches a certain level, when he has sprouted many branches, he must make sure that this growth is matched in his roots – in his actions in the world of action. If he neglects his roots, he will lose his stability and balance, and will likely be uprooted.

All parts of the tree – its long branches, green leaves, and sweet fruit – grow only by virtue of the roots. The roots are not visible, not lovely, and not tasty, but they are set in the ground and connect it to

10. From the blessings that precede the *Shema* in the Evening Service.
11. Deuteronomy 32:47.
12. *Avot* 3:17.

the rest of the tree. Tree roots are among the strongest things that exist; they can even split rock. The branches, with all their magnificence and glory, lack such strength.

Man should learn from trees and always maintain the right proportion between his wisdom, dreams, and aspirations on the one hand, and his practical life – his activity in and hold on the world – on the other.

This principle applies also to the life of the nation as a whole. The branches represent the leaders, who must realize that without roots – without caring for the margins of society, for the children and for the underprivileged, and without a hold in practical life – there is no chance of survival for the upper echelon. For every branch that shoots upward, the people as a whole and each individual must put down roots below.

THE CASTING OF LEAVES

When observing trees, one may notice that a tree that looks sizable and promising in the summer looks much less impressive in the fall. After all the leaves have fallen, all that remains is the trunk and a few branches. The mighty oak is tall and beautiful, but come autumn, it looks like a dead log, and some people might even cut it down. If, however, it is known that it is a living tree, which in due time will foliate once again, people will not give up on it so quickly.

The same thing may happen to a human being. A person may reach the autumn of his life, when everything dries up and falls away. Everything he thought he had attained, accomplished, built, and grown is blown off in the wind, and he is left like an empty vessel. In such a situation, one must remember not to cut down the tree; it will grow back again, if only given the time and the opportunity.

Many people faced with such a predicament are deterred from moving forward. They think that something in them is dead, and that they cannot possibly be revived. A person may give up on himself entirely, just because his vitality is quieted for a year or more. It thus happens that people commit sins, fall, and lose themselves merely because of the thought that "I am a withered tree."[13] In reality, however, a tree, after losing its foliage, can revive and become no less beautiful than before.

13. Isaiah 56:3

This process of withering and revival is part of the tree's nature; it casts off its leaves, but is rejuvenated in due time. Time is similarly necessary for the rebirth of a human being; we cannot expect that one who went astray will awaken immediately to renewed growth. If the slumber of a tree lasts half a year, that of a human being may last much longer. Recollection that this period eventually ends and is, in fact, followed by renewed bloom is encouraging and life-giving.

Purim

"Your Miracles Which Are with Us Daily"[1]

THE MEGILLA – WITHIN THE LAWS OF NATURE

In our liturgy on Purim, we emphasize the miraculous nature of the day's event. We add the *"Al HaNisim"* ("For the Miracles") prayer in the *Amida* and in the Grace after Meals, and before reading the Megilla we recite the blessing, "Who performed miracles for our fathers." Yet there does not seem to be even one miracle in the entire *Megillat Esther*! The Megilla describes a sequence of events that, to be sure, makes an outstanding narrative, but the whole story can be explained in a this-worldly manner, without recourse to miracles and wonders.

Some narratives are written with deliberate gaps and omissions, but the story of the Megilla has no holes. In the Megilla, all the stages of the story can be clearly seen, and one can grasp how they are each built upon the other. The narrative structure is complete, the story unfolds naturally and comprehensibly from beginning to end. There is no narrative climax, no miraculous event at the peak of the narrative. All the details are closely knit together, and all the vicissitudes can be explained rationally.

One might argue that some of the events in the Megilla are

1. From the *Amida* prayer.

illogical, perhaps even miraculous, but upon examination, it becomes clear that they in particular are most lucid and logical.

MORDEKHAI'S PROMOTION

Esther did not become a savior as an afterthought, but was rather planted in the palace, as can be seen from Mordekhai's words to her, "Who knows, perhaps you have attained to royal position for just such a crisis."[2] Mordekhai the Jew, who sat in the palace gate and lived in the royal court, arranged in advance that he would have a secret agent in the king's palace. Mordekhai belonged to the upper echelons of the Persian government – in his own right and as the representative of the Jews. He was a politician with a long-term strategy, and he prepared the ground for the time when he would reach a position of power.

The incident of Bigthan and Teresh, which at first appears entirely irrelevant to the main plot, was similarly part of a well-planned strategy. Mordekhai's report demonstrated loyalty to the crown and was a good investment in establishing the right connections that could be used in the future to open a channel through which to reach the king.

THE KING'S RING

The fact that the king grants unlimited power to others – first Haman and then Mordekhai – appears strange, but in fact was based purely on political motives. The government in the Persian kingdom was autocratic, but although the king had unlimited power and authority, he could not deal with all the complex affairs of the kingdom even when he was sober and not preoccupied with his lusts. The policy of the Persian kings was therefore to appoint deputies, to whom they granted the power and authority to sign on anything in their name.[3]

Obviously, such deputies posed a danger to the king more than anyone else in the kingdom, and the king could not allow anyone to grow too strong. One of the ways of dealing with this problem was to replace these powerful deputies from time to time. In addition, the policy was

2. Esther 4:14.
3. This practice was widespread in other kingdoms as well. For example, an identical relationship existed between Joseph and Pharaoh, the king of Egypt.

to choose people of foreign origin for these roles, as they had no base of power or support in Persian society. Such people could be relied upon because they would do everything they could to further the interests of the king who promoted them, and they could not seize control, for they did not have popular support. When such a person achieves a victory, it is the king who profits, and when he suffers a defeat, the defeat is at his own expense.

Haman thus reached a position of power because he was an Agagite – a foreigner, a social nothing. Evidence of this can be adduced from the fact that hanging him was a simple matter; no one protested his execution. For this same reason, Mordekhai reached such a position as well; he, too, was a foreigner – a Jew.

ESTHER'S MANEUVER

If we examine Esther's actions, we discover the same consistency and clarity that characterize the whole narrative.

In the extremely dangerous game that Esther plays, on which she stakes her life, she attempts to portray Haman, the most important man in the kingdom besides the king, as too important and too powerful. Ahasuerus need not be especially smart or suspicious to feel uncomfortable at the party she throws, to which only one other man besides himself is invited – his ambitious deputy. Haman's fall upon the couch is another drop in a bucket that is already overfull.

Haman, on his part, commits a double error. First, he errs in his interest that Ahasuerus kill Mordekhai. At this stage of the narrative, although the king does not yet know Mordekhai personally, he is sure of Mordekhai's loyalty. Haman's second error is his suggestion for what should be done for "the man whom the king desires to honor."[4] In a country like Persia, where the king was considered a semi-divine being, the suggestion that someone else should be allowed to ride on the king's horses and be attired in royal garb is simply astounding in its brazenness; it is tantamount to sedition.[5] Haman thus greatly increases Ahasuerus' suspicions of him and hastens his own end.

4. Esther 6:6–9.

5. Even according to Jewish law, which hardly deifies the king, no one except the king

Haman's hanging at Ahasuerus's command is likewise logical and to be expected. In fact, it would have been surprising had Haman not been executed; he became a candidate for the gallows the moment he was appointed – ever since the king promoted and advanced him above all the officials, his hanging was only a matter of time. When such a man becomes too powerful, his demise is part of the natural course.

EXTERMINATING AND SAVING THE JEWS

Even the plan to exterminate the Jews is natural for King Ahasuerus, and the same goes for saving them.

In Ahasuerus' view, the wine feast is an important matter, while politics is something minor and peripheral. When Haman complains to him about the Jews, Ahasuerus hardly knows what he is talking about. He does not care and it does not interest him whether thousands of people are killed. His main concern is the royal treasury, and if Haman promises to underwrite the cost of the bottles of wine for the rest of Ahasuerus's reign, he has no reason not to agree.

When Haman is hanged, his property is presumably confiscated for the king's benefit. Since the king will receive the money pledged in any case, he does not have to kill the Jews as Haman had planned. In fact, it is better that they should remain alive and continue to pay taxes!

NO MIRACLES

All the points that we have raised – and one can cite many others – teach us the extent to which the Megilla is written as a story in which all the events are clear, natural, and consistent.

Of course, the sense of God's presence pervades the narrative, despite the absence of His name from the Megilla. There is fasting, there is prayer and lamentation, and there is faith in deliverance – but there are no miracles. The contrast with the other stories of the Bible – replete with miracle narratives, a large portion of which involve deviation from the laws of nature – is striking.

---

himself may ride on the king's horses, and when the king dies his horses are killed or disabled.

This point can be brought into sharper focus by comparing the miracle of Purim to that of Ḥanukka.

Ḥanukka and Purim are similar in that neither is a festival by Torah law, and "*Al HaNisim*" is recited on both holidays. On Ḥanukka, we elaborate: "You delivered the strong into the hands of the weak, the impure into the hands of the pure, and the arrogant into the hands of those who occupy themselves with Your Torah." The main focus is the military victory, a victory that is remarkable in that those who were not supposed to win won nevertheless. While the miracle of Ḥanukka was not a miracle in the sense of the breaching of the laws of nature, there is a wondrous aspect to it.

By contrast, nothing appears wondrous about Purim. It is a story that could – and, in some aspects, must – happen all the time.

NES AND PELE

To explain the miracle of Purim, which we have celebrated for almost Two and a half thousand years, we must distinguish between two kinds of events: *nes* and *pele*.

A *pele* is something out of the ordinary, unnatural, not in keeping with the way of the world. A *nes* is generally defined this way as well, but a *nes* is not necessarily supernatural (and conversely, a supernatural event need not be a *nes*).

These two concepts may overlap, but they are certainly not identical. We may say that a *pele* is what does not lend itself to logical explanation, whereas a *nes* is a significant event, whether it occurs within the framework of the laws of nature or outside of that framework. The essential element of the *nes* is its significance; its naturalness or supernaturalness is merely the mechanism of the occurrence. On the theological level, it can be said that to omnipotent God, it makes no difference what the mechanism of the *nes* is; hence, to us, too, it should make no difference. What matters is what happened, not how it happened.

This entails a change of conception, for even an event that occurs in keeping with all the laws of nature can still be deemed significant. This is, in fact, the implication of the "*HaGomel*" blessing recited in thanksgiving for deliverance from danger. It is not that the recovery from illness, for example, was miraculous, but that it was significant, and what is significant is what becomes *nes*-like. The definition of a *nes* hinges not on the rarity of the occurrence and its implausibility, but on its importance. When an occurrence has significance, it enters the category of a *nes*, even if it has no miraculous aspect.

Three times a day, we say, "We will give thanks to You and declare Your praise...and for Your miracles (*nisim*) which are with us daily." What are these daily miracles? After all, not every day does one experience the miraculous abridgement of a journey, nor does manna fall from heaven for everyone. Strange and incomprehensible events do not occur every day. Clearly, the reference is to miracles in the sense of significant events; such events occur literally at every moment, and for them we must give thanks.

This is one of the reasons for the sages' statement that even if all the festivals are nullified, Ḥanukka and Purim will never be abrogated.[6] Ḥanukka and Purim are unique because they are festivals on which we celebrate and offer thanks for "non-miraculous" miracles.

Some have termed this type of miracle a "hidden miracle," but in truth, it is not a hidden miracle. The miracle is actually quite revealed, since the definition of a miracle hinges on the fact of a great deliverance for Israel.

In *Megillat Esther*, all the developments are explained in great detail. All the parts are on display; nothing is missing. Everything appears in such a way that it has a precise cause and effect, and every event is connected to the one that follows in a logical fashion. Every part stands in its natural place; every twist leads in a certain direction. And yet, every aspect is miraculous.

PRAYER – FOR WHAT?

As we noted, although God's name does not appear in the *Megilla* at all, reference is made to God indirectly. Esther directs Mordekhai to pray and to fast, and says that she and her maidens will also fast and plead for God's aid. When the characters want certain things to happen, it is necessary to pray for God's help.

But when they pray and seek God's assistance, their intention is

6. The Midrash on Proverbs 9.

not that lightning should suddenly descend from heaven and kill Haman, nor that Ahasuerus should suddenly turn into pickled herring.

Thus, right after the fasting and the lamentation, Esther puts on the most beautiful apparel that she has and tries to attract Ahasuerus to the best of her ability. On the one hand, she relies on God's help; at the same time, nature follows its usual course. There is no attempt to alter or shift the ways of nature. Mordekhai and Esther petition and pray precisely for "Your miracles which are with us daily," not for wonders and a change in the order of nature.

Experience of past generations shows that after supernatural wonders, things return to the way they were, and no significant changes are affected. In this respect, it is precisely the realistic miracles that can lead to the positive result and genuine change of "The Jews confirmed and accepted,"[7] when they confirmed anew what they had accepted at Sinai.[8]

An extraordinary phenomenon is perhaps remembered for a long while, but as a curiosity, and no more than that. The people who saw the fire descend from heaven in the time of Elijah surely spoke of the event for years afterward, but the event had little influence. By contrast, it is the miracles that "are with us daily" that affect the significant changes.

Although the wondrous miracles occur by the direct intervention of God's supreme power and without human intervention, it is clear that the second type of miracle is no less important. The main thing is that there should be a *nes* – that something should happen, without it necessarily being extraordinary.

OTHER MIRACLES

In the time of the First Temple, miracles generally occurred in an unnatural way. Israel's deliverance in the days of Hezekiah came about when all of Sennacherib's soldiers turned into a pile of corpses overnight. This was an entirely wondrous and miraculous deliverance, but the Jewish people did not ultimately become more attached to the Torah as a result.

In the time of the Second Temple, there were far fewer wonders, but there were many "natural" miracles. Because these miracles were

7. Esther 9:27.
8. *Shabbat* 88a.

miracles that required that people pray for them, they are remembered and observed.

Natural miracles did not cease in the time of Mordekhai and Esther and in the time of Mattathias and his sons; rather, they continue throughout the generations. In these times, God in effect says, "I no longer wish to show you miracles that even a simpleton would notice, declaring, 'Look! It's a miracle!' Now you will see miracles that you will have to examine and study."

Apparently, such miracles have a deeper effect. The "confirmation and acceptance" of the Jews in Mordekhai's time endures, while the influence of "HaShem alone is God"[9] was only temporary.

THE FADING SENSE OF MIRACULOUSNESS

As soon as one gets used to something, its miraculous nature fades, along with the sense of wonderment.

In the wilderness, the people of Israel within a short time grew accustomed to the manna and were no longer amazed by its daily fall from heaven. When Eve gave birth to Cain, she exulted, "I have made a human being together with God!"[10] Every subsequent birth is no less of a miracle, but since it has become a common event, we tend to take it for granted.

It can be argued, then, that what we term "supernatural" or "miraculous" is simply something that we are not yet accustomed to. The truth is that it does not matter whether the occurrence is considered "natural" or "supernatural;" what is important is how we perceive it.

We recite many blessings over things that to us seem ordinary and routine – opening the eyes upon awakening, the ability to stretch and stand erect, the ability to get up and walk, and so forth. These things seem ordinary because, in the midst of the routine, their significance tends to get lost, even though in truth it remains ever in place.

As a rule, we discover the great importance of routine things only when we are deprived of them. It is only when one's leg hurts, making

9. I Kings, 18:39.
10. Genesis 4:1.

walking difficult, that one realizes the significance of the blessing "Who makes firm the steps of man."

When the people of Israel walked on dry land, they never sensed that there was anything miraculous about it. Only when they walked "on dry land in the midst of the sea"[11] did they appreciate the miracle that even the mundane aspect entails. We often need the extraordinary to restore to us the sense of the significance of ordinary things. When we see something that occurs under unusual circumstances, we reacquire the ability to see also the miraculous within the routine and the usual. The sudden shift is necessary to enable us to view what the routine covers up, to once again see what is truly important and what is not.

A NEW OUTLOOK ON REALITY

The miracles that God conveys in the ordinary course of nature, unfolding naturally and understandably, are the miracles that have the greatest effect on us. The Creator reveals Himself in all His glory precisely through the reality in which He creates, animates, and grants all of existence – and yet cannot be seen. In this sense, it is precisely nature and the natural mode of God's rule that reveal the heights of divine creativeness.

A similar phenomenon can be observed in historical processes. There are minor events that are forgotten because they play no role in shaping the future, there are major events and major figures that history remembers, and there are even greater matters which are so basic that we cannot define what they are and who was responsible for them. We do not know who first began to use fire or when, who invented the wheel and how. Paradoxically, the things that truly changed the world – the development of the earliest inventions and the evolution of our primary concepts – are the things about which we know nothing.

In this sense, nature as a whole is the greatest creation, for like every great creation, it is utterly unappreciated.

In order to be influenced by such natural miracles, one must be able to identify them; one must open his eyes and pay attention. The very fact that one makes an accounting of the events of his life, that he weighs

11. Exodus 15:19.

everything, large and small, and sees "Your miracles which are with us daily" – this elevates a person above and beyond his former station.

This rectification of the power of observation occurs on Purim, in the context of the theme of *venahafokh hu*, "and the opposite happened."[12] A person in a state of *nahafokh hu* is one who exists within a reality that follows the course of nature and the world order, but at the same time can assume a different way of looking at that reality, thereby uncovering the divine that conceals itself there.

This illumination of "Your miracles which are with us daily" is what we take with us from Purim onward.

12. Esther 9:1.

Scroll of the Exile

THE MEGILLA AS A MODEL

Purim is an anomaly among Jewish festivals. It differs from the other holidays in halakha, customs, and historical attitude, but most clearly in its original source – *Megillat Esther* itself. The anomalousness of the customs of Purim and *Megillat Esther* stand out all the more in comparison to Ḥanukka, the festival closest to Purim both chronologically and in meaning.

The books of Maccabees, although not included in the Biblical canon, belong to the conceptual and stylistic framework of the books of the Bible in terms of the nature of the narrated events, the character of the heroes, and the nature of the national-religious conflict in the background. In contrast, *Megillat Esther* is on the other side of the gulf that separates the sublime from the ridiculous. Its heroes are the inflated and light-headed Ahasuerus, the wicked and petty Haman, the beautiful Esther, who rises to glory as a sort of prototype of the Cinderella fairy tale, and Mordekhai the *tzaddik*, who becomes entangled in the intrigues of the royal court of an Oriental tyrant.

The commentators have noted the fact that nowhere in *Megillat Esther* is God's name mentioned, not even by epithet. It is no wonder, then, that our sages in the Mishnaic period were divided on the question of whether this book should be included among the Holy Scriptures.[1]

The explanation of all these peculiarities can be encapsulated in one point: the Jewish People in exile. Purim is the festival of the *galut*, and *Megillat Esther* is the book of the *galut*.

Megillat Esther is the prototype, the basic pattern of the Jewish People's life in exile. The story of *Megillat Esther*, its characters and events, seem to form a simplistic melodrama, an unrealistic legend. They take on true, serious, and even tragic meaning, however, when viewed within the totality of Jewish history – not just as a depiction of Mordekhai and Esther's period, but as part of the Jewish People's history in all the years of its exile.

Ahasuerus, the great king "who reigned over a hundred and twenty-seven provinces,"[2] "on the mainland and on the islands;"[3] who most of the time is preoccupied with feasts and with harems; who, out of ludicrous self-importance, proclaims edicts on every imaginable subject; who, unthinkingly and without regard to all the consequences entailed, decrees "to destroy, massacre, and exterminate all the Jews"[4] – is he a product of the imagination? In fact, there is almost no generation in which we do not encounter him, going by a different name, in a different country, and in other garb. Perhaps Ahasuerus in and of himself is a ludicrous and unimportant personality, but he symbolizes the fact that even an exceedingly foolish and weak tyrant can bring terrible disaster upon the Jewish People in *galut*.

The same goes for Haman, a character ornamented by the *Aggada* with additional stories about having been a barber for twenty-two years.[5] This nobody emerges as the de facto head of state and decides that personal animosity, superstition, or any other nonsense justifies harming the entire Jewish People. There is no need to search far afield in order to find this Haman again and again, very real and very menacing.

---

1. *Megilla* 7a.
2. Esther 1:1.
3. Ibid. 10:1.
4. Ibid. 3:13.
5. *Megilla* 16a.

In our eyes (and even in some passages in *Megillat Esther* itself, not to mention its Midrashic ornamentation), Haman is a comic figure. In our history, however, this figure is accompanied by a great deal of blood and tears. Haman's calumny – "There is a certain people, scattered and dispersed among the other peoples ... whose laws are different from those of every other people; they do not obey the king's laws. It is not in your majesty's interest to tolerate them"[6] – has not been improved upon much over the 2,500 years that have elapsed since then. With minor variations, it has been repeated in our time as well by various "Hamans" – Nazis and Communists, Moslems and Christians, all over the world. We no longer laugh at the worthless character of this demagogue, who was a barber and a bathhouse attendant; rather, we are scared of him.

We could elaborate and show how the bizarre, astonishing, and absurd story of *Megillat Esther* – which would have been funny had it not been so tragic – reoccurred, generation after generation, in various places in the world; how the Jewish People's deliverance was set in motion by those with the courage to intercede; how women like Esther or those of lesser eminence and stature served as props of salvation and deliverance.

Our sages have already stated that the heroes of the *Megilla* are not just characters in and of themselves: "Ahasuerus is the first of all sellers; Haman is the first of all buyers."[7] The *Megilla*'s personalities serve as prototypes for hundreds and thousands of others like them.

THE STORY OF THE GALUT

All these troubles stem from the fundamental evil of Israel's exilic existence. In exile, Israel is a people without real support, a people whose merits will always be overlooked and whose shortcomings will always be emphasized. Every whim of the ruler and every change of mood will always be directed against the eternal scapegoat.

The *galut* is a distinct period, a new era in Jewish history, different from all that we had known and experienced before. It defies a mere political definition of whether the Jews are in the Land of Israel or outside of it. Rather, *galut* defines an essential, inner part of our being: Is

6. Esther 3:8.
7. *Esther Raba*, introduction, s.v. 10, Rabbi Berekhia.

the *Shekhina* in its place, or is the *Shekhina* in exile, hiding elsewhere and in another form?

For this reason, Purim is a festival that is connected to the mystery of the "hiding God," Who hides in all things and is found on all sides simultaneously. This aspect of Purim is expressed symbolically by the name "Esther," in the sense of *hester*, hiddenness.

Megillat Esther, then, is the *Megilla* of the divine "hiding of the face," the *Megilla* of the Jewish People in exile, where the most dreadful threats to its existence begin, as it were, with comedy, and where the miracles that occur in the process of its deliverance likewise stem from the nature of the *galut*.

The story is told about the grandson of one of the Hasidic Masters, who came crying to his grandfather. "What happened?" asked the grandfather. The boy explained that he was playing hide-and-seek with his friends, but when he went to hide, no one came to search for him! Upon hearing this, the grandfather began to cry as well. For that is exactly what God says: "I am hiding, and no one comes to search for Me!"

One who hides wants others to search for him. When he announces that he is hiding, he is saying: "Perhaps you do not see me, but you can be sure that I am here."

This conception is the antithesis of the one expressed by several philosophers, that if the divine cannot be seen or recognized, the implication from our standpoint is that He does not exist. *Megillat Esther* teaches us that while it is true that we do not see or perceive God, that does not mean that He is not present; on the contrary, He is present all the more.

This is the complexity and the power of Purim compared to the other festivals. On Purim, we do not celebrate God's revelation, but His existence; we celebrate the fact that He exists, even though and because He is hiding. For what is invisible, what is hidden, is certainly higher than anything revealed.

Among the melodies of the Chabad Hasidim, there is a melody to the words "Indeed, You are a hiding God." Surprisingly, it is not a sad melody, nor a melody of longing, but rather a joyful melody, as if to say, "Indeed, You are a hiding God, but we know that You are present."

Purim is a festival of the exile, for its message is that amidst the darkness and the shadows, amidst the persecution, the difficulties and the uncertainty – there, too, God is present. This tension is what creates the burst of joy on Purim.

In the midst of revelation, when one proceeds from level to level, there is a calm, progressive process; one sees, hears, and attains certitude. On Purim, however, in the midst of the exile and hiddenness, there is an element of surprise. One feels that he neither sees nor hears; one searches – and suddenly, one finds. At that point, there is an outburst of joy that is not to be found when life is calm and orderly, like a love story that is all the more thrilling and moving because there is a period of remoteness and uncertainty.

In this sense, *Megillat Esther* is the story that accompanies us in *galut* and stays with us until *galut*'s end.

"*Galut*" is a process, a long period of concealment in which we search in darkness, and where occasionally a real find turns up that elicits a special burst of revelation and joy. For such a find is a discovery of the hidden, a revelation of the concealed.

Only indestructible faith and profound insight, with a vision of the Jewish future through the generations, could have brought about the *Megilla*'s inclusion in the Holy Scriptures. For the *Megilla* is the epitome of Jewish life in *galut*, of the greatest expression of the faith that beneath all the external causes, the Guardian of Israel is revealed.

The *Megilla* teaches that the Jewish People must learn to live a life of this kind, and that it must hope for miracles of this sort. We long not for the miracles in Egypt and at the Red Sea, which were accomplished by "a strong hand and an outstretched arm,"[8] but miracles within the twists and turns of history. And through it all, we are to maintain the faith that "relief and deliverance will come to the Jews."[9] In times of distress, assimilation and disguise will not avail even those Jews who are in the king's palace, and yet in spite of everything, there is still hope.

The story of the *Megilla* continues as long the *galut* lasts, and as long as the world operates as it does now – with God's face hidden and

8. Deuteronomy 26:8.

9. Esther 4:14.

His name left out. Would that the days soon arrive when we will no longer perceive the grave aspect of the *Megilla,* when we will be able to read the *Megilla* in a truly joyful mood, knowing that now it is only a legend from days that will never again return.

The Jews Confirmed and Accepted

AN ASTONISHING FESTIVAL

The "personality" of Purim incorporates two aspects that do not appear to be in harmony with one another.

On the one hand, the days of Purim seem to be ranked lower than the other festivals. The observance of most Jewish festivals is mandated by the Torah, and their obligations are defined and established. The observance of Purim, however, is derived strictly from *Megillat Esther*, and its various laws and customs are of Rabbinic origin.

On a deeper level, the miracle of Purim is incomparable to the miracles in the Torah. Nothing about the Purim miracle transcends nature. The entire miracle is clothed in a natural and material garment; the course of events seems plausible, credible, and natural, and the intervention of Providence is far from apparent.

On the other hand, our sages go to great lengths in their praise of the festival of Purim, to the point of saying that in the future, all the Prophetic Books and the Writings will cease to be used except *Megillat Esther*,[1] and that even if all the festivals are abrogated, Ḥanukka and

1. Jerusalem Talmud, *Megilla* 1:5.

Purim will never be nullified.[2] The sages conveyed that Purim's greatness exceeds initial and superficial appearances.

An additional aspect of Purim that requires clarification is the nature of its laws, some of which are astonishing. Although the Torah obligates us to rejoice on all the festivals, on no other holiday is there a mitzva, as on Purim, "to become intoxicated … until one does not know."[3] What is it about Purim that justifies this special and anomalous rejoicing?

The answer is implicit in the question – it must be that Purim has deeper significance; more than what meets the eye. Purim is not simply the festival of Israel's deliverance from impending physical danger; rather, there is hidden meaning in the external events that occurred during the days of Purim.

THE REDEMPTION FROM EGYPT

In order to understand the full meaning of the exalted illumination that was and is revealed on the days of Purim, we must compare it to the revelation of the "first redemption," when our ancestors were redeemed during the exodus from Egypt.

The divine revelation of the Exodus began with the ten plagues, continued with the great revelation at the splitting of the Red Sea, where "maidservants beheld what even Isaiah and Ezekiel never saw,"[4] and concluded with the most sublime revelation of all, the Giving of the Torah on Mount Sinai. There, the divine revelation was exalted and out of all proportion to the Jewish People's spiritual level at the time.

Egypt (*Mitzrayim*) was not just physical exile in which the bodies of the Jewish People were afflicted. Egypt was spiritual distress and narrow straits (*meitzar*), where the Jewish People was on such a low level that they resembled the Egyptians in almost everything: "These were idolaters and these were idolaters."[5]

The only thing that distinguished Israel in that period was their deep and boundless faith, like that of our patriarchs Abraham, Isaac, and

2. The Midrash on Proverbs 9.
3. *Megilla* 7b.
4. *Mekhilta DeRabbi Yishmael, Beshallaḥ, Masekhta DeShira,* 3.
5. *Vayikra Raba* 21.

Jacob. This faith was fundamental and essential, but not conscious. In Egypt, a Jew could be a believer without his faith contradicting, to his mind, the idolatry he imbibed from his surroundings. Nevertheless, the Jews in Egypt possessed the readiness and ability to receive the outpouring of God's benevolence when it would eventually come.

And the outpouring indeed came. When the merit of the patriarchs was aroused, when it was God's will to hasten the redemption and take His people out of Egypt, it was a time of illumination and revelation in all worlds. Not only was the Red Sea split before the people of Israel, but all worlds were opened up, revealing the whole dimension of mystery and hiddenness. When God descended to take His people out of Egypt, the divine light, which cannot ordinarily be perceived or appreciated, was revealed on earth.

Obviously, the miracles of Egypt did not occur in the ordinary course of nature, for all of nature melted, fled, and withdrew "before the God of Jacob."[6] The revelations were extremely powerful, and therefore too great for the receivers to truly grasp and understand. The maidservant at the sea, Israel's humblest and lowliest, suddenly was privileged to behold sublime visions that in later times would not be attained even by the prophets! The pinnacle was the Giving of the Torah, the highest of all the revelations, when God descended and revealed Himself to His entire people and everyone was privileged to reach the level of prophecy.

HE OVERTURNED UPON THEM A MOUNTAIN OF INTIMACY

Our sages relate that the Holy One, blessed be He, overturned Mount Sinai over the people of Israel like an inverted cask so that they should accept the Torah.[7] This midrash clearly cannot be understood according to its simple meaning, for in our prayers we say, "And His kingship they accepted upon themselves *willingly*." It is impossible that God coerced Israel to accept the Torah. What, then, is the meaning of the symbol of the mountain overturned upon their heads?

The mountain overturned over them was a mountain of abundant love and intimacy, not one of coercion. In the midst of an unparalleled

6. Psalms 114:7.
7. *Shabbat* 88a.

and never-to-be-equaled sublime vision, the people of Israel accepted God's kingship and commandments willingly and lovingly. But that very intimacy constituted constraint, for who could be so near to divine revelation and not accept it willingly? Who could behold the living God speaking out of the fire and not experience self-nullification, the nullification of all one's whole self in the midst of cleaving to God?

It is understandable that constraint was necessary. Without some element of compulsion, had they progressed slowly and steadily instead of making an immediate commitment, the people could not have attained those sublime revelations. God's hand was required to carry and uplift the people beyond their true level to a higher and more exalted state.

However, such a jump can last only as long as the "constraint" of the revelation endures. When the revelations at Sinai wore off, the people could not remain on their elevated level, and their fall through the sin of the golden calf immediately followed.

The revelation at Sinai demonstrates that even if supreme revelations descend from above, and even if people are receptive to these revelations, this does not constitute a true hold in godliness. The relationship to God is not yet stable or fully developed, and its existence depends on continued divine emanation. Since the basis of the world is precisely hiddenness, however, these revelations cannot continue forever. After the revealed light comes darkness, and with it is likely to come a fall and instability.

AWAKENING FROM BELOW

The state of things was entirely different in the time of Persia and Media. Then, too, the majority of the Jewish People lived in exile, which always constitutes a lower level of Jewish existence, and there, too, came a moment of illumination and awakening. This time, however, it was an awakening of an entirely different sort.

The decrees of Haman and Ahasuerus were designed to bring about the Jewish People's annihilation. More than a war for the people's physical annihilation, it was a war for spiritual annihilation, a war of Amalek's descendants against the Jewish People's spirit. At such a time, when the verse "I will utterly hide My face"[8] becomes a full-fledged reality, when it seems that "God has forsaken the land"[9] and that the world operates by the laws of "survival of the fittest" – this is the time of the greatest test.

In the days of Mordekhai and Esther, Amalek – Haman – was at the height of its power. Amalek was the actual ruler, with Ahasuerus consenting privately to what Haman proposed openly. Amalek, ruler of the world, wanted to break the Jewish People, to exterminate it. The Jew's life was no doubt darkened in those days, when it appeared that all were against him, when there was no way to escape the decree. As opposed to the light of the revelation at the time of the Exodus, here there was redoubled darkness, outer darkness as well as inner darkness, uncertainty and inability to act against the decree.

Precisely at this time, when Amalek threatens to conquer the whole world and it appears that it indeed has the power to do so, the inner spark intensifies, the spark that is truly "a part of God from on high" in the soul of the Jew. Suddenly, Amalek has no place in the Jewish soul, and the Jew rejects the temptation offered by Haman to become like him. The Jew is ready to give up everything in order to maintain his Judaism.

The people's willingness to give up their lives rather than renounce God and faith in Him and in His Torah was a more profound and inward recurrence of the acceptance of the Torah. The *Megilla* describes this willingness: "The Jews confirmed and accepted"[10] – they confirmed anew what they had accepted at Sinai.[11] The Torah that was given by way of compulsion at the revelation at Sinai was reaccepted wholeheartedly under the shadow of Haman, despite all the hiddenness and darkness. Here, there was no coercion in the form of a mountain of love. On the contrary, all the forces fought against the Jewish People and their faith; yet the Jews nullified their personal existence – as human beings, as

8. Deuteronomy 31:18.
9. Ezekiel 8:12.
10. Esther 9:27.
11. *Shabbat* 88a.

individuals desiring and craving life – and returned to a state of "confirming and accepting."

This inner commitment of all members of the Jewish People, great and small, constituted an "awakening from below," and correspondingly – "as face answers to face in water"[12] – a profound and exalted revelation came down from above.

This new revelation was actually more exalted than even the revelation at Mount Sinai; it was a revelation of such scope that it could be revealed not only supernaturally, through the signs and wonders as at the Exodus, but also within physical nature. The ordinary forces in the world, which in and of themselves belong to the aspect of the concealment of God's name, likewise attained revelation, and the miracles which brought about Israel's redemption occurred within nature itself.

YOM HAKIPPURIM – KE-PURIM

The fact that this revelation was the result of the greatest possible self-nullification to God's oneness, and that the revelations of Purim, in their deepest sense, are considered a completion of the revelation at Sinai, explains the greatness of the day. We can now understand the well-known enigmatic saying equating the holiest day of the year, Yom Kippur, to Purim: "*Yom Kippurim – ke-Purim.*"

How can it be that Yom Kippur is merely an imitation of Purim? Once we understand how profound the Purim revelations were, how the Jewish People reached the pinnacle of self-nullification to divinity and thereby the heights of revelation, the comparison becomes clear. On Yom Kippur, the Jew attempts to reach the same exalted levels that were attained then, during the days of Purim.

The original revelations of the festival reappear each year upon Purim's arrival. It is thus understandable that our sages praise and exalt these days, declaring that they will never be abrogated. On Purim, we triumph over Amalek, not only the physical Amalek in the form of Haman, but also the spiritual Amalek, the inner temptations of heresy. Our victory indicates that Amalek has no power over the Jewish People.

12. Proverbs 27:19. The simple meaning of this expression is that what a person feels toward his fellow man is reflected in the way that his fellow man feels toward him.

Because of these revelations within Jewish souls and in supernal worlds, the joy on Purim is greater than that of the other holidays and festivals, for the revelations of Purim are more exalted than those of any other festival.

Preparing for Drinking on Purim

Our sages have taught us that *Yom HaKippurim* is *ke-Purim*, like Purim.[1] Neither day is a regular, normal continuation of ordinary life. On both holidays, we behave as though we are not ourselves. On Yom Kippur, we overhaul our personalities and repent, and on Purim we diverge from our ordinary state of mind – we drink and become intoxicated "until one does not know."[2]

However, there is a basic difference between these two departures from the norm. Yom Kippur is intrinsically a day of forgiveness and pardon, and "the essence of the day effects atonement"[3] even without man's inner work and preparation. By contrast, the departure from constraint on Purim requires extensive preparation beforehand. The loss of lucidity, ironically, must be accomplished with awareness and knowledge of what one wants to achieve through this divergence; otherwise, no profit results. All that will remain of Purim is a headache and soiled clothing.

1. *Tikunei Zohar, tikun* 21, 57b: Purim is named after *Yom HaKippurim*.
2. The old joke is that on Purim, the Jews pretend to be *goyim*, and on Yom Kippur, the *goyim* pretend to be Jews.
3. Mishna *Yoma* 8:9; *Yoma* 86a.

(And what a pity to go through all the trouble, since one could suffice with the halakhic "until one does not know" – namely, sleep![4])

BEHIND THE MASKS

Although there is no explicit source for the idea in Scripture, part of the theme of Purim is masks.

In *Megillat Esther*, the *Megilla* of concealment, there are quite a few disguises. Our sages relate that Haman actually was the bathhouse attendant and barber of Kfar Kartzum, who disguised himself as "the great Haman."[5] Esther, too, disguised herself, in that she did not reveal her nationality to the king.

Most importantly, the miracle of Purim itself is in disguise. The miracle of Purim is one of deliverance, but it is hidden behind a mask; everything appears ordinary, as though accomplished by natural means.

The world itself has a disguise – nature. In the literature, it is written that *teva* (nature) is so called because the true content sinks (*tovea*) in it and is lost. Externally, one sees only the outer aspect and not what lies inside.

That is why one must become intoxicated – in order to see the miracle of Purim, to see what lies behind the masks.

The miracle of Purim was not completed by the fact that many of the people of the land professed to be Jews, for that, too, was in truth only a mask. On Purim, the masks are removed from the Jews themselves. A decree of Ahasuerus was necessary to compel the Jews to remove their masks and decide that they were Jews, so that everyone should tear off the masks (*masekhot*) that conceal (*mekhasot*).

THE BENEFIT OF DRINKING

Physiologically, alcohol acts as a depressant, slowing one's vital activities. (An extreme case of this effect can be observed in one who drinks a large quantity of alcohol and falls asleep. It is difficult – if not impossible – to rouse him.)

The depressant effect is gradual. In the first stage, alcohol low-

---

4. *Shulḥan Arukh, Oraḥ Ḥayyim* 695:2.
5. *Megilla* 16a.

ers the functioning of the "control centers" in the brain, which inhibit a person from doing certain things, whether positive or negative. This creates an opportunity for those things – which generally are dormant – to be expressed. In and of itself, the alcoholic drink has no message; its whole task is to enable other things to emerge.

Intoxication leads to a wide range of reactions. Some people become happy, while others cry. One person may emit all the foulness of the world, only holy things spring forth from his friend.

In order for intoxication to be beneficial and not just make one uglier and despicable, it is important to decide beforehand where one wishes to end up through the intoxication and in what manner one wishes to depart from constraint. One must have in mind ahead of time where this outburst should lead, planning the manner in which to release his chains and depart from habitual patterns of behavior.

According to the halakha, there are cases in which it is sufficient to begin an act with a certain intention in order for the entire act to be considered as having been done with that intention, and the same applies to intoxication. One's accomplishment depends on his intention before beginning to drink.

If one's intention is to drink for the sake of drinking, for the sake of boisterousness or in order to fall asleep as quickly as possible – these will be the goals ultimately attained.

If, however, the intention is to enter a state of intoxication so that something profound should emerge – even if one does not know beforehand exactly what that something will be, as Purim is, after all, the day of mystery and not knowing – then this is a unique opportunity to function above the plane of the ordinary intellect.

A person must remind himself: Now I am transcending the bounds of knowledge and logic. I now have the opportunity to transcend my ordinary limits. I can use the opportunity of Purim to open things that I cannot touch all year round.

BEYOND THE LIMITATIONS OF THE INTELLECT

Many times in the course of our lives, we are afraid to take initiative. We must make decisions, but we haven't the time or the courage to make them. Since life never stops on its own, everything continues, and there is no point at which this cycle can be halted. We form fixed notions of ourselves: "I am thus and thus. Everyone knows me as such, and that is also the way I must be."

On Purim, we have the opportunity to emerge from our immobility, since everything is moving and shaking.

This applies not only to the realm of fulfilling mitzvot and serving God, but to all areas of life. We need the assistance of something that will move us, that will give us the courage to make a change. Although the courage gained from drink is not genuine, after a decent gulp one gains sufficient courage to resolve to change one's life from now onward.

The story is told of someone who went to his *Rebbe* on Purim and said to him, "*Rebbe*! I would like to ask you for something!"

The *Rebbe* asked him, "By what right?"

The man answered, "It is written in the halakha that on Purim, 'Whoever puts out his hand to beg – we give to him.' Therefore, I now request that the *Rebbe* give me!"

The rule that on Purim "whoever puts out his hand to beg, we give to him" – applies to the spiritual as well as the physical. On Purim, one can turn to God and put out one's hand to Him in a request for spiritual growth, because Purim is a day of abandon on which one is authorized and entitled to depart from constraint.

Sometimes, a person is anxious about the consequences of the inner changes that he would like to adopt. Who among us has not asked himself, "If I begin to attain all sorts of heights and levels, who knows where I might end up?" So, too, when we pray or engage in serving the Creator, we become apprehensive. "I might, God forbid, turn into a respectable person!"

Purim is an opportunity to undergo inner metamorphosis, to make resolutions that we previously avoided because of all sorts of fears generated by the mind. The lack of lucidity on Purim may afford the possibility of committing all the transgressions I ever wanted to commit; on the other hand, it also presents the opportunity of doing all the mitzvot that I ever wanted to do, but did not dare.

Purim is the time to make a leap to a different side and to remain there on the day after. The departure from constraint is not just for the duration of the intoxication; it is an opportunity to extricate oneself, since in any case one is not on the usual course of life. Purim is the impetus to change; after Purim, we hope to find ourselves in a different place.

RELEASE FROM INHIBITIONS

During the course of the year, there are many things that we would like to do or say, but we do not do or say them – sometimes because they are impolite or not nice, and sometimes because we are not sure that this is what we truly think. In the course of the year, I might want to say to someone, "Every time I see you, there is light in my heart," but I cannot say these words to him; we know each other too well, and it is difficult to verbally express the fact that we are dear friends.

When Purim arrives, statements of a different kind altogether suddenly emerge, statements of real value. On Purim, I can tell my friend what he means to me. Tomorrow, we both will have forgotten the tipsy conversation, but some memory or trace of it always remains.

On *Yom HaKippurim*, one can say, "Now, time has no meaning. The clock can be turned back, and I can act as though I never sinned." Similarly, on Purim I can say anything and do anything, as though it were a new world.

Purim is a day of exceptional rejoicing and revelry, the only day on which a Jew is permitted to lose his composure and awareness in order to open new doors. On Purim, we remove our masks, and it is impossible to know beforehand exactly what lies beneath. What will be revealed depends primarily on the question of how we enter the holiday. In what kind of *pur*, lottery, are we participating? Is the question which prize we will we receive, or only how much will we lose? Choosing the right lottery, the one that transcends the bounds of human knowledge and logic, allows us to make resolutions that transcend our limits.

What lies beyond the doors of our souls, doors that ordinarily remain closed? That depends on how we prepare ourselves before opening them.

Obliterating Amalek

YOU SHALL OBLITERATE THE MEMORY OF AMALEK

Throughout the generations, the Jewish People has suffered from the heavy blows of many enemies who oppressed and assaulted us. Nevertheless, we are commanded to exact revenge from and totally destroy Amalek alone – a command that is not directed even against the seven nations of Canaan.

Amalek is "deserving" of such special treatment due to the degree of its hatred for the Jewish People, a hatred that has no cause or reason. Amalek's attack on Israel's camp in the wilderness defies logic. Only an irrational, baseless hatred could have motivated an attack on such an enormous camp. Hatred deprives the enemy of his ability to think rationally.

Balaam's prophecy, "Amalek is the beginning of the nations,"[1] alludes to the fact that in Amalek, there is something beyond ordinary alienating hatred, beyond the rule that "Esau clearly hates Jacob."[2] Amalek harbors hatred that leads to actual assault.

1. Numbers 24:20.
2. *Sifrei* 69.

Amalek's hatred of Israel stems from the clash of two forces that are always at odds with each other.

The Jewish People are endowed with an innate consciousness and faith. Even when it appears that all hope is lost, that the world is arbitrary, the Jewish People maintain their faith. This faith has neither rhyme nor reason; it is without rationale. The Jew himself does not know why he believes, but he does so nonetheless. This is the stubbornness of faith, which reaches to the very root and foundation of the Jew. The Jewish People is indeed a "stiff-necked people,"[3] in which is latent the resolve not to submit to the world and to the forces of evil, but to hold fast always to God and His Torah.

Conversely, Amalek is the nadir, the basest of the forces of evil. Wherever there is feebleness of mind, whenever a Jew fails to see before him the way of God, Amalek appears. The danger of Amalek is especially great when a person proceeds on faith alone, without understanding and without experiencing his faith with true, living feeling.

"God will be at war with Amalek throughout the generations"[4] refers to the eternal war of faith against heresy, the war of the godly forces, the bearers of light in the world, against those who stand for doubt and feebleness of mind. This war continues as long as Amalek exists in the world in any form, as long as the seed of Amalek – the seeds of doubt and indifference of heart sown in the world by Amalek – still remains in Israel's heart.

Haman's hatred stems from this same Amalekite root. Of course, the *Megilla* relates how Mordekhai personally angered Haman, but Haman's generalization to include all of "Mordekhai's people"[5] points to prejudice – a basic hatred of Israel. Haman's contentions, like the anti-Semitic contentions in every generation, are perhaps factually correct – "There is a certain people, scattered and dispersed among the other peoples... whose laws are different from those of every other people; they do not obey the king's laws."[6] But his struggle against the Jewish People

3. Exodus 32:9 et al.
4. Ibid. 17:16.
5. Esther 3:6.
6. Ibid. 3:8.

does not stem from these reasons, but from a basic hatred toward those who belong to another pole of existence. Haman and his cronies stand on one side, and the Jews on the other, the side of faith.

THE ROOT OF EVIL

There is a book entitled *Conversations with Hitler*, written by a man who was a former member of the Nazi party and friend of Hitler, of accursed memory. In one of the conversations recorded there, the two of them are speaking of the Jews, and the author says to Hitler, "Between the two of us, both you and I know that all the contentions against the Jews are false. Why, then, do you hate them?"

Hitler's answer is, "I cannot forgive the Jews, because they invented morality."

Such a statement is prototypical of Amalek. Their hatred is not a result of a wrong committed against it, but rather antagonism toward the essence of the Jew, who symbolizes the Holy One, blessed be He – "these are God's people."[7] That is what infuriates Amalek. Amalek would like to uproot God from the world, and because it cannot do so, it turns to God's representatives on earth – the Jewish People.

Ishmael is angered by the prohibition "You shall not steal," and Esau is troubled because of "You shall not murder." Amalek, however, objects to the principle "I am God." Every nation symbolizes a different character defect, whereas Amalek, "beginning of the nations," represents the fundamental defect, the complete opposite of holiness.

Amalek's hatred transcends sense and reason. Just as love endures when it is not dependent on external factors, Amalek's hatred is not dependent on anything, and therefore never ceases to exist.[8]

Most people sin because, due to a mistaken notion or a spirit of folly, the transgression seems good in their sight, not because of an intrinsically evil will. Amalek, who hates for the sake of hating, possesses such an evil will; he adores the root of evil, which must be eradicated from the world. Amalek is defined as evil itself, and for that reason it belongs to the category of the world's imperfect existence.

---

7. Ezekiel 36:20.
8. Cf. *Avot* 5:16.

As a response to this total hatred on the part of Amalek, the Jewish People's total war against Amalek was born; "God has set the one opposite the other."[9] All other wars that the Jewish People were commanded to wage had a reason. Their war against Amalek, however, a war of total annihilation, transcends reasons. As long as intrinsic evil exists in the world, the world is not yet complete. Only when evil – the seed of Amalek – is eradicated will God's throne and name be complete, and will a different world emerge, a world in which "God is one and His name is one."[10]

THE WAR WITHIN US

In the inner life as well, the eradication of Amalek applies at all times, in every generation, and within every individual. This battle is essentially no different from the external eradication of Amalek.

The numerical equivalent of "Amalek" is the same as the word *safek* (doubt), alluding to its inner nature. Legitimate doubt – when there is something that a person does not know conclusively – is removed when the matter in question becomes clear and when he deals with the problems that it raises. Amalek seeks to encourage and perpetuate doubt, and thus attempts to halt any effort to deal with doubt and resolve it.

Amalek accomplishes this through the disengagement of thought and feeling. Were the heart to feel all that the mind understands, there would be no room for doubt at all. In practice, however, insights grasped clearly in the brain are obscured when they descend to the emotional realm – and there, doubt is given a foothold. A person's life is full of exalted emotions and profound thoughts, but the transition between thought and feeling and between feeling and action involves enormous difficulties – the inner war against Amalek.

The disengagement of mind and feeling does not pertain to Amalek alone. In fact, it is a universal human problem, which the Kabbala terms "*meitzar hagaron*," "constriction of the throat." The centers,

9. Ecclesiastes 7:14.
10. Zechariah 14:9.

the brain and the heart, are not linked; there are barriers between them[11] that prevent a connection and separate understanding from feeling and enthusiasm.

The disengagement of understanding and feeling is the source of all the evil that human beings perform. A person may know with certainty that a particular deed is not good, but do it nonetheless. Conversely, there are deeds that we know should be done, but our hearts remain unmoved and do not encourage us to do them.

At times, this disengagement also protects us. If everything that occurred to the mind were to lead to immediate action, we would fall into all sorts of foolishness. The barrier between mind and heart creates a problem on the one hand, but provides balance and protection on the other, and is therefore a problem that is difficult to resolve.

Amalek seeks to institutionalize this disengagement, and thus create permanent skepticism, *safek*.

CONTRARIETY

While this type of doubt is the provenance of all mankind, there is a second kind of doubt that belongs to Amalek alone. This is the level of "the root of Amalek," doubt that requires no arguments to maintain, but which stands on contrariety alone. This is the doubt of "one who knows his Master and yet intends to rebel against him"[12] – the recalcitrance that brings one to ask in every situation, "So what?" "But why?"

For example, it occasionally happens that we forget how to spell a certain word. We try to remember and go through all the possibilities, but we cannot recall. In such a situation, even if someone were to try to help me and tell me the correct form of the word, I will never be sure of it, because the doubt has already taken hold of me. Without any rational explanation, I become so suspicious that it almost drives me crazy.

The mechanism of Amalekite doubt is built the same way. It does not rest on logic. A completely nonsensical idea enters my mind, and I cannot free myself of it, no matter how hard I try.

11. In Hasidic thought, these barriers are referred to as "Pharaoh's chiefs" – the chief butler and the chief baker (see Genesis 40).

12. *Sifra Beḥukkotai* 2.

Jewish faith teaches that there is a divine power that directs the world; that God's power pervades the universe – God watches over everyone at all times with His providence. Amalek, on the other hand, injects coldness into our hearts, the feeling that one need not get so excited, that one can take the world less seriously. From the Amalek within us sprouts the doubts, the concerns, the conjectures – "Maybe...," "Perhaps..."

Even at the greatest heights, when a Jew attains full awareness and perception of the divine light which pours over him, Amalek stands in the way. With recalcitrance and defiance encompassing all the forces of evil, Amalek whispers, "Perhaps all this is nature, for everything is nature; there is no divinity in the world."

At some point during childhood, it occurs to many children that their parents may not be their real parents. Such a thought usually stems from the fact that the child feels slightly alienated, and on this he builds theories and castles in the air. Similarly, Amalek, through foolish and unfounded ideas, succeeds in creating doubts about faith. The doubt is not created on a particular basis or because of a particular argument, but due to the very existence of the world of chaos, and if it is allowed room, it will grow.

REMOVE YOURSELF FROM DOUBT

How can we deal with the doubts of Amalek? Not for naught is the struggle against Amalek called "obliterating Amalek." To obliterate the memory of Amalek means to erase it completely. The way to deal with Amalek is by ignoring it and its questions.

Amalek is intrinsically incapable of being persuaded, for its arguments do not stem from the realm of cause and effect. Were they to stem from logic, the moment I would deal with the cause and reject it, the effect would be mitigated. The complete obliteration of Amalek is achieved only when "with their own eyes they will see,"[13] when there will be absolute certainty through inner insight.

The *Zohar* writes[14] that questions and objections in the Talmud

13. Isaiah 52:8.

14. *Raya Meheimna*, *Naso*, 124b.

come from the same root as impurity. The questions of the Talmud are different from those of Amalek, however. The Talmud questions, contradicts, and demolishes for the sake of construction; a subject is taken apart and broken down in order to be reconstructed in a corrected and more solid form. The questions in the Talmud are built upon the relations between different parts of reality, and they serve to harmonize these parts with one another. The purpose of Amalek's questions, in contrast, is not to clarify how to act in the world. Indeed, the question itself is secondary; its purpose is to enter into conversation with a person in order to undermine his opinions and beliefs.

King Saul's life story reflects this matter clearly. Instead of eradicating Amalek immediately and decisively, in the way that Samuel dealt with Agag, Saul chose to "negotiate" and compromise with Amalek. A comprehensive analysis demonstrates that Saul's entire life was full of doubts. He killed the priests of Nob because of his doubts about their loyalty, and he pursued David even after admitting that David would reign after him.[15] Doubt gnawed at his mind to the point that everything that occurred took on the appearance of doubt. Not even thoughts of repentance could extricate him from this state of mind.

CLARITY IN DAYS TO COME

Many sources explain that the words "you followed Me in the wilderness, in a land not sown"[16] describe a situation of basic unclarity, a situation in which Amalek can take hold. Amalek can harm only "those lagging to your rear,"[17] those people in whom it has already made a stake.

Doubt does not take hold when there is clear truth, when people see "with their own eyes." Such complete clarity characterized the revelation at Sinai, when there was direct contact with God. In the Torah of Moses, there are no questions, for it is perfect. Moses did not have

15. I Samuel 24:20.
16. Jeremiah 2:2.
17. Deuteronomy 25:18.

to deal with doubts, because he could turn directly to God – "Stand by, and let me hear."[18] Only after his death did laws begin to be forgotten.[19]

So, too, the days to come will bring the fulfillment of "And all flesh will see that God Himself has spoken"[20] and "I will remove the spirit of impurity from the land."[21]

Until the time of that clear vision comes, there is the festival of Purim, the festival of the war against Amalek, a festival that is not based on the rational. Moreover, the very nature of one of the day's mitzvot is loss of lucidity.

Amalek cannot be beaten with the help of the intellect or by means of argument and persuasion. Amalek must be approached on a plane unrelated to the intellect, where one rejects and does away with Amalek entirely – to remove oneself from doubt.

18. Numbers 9:8.
19. See *Temura* 16a.
20. Isaiah 40:5.
21. Zechariah 13:2.

Pesaḥ

A People That Dwells Apart

"HE PASSED OVER"

The meaning of the festival of Pesaḥ is multifaceted, not only because of the varied mindsets of those who celebrate the day, but because the festival itself contains numerous and diverse aspects. Still, although the festival has been crowned with many names – both in the Torah itself and in popular speech – the fact that the most widespread and accepted name is still "the festival of Pesaḥ (Passover)" lends greater weight to the special meaning that lies in this particular aspect of the holiday.

The source of this name appears in the Torah – "He passed over [*pasaḥ*] the houses of the people of Israel in Egypt when He struck the Egyptians, sparing our homes."[1] The event that it recalls perpetuated the miraculous pattern of the ten plagues, accentuating one particular aspect – the distinction between Egypt and Israel. This idea was expanded and crystallized on the night of Pesaḥ, becoming a comprehensive idea expressed by the festival of Pesaḥ throughout the ages: the difference between Israel and the nations.

The exodus from Egypt was an emergence from bondage to freedom, marking the beginning of the formation and development of

1. Exodus 12:27.

the Jewish People. At the same time, however, the Exodus constituted a change in the nature of the Jewish People, the beginning of Israel's separateness and distinction. The Jewish People became "a people that dwells apart, not reckoned among the nations."[2]

When the earliest anti-Semites claimed the existence of "a feeling of hatred that the Jewish People harbors toward all the nations," they hit upon this very same point, despite distorting its inner meaning. Not for naught did they regard the Exodus as an event that established the eternal isolation of the Jewish People, the fact that it is always, in all generations, the "other."

The Jewish People's otherness, its apartness, is not a manifestation of hatred toward the world, but it undoubtedly underlies the alienation felt by the Jewish People throughout the generations, both while dwelling in its own land and while living in exile. Already in Second Temple times, Greek authors write about this otherness of the Jews, clearly indicating that this quality is not an exilic "defense mechanism" but an intrinsic part of the Jewish spiritual character.

THERE IS NO ESCAPE FROM THE SINGULARITY

In every social group in the world and every nation, there is a sense of difference between "us" and "them," but in the case of the Jew, this feeling not only is more developed but also has another level of meaning.

The concept of God choosing Israel as His people differs from the nationalism of other peoples, for, among other reasons, it is not necessarily connected to national pride. Even those among Israel who make a great effort to imitate and be like others sense the same apartness and foreignness. In fact, sometimes this feeling is accompanied by a sense of helplessness and even embitterment. Why does it have to be this way? Why do we have to be other and different? Whether this phenomenon expresses itself in a sense of superiority and pride or by forced and forlorn loneliness, the very same feeling of apartness and distinction exists. This sense of abnormality, then, does not depend strictly on Israel's distinctive manner of existence, but is intrinsic to Israel itself.

Resentment of Jewish distinctiveness has always been an active

2. Numbers 23:9.

force within the Jewish People: "Let us be like the nations, like the families of the lands."[3] The desire to be "like all the nations" not only exists in the form of resentment of or rebellion against the religious character of the Torah's commandments, but has also entered the framework of Judaism itself. The appointment of a king is connected with the aspiration to build social structures that will be closer to what is acceptable among the surrounding nations.[4]

The attempts at assimilation over the course of history all boil down to the desire to negate this feeling of distinctiveness. The German and French "members of the Mosaic religion" did not consciously intend to renounce their Judaism, but they tried to make this Judaism similar in its form and essence to other religions, to remove from Judaism its foreign character, and to put it into a framework that would conform to the conceptions of other nations. This was and is the goal of all the attempts to westernize the Jewish People – to pour the Jewish content into vessels that have no aspect of distinctiveness or foreignness.

The fact that such attempts always end in the abandonment or distortion of content attests to how impossible these attempts are. Not only is the existence of distinctive content vital to the Jewish People, but so are the distinctive and singular forms through which this content is conveyed.

The contrast between Israel and the nations is therefore essential and necessary (although it need not necessarily express itself in mutual hatred). The Jewish People cannot be like the other nations and at the same time be itself. In this regard, it does not matter whether the Jewish People, in being itself, wishes to keep the mitzvot or to violate them. At all times, even at a time of casting off the yoke, the Jewish People is different; the saying, "'In all your ways know Him'[5] – even for a matter of transgression"[6] is strangely fulfilled.

3. Ezekiel 20:32.
4. This is apparent not only from the people's request for a king at the time of Samuel, but in the Torah's command itself.
5. Proverbs 3:6.
6. *Berakhot* 63a.

ON THE OTHER SIDE

The designation of the holiday as "Pesaḥ" originates from the account of the plague of the firstborn, but its meaning extends far beyond this historical event. The passing over, the leap, and the distinction between Israel and the nations have become central motifs of our existence in all times. What is true and applicable for the whole world ceases to be applicable and meaningful for the Jewish People. In the case of Pesaḥ, the distinction is reflected in a calamity that befalls others but does not befall the Jewish People, but that is only one expression of the idea that is reemphasized time and again during Pesaḥ – the idea of the Jewish People being the "eternal other," and the curse and the blessing that this entails.

The festival of Pesaḥ is the day on which the family gathers together as a distinct unit, a special group performing an ancient ceremony that repeatedly stresses national unity alongside the fact that the Jewish People is always separate and distinct – in moments of ascent and triumph as well as in moments of defeat and descent. As the Midrash says about our first patriarch, Abraham: "The whole world stands on one side and he stands on the other side."[7]

7. *Bereshit Raba* 42:8. The Torah (Genesis 14:13) calls Abraham *Avram HaIvri,* which literally means that he came from the other side (*'ever*) of the Euphrates; the Midrash adds another layer of meaning to this.

Exile and Redemption

"I will show you wondrous deeds, as in the days when you went out of the land of Egypt."[1] On the basis of this verse, the Midrash[2] and *Zohar* explain that the exodus from Egypt is the model of and gateway to the future redemption. In the same way, the exile in Egypt is the archetype of every exile and all bondage.

Exile and redemption as represented by the Egyptian exile and deliverance from it are part of a protracted process in every generation. The life of the Jewish People goes through great cycles of exile and redemption. Hence, the study of these concepts relates not only to the external phenomena and visible effects of things, but also to their inner meaning and spiritual essence.

Exile and redemption appear in different forms and on various levels of depth throughout all of reality. As one delves deeper into the spiritual aspect of the external phenomena, one finds deeper and more inward cycles of exile and redemption. The Jewish People's exile from its land is the larger, overt and manifest exile, but deeper is Israel's exile

1. Micah 7:15.
2. See *Shemot Raba* 15:11.

within its own self – that is, the exile of the spiritual essence within the corporeality of the world, the exile of the divine soul within the concealment of the animal soul and the body. Still deeper is the exile of God's *Shekhina* within our world, the exile of the Divine Light within the material world that conceals and obscures.

"WE WERE LIKE DREAMERS"

In the broadest sense, exile is an incorrect relation between things. Whenever the relations between the parts are not as they should be – when the lofty do not stand in their high place, and the lowly are found up above – that is exile. According to this understanding, exile not only relates to Israel's exile from its land and its servitude, but to the very order of the world in its existing state. The world, too, is essentially in exile.

Exile expresses itself in the fact that, at first glance, the existing state is in good order, whereas inwardly this state has a fundamental flaw, an irresolvable contradiction.

For this reason, the symbol of exile is sleep – the dream. "I am asleep, but my heart is wakeful:"[3] "'I am asleep' – in exile."[4] A dream is a combination of what is apparently regular and orderly with what cannot possibly be correct. The dream incorporates worldly events and phenomena that could stand on their own, but which are not combined properly and perhaps are even combined completely illogically. Nevertheless, a dream is characterized by the inward feeling that everything in it is correct; the impossible becomes existing and understandable reality.

The period of exile is nothing but a long nightmare in which the Jewish People "dreams" that its unnatural existence is possible and tolerable, that it is somehow comprehensible. "When God returned the captivity of Zion, we were like dreamers"[5] – when we examine the period of exile in retrospect, we will understand that throughout that period, we lived as if in a dream.

In spite of its unfeasibility as true existence, however, the dream affords profound possibilities; it enables life to carry on, even under the

3. Song of Songs 5:2.
4. *Zohar, Emor,* 95a.
5. Psalms 126:1.

worst of conditions. Were it not for the dream's ability to contain within it irreconcilable contrasts, the soul's existence in exile would be impossible. A dream-like quality is added to the pain of exile – the ability to integrate, in spite of everything, the true inner will of the soul with the strange reality, which the soul can neither accept nor tolerate.

Such is Israel's exile among the nations, and such is the soul's descent into the body. Moreover, the creation of the world in general is entirely a process of exile. The Jewish People's exile among the nations is an expression, an end point of a process that includes all of existence.

ASPECTS OF EXILE

On the individual psychological level, most people live in a state of exile. During prayer and while serving God, the individual leads an exalted life. When engaged in Torah study or in prayer, he avows that his physical life, the life of the body, is secondary and of little importance for his true, inner life, the life of the spirit and the soul. At such times, a person earnestly thinks that his life is dedicated to drawing near to God, to transforming himself into a receptacle for the Divine Light.

However, after the prayer concludes and when he is not engaged in Torah study, this same person leads a completely physical life. All his desires and aspirations are like those of any ordinary person; materialistic and physical motives and goals determine his way of life.

The life of such a person is conducted within a dual framework, full of inner contradictions. Yet he himself is totally unaware of the existence of such contradictions in his life. As in a dream, he accepts the existing picture of reality; he fails to understand that this situation is illogical and impossible.

The exile of the entire world, the concealment of the *Shekhina* – is an even deeper and broader dream.

The world cannot detach itself for even one moment from the divine life that fills all worlds and vitalizes them. All of the world's creatures – the exalted ones who recognize God's greatness, as well as those who are able to forget His existence or even deny it – live only by this power that flows in them.

But the world is not aware of the beneficent outpouring that vitalizes it; the world does not sense that its existence depends on the ever-renewed will of the Creator. Every existing thing in the world considers itself the center, as though it exists in its own right, without any connection to divinity. The divine power, which is life's essence and the true "I" of everything, hides and is concealed within its many coverings, and reveals itself in forms that are neither real nor natural.

The prophet exclaimed, "Should an ax boast against he who hews with it?"[6] This is, in fact, what everything in the world does to a certain degree when it feels that it is not dependent on the outpouring of God's benevolence or that it is not a part thereof. The world dreams that it is separate from divinity and able to stand on its own.

FOR LACK OF DA'AT

What makes it possible for this dream life to continue? Why do the individual, the people, and the world not awaken from this strange state? Moreover, what is it that creates the dream?

The answer is that all exile is a sort of "*Mitzrayim*" (Egypt), a world that is limited and constricted, a world of *meitzarim* (narrow straits) and bounds. Within this constricted world, the exalted faculties of the soul are paralyzed – as a result of distress, due to the inability to develop, and because of a reality that is antithetical to true life.

Exile is based on a lack of *da'at*, the faculty that connects abstract intellectual understanding with real and emotional life. As long as there is insufficient spiritual strength to draw conclusions from reality, life remains in the realm of a "dream." Everyone knows and understands that this state is strange and cannot be truly understood, yet everyone continues the same way of life and with the very same approach to it.

Since the faculty of understanding is not active in the soul, the soul's exalted faculties are in a state of concealment – in other words, in exile. What manifests itself in the soul, in the people, in the world, is only the external aspect, the outer shell of things, while the inner, exalted aspect remains hidden. This is not to say that in a state of exile there is no ability whatsoever to understand and comprehend, but that the understanding of exile remains detached from real life. The mind

6. Isaiah 10:15.

grasps in abstract that things are not as they appear externally, that there is inner meaning, but this grasp falls short of true awareness.

To be sure, in no state of exile does the concealment reach such a degree that it completely hides and extinguishes the form of the inwardness and its true essence. Nevertheless, what manifests itself is not the conscious element but only a more basic component, which it is entirely impossible to conceal – the power of faith.

On the one hand, faith is a basic, fundamental, essential faculty of the soul, for it expresses the stable element to which nothing can happen, which can never break down. However greatly the darkness and concealment intensify, the power of faith will always prevail, for faith is the manifestation of the very life-force that pervades everything.

On the other hand, precisely because faith stems from such a lofty source, it manifests itself within the soul and consciousness in ways that are not high and lofty. Since it transcends *da'at*, *da'at* cannot evaluate or judge it. Hence, faith is liable to also reach levels in no way sanctioned by the intellect. Since faith's discernment is not rational, it happens that "a thief, at the entrance of the breach by which to break in, calls on the Merciful One for help,"[7] without feeling any contradiction between the request for God's assistance and the act he is about to commit.

Intrinsic to exile, then, is the decline of the power to distinguish between things, the nullification or concealment of wisdom, which is the power to evaluate deeds and external manifestations in accordance with their inner meaning. This inability to distinguish between things can create a situation in which one behaves in contradictory ways, without sensing that they cannot be combined.

Thus, exile is a dream that contains within it its own solution, a state that appears to be strange and unrealistic, and yet nevertheless exists.

THE PURPOSE OF EXILE

The Midrash provides a rationale for the existence of exile:

> The Holy One, blessed be He, exiled Israel among the nations only so that proselytes might join them. As it says, "And I will

7. *Berakhot* 63a (cited in *Ein Ya'akov*).

> sow her for Myself in the land."[8] Surely a person sows a *se'ah* in order to harvest many *kor*![9]

The rationale "so that proselytes might join them" may be understood not only according to its plain sense, but also in an inward, spiritual sense, by focusing on the *midrash*'s metaphor: "And I will sow her for Myself in the land."

On the one hand, the kernel that is sown in the ground stays there until it decomposes; its appearance and all its qualities disintegrate almost entirely, and it no longer retains its own independent existence. On the other hand, the seed is the beginning of new life, from which an entire tree will grow. Indeed, the addition vastly exceeds the principal investment.

It is no coincidence that the sowing of the kernel precedes the growth of the tree; the decomposition of the seed is a necessary stage in the tree's growth.

Similarly, exile is not an accidental stage, merely a punishment that comes before the redemption. Exile is the necessary preparation that must precede the redemption; there can be no redemption without exile. Abraham was told, "Your descendants will be strangers in a land not theirs … and then they will go free with great wealth."[10] In order for there to be an exodus from Egypt with its exalted revelations, the people of Israel must first go down to Egypt and be enslaved there.

The whole kernel, fully ripened, is a complete, closed, and unique unit of life. Yet, despite its individual perfection, it cannot bring its contents forth unless it bursts out of its bounds and draws life from beyond itself. It must gather a wealth of life from the earth, utilizing the earth's almost unlimited growing power. This power flows within the limited kernel until the tiny kernel metamorphoses into a giant tree. Toward this end, the kernel must first decompose, lose its identity, and subordinate itself to the general forces in the earth. Without decomposition of the seed itself, it will not be able to activate the system dormant in it.

---

8. Hosea 2:25.
9. *Pesaḥim* 87b; *Zohar* 244a. A *kor* is approximately 30 *se'ah*.
10. Genesis 15:13–14.

The seed bears within it the message; it is the husk and casing of the genetic code. In order to preserve the inner point and pass it on, the seed must be split open, at the expense of its own independent existence. Hence, the kernel must be buried in the ground and therein lose its whole external form. When only a latent spark of the kernel's essence remains, then it begins to draw the earth's force, and then it can rise and grow into a majestic tree.

The concept of the "seed of Israel" expresses not only the continuity of the Jewish People, but also its influence on the world, its status as the world's inner essence, a point that provides purpose and directs the whole. When God "sows" Israel among the nations, he "invests" in the world, so as to ultimately transform all of existence into a new and holy reality.

The redemption – even though it appears to be a new and complete stage, totally unconnected to the preceding exile – is actually the necessary continuation of the exile. Just as both night and day are necessary, although night is dark; just as we experience sleep and awakening, and one cannot live in a state of constant wakefulness – so, too, every redemption must be preceded by a period of exile. As long as the fetus is in the womb, it is without full sensation and lives a confined, limited, and strange life. During its gestation, it undergoes the change from something of no substance, from a drop devoid of full-fledged life, to fully developed human existence.

When the stage of preparation ends, redemption arrives, revealing to all eyes what emerged and developed secretly under the yoke of exile. The more bitter the exile and the longer it lasts, the more complete is the consequent revelation of what was done in secret – namely, the most exalted redemption.

Redemption is a transition to a higher stage of existence, and for the sake of this ascent, descent is required. To accomplish redemption, it is necessary to nullify the existing "I," who recognizes and understands, and descend to the lower stage of faith without *da'at*, of a dream unconnected to reality. Precisely from out of the descent, from out of the seemingly low reality of the external conditions, the existence of man, the life of the people, and the essence of the world will draw forth a fresh profusion of higher levels.

REDEMPTION OF THE WORLD

The Jewish People, aside from being a collective of individuals, is the inner essence of all of existence. The task of the Jewish People, like the seed sown in the earth, is to change and direct the force of reality, to promote the growth of a towering tree with many branches. The Jewish People's concern is to change the whole world and make it more "Jewish," to make it a world that reflects the essence of Judaism – *Shekhina* and sanctity.

Exile is actually a process of transformation, which in kabbalistic and Hasidic literature is called "selection and elevation of the sparks" or "rectification of the Universe of Chaos." Within exile, there is a point of holiness that acts in the very midst of things in order to change and transform them, so that they, too, will pertain to holiness.

The world of exile, the Universe of Chaos, is not a world of emptiness and nothingness, but a world whose contents are not properly arranged; it has no structure of orderly systems. It is a confused human world that does not know its purpose or goal. In such a world, everything is equally possible and impossible.

The process of redemption, of emerging from exile, is a learning process. The world must learn in order to know what it is, what the forces affecting it are, and what their inner nature is. In a certain sense, this process resembles that of psychoanalysis. The world suffers from a psychological complex – it thinks that it is a world, that it is a separate entity existing in its own right. For it to be cured, it must be told the truth – that everything is Godliness, that "there is none besides Him."[11] It is the task of the Jewish People in exile to teach the world the truth.

REDEMPTION FROM EGYPT

Egypt is called "the nakedness of the earth,"[12] the lowest and basest place in the world, because it represents the quintessence of earthliness – the

11. Deuteronomy 4:35.
12. Based on *Kohelet Raba* (1:4): "R. Berekhiah said in the name of R Shimon b. Lakish: Whatever the Holy One, blessed be He, created in man, He created in the earth… Man has nakedness, and so has the earth, as it says: 'You have come to see the nakedness of the land' (Genesis 42:9)."

concealment of Godliness. Egyptian culture does not perceive or recognize God's existence; instead, it postulates the existence of a world that stands on its own, separate from divinity.

The name "*Mitzrayim*" (Egypt) is interpreted as the plural of *meitzar* – narrow straits containing all kinds and degrees of exile and degeneration. The name of the Egyptian king signifies the same idea: ⊠⊠⊠⊠ (Pharaoh) is an anagram of ⊠⊠⊠⊠ (the back of the neck), the opposite side. Pharaoh – by opposing God, who sustains all of existence – represents anti-existence.

The prophet Ezekiel describes Pharaoh as "The great monster that sprawls in its channels, who says, 'Mine is my Nile, and I made myself.'"[13] Pharaoh maintains that the only existence that is not in doubt is his own; hence, the Nile is mine, the forces that operate in the world and drive it are mine, and all of existence belongs to me. All that remains, then, is to reach the conclusion of ultimate darkness and degeneration – "I made myself," or in other words, "I am God."

Opposite Egypt stands the Jewish People, the smallest of all nations. By its very existence, it bears the divine truth; it is the people that represents the divine presence in the world. Israel's descent to Egypt stems from the need to master Egypt and attain the greatest victory of light over darkness.

The victory over Egypt is the model for the whole range of relations between Israel and the nations, between the divine soul of the Jew and the world to which it has descended. The exodus from Egypt shattered the idea that the world is autonomous and that it exists independently, for its own sake. The victory results when, from out of the darkness of this world emerges the preeminence of the light; when it becomes clear that the exile was but a dream, and the true reality is revealed for all to see.

13. Ezekiel 29:3.

From Servitude to Freedom

On Seder night, we observe a vast array of customs and symbolic rituals through which various elements connected to the Exodus come to the fore. Yet, for all the rich diversity of the Seder night, there is one central motif: "Once we were slaves to Pharaoh in Egypt; now we are free."

The concept of freedom is expressed in the Haggada through ritual and symbolic acts, through poetry, and through the overall atmosphere. The Seder participants recline, as is the custom of free people; they drink four cups of wine to emphasize the bounty, free choice, and ease of liberty. The text of the Haggada itself reiterates in different forms and various ways this one central idea: We are free.

SLAVERY OR LABOR

It would seem that there is nothing easier to understand than the meaning of slavery. The superficial image of suffering and degraded slaves, beaten and afflicted, is clear. The slave performs hard labor under the watchful eyes of overseers and supervisors, who make sure that he faithfully fulfills his daily quota of work. The slave's wage is low and his labor is great. But is that the essence of slavery?

The reality of life in this world is that almost everyone, although free, labors hard and with all his energy in order to earn his livelihood. At any given time, only very few do not work under the pressure of time and non-optimal conditions; it is rare to find someone who does not suffer from the necessity of working hard to meet expected quotas and the oppression of those in charge of them. The whip of the struggle for subsistence is applied almost constantly to the backs of the workers. Throughout the generations, most people have worked hard and yet brought home only enough to meet their basic needs.

The ratio between labor and rest, work and ease, changes from place to place and from one profession to another. Ultimately, however, the life of a free person is similar to a life of servitude – even hard labor. Both are composed of a certain combination of these two elements, work and rest.

The essence of slavery, then, lies not in its outer manifestations, but in its inner content. The hardship and suffering entailed in labor are not what create servitude, just as wealth and prosperity do not define freedom. The essence of slavery lies in the fact that the slave's labor is done entirely for others. The one who determines the purpose of the work is not the worker, nor are the worker's desires and aspirations expressed through his work. The other, superior person determines the purpose and sets the goals; the slave is forced to always do the will of the enslaver.

What the slave is compelled to do is of little import. It makes no difference whether the slave performs hard labor with mortar and bricks or sits in an air-conditioned room and writes literary essays. Even in the latter case, he would still be a slave.

Pharaoh understood this quite well. When he feared the people of Israel's growing strength in Egypt, he expressed the concern that they might attain self-identity "and fight against us and leave the land."[1] To ensure that the people of Israel remains in Egypt, Pharaoh must prevent the formation of self-identity, so he forces the people to occupy itself with things that are not its own concern – "to afflict it with their burdens," the burdens of the Egyptians. "And the people built store cit-

1. Exodus 1:10.

ies for Pharaoh, Pithom and Raamses."[2] These projects may have been important, and the work on them helpful and productive, but this work was for Pharaoh and for Egypt. Hence, Israel's employment in this work transformed the people into slaves – a people that produces for others and does their work.

Even one who barely toils can be a slave, and even one who labors endlessly may be free. Israel's passage into its own land and devotion to its own goals do not exempt it from the obligation to work. In fact, the new objectives may entail difficult and exhausting labor. The difference between the work of the slave and that of the free person is not in the difficulty of the work nor in a higher wage for the labor, but in the work's purpose and goal. The free man works for his own purposes and goals, for his own sake.

"ONE NATION FROM THE MIDST OF ANOTHER"

Servitude begins with the slave doing the work of others, who determine his way of life and his objectives. But servitude can go deeper than that when it ceases to be merely external toil and is internalized.

As long as the slave feels that as an individual or as part of a nation, he has his own independent aspirations – as long as he feels the suffering of his servitude, recalling that he is compelled to do the work of others despite his own goals – he is not yet completely enslaved. When the slave forgets that he is a person and begins to identify with his servitude, then the servitude has penetrated his soul. At that point, he loses his independent existence.

The prophets and our sages emphasize that, little by little, the people of Israel ceased to feel the servitude and began to identify with the work and with the Egyptians. At that point, they lost their status of independent beings.

Identification with the Egyptians does not mean that the Jews become full-fledged Egyptians, for the Egyptians (of old, or their successors in every generation) do not want to give the Jews that "privilege." But when the Jews begin to aspire to the same things as the Egyptians,

2. Ibid. 1:11.

when they regard the work imposed on them as their objective in life, they thereby subscribe to the Egyptian people's aims and aspirations.

One who has no volition of his own – whether because slavery has dulled and broken his spirit or because he has not developed an independent personality – cannot be truly free. Such a person has no essential character of his own, and he will not become free even when the yoke of bondage is eventually removed from him and he ceases to be a slave. Instead, he merely becomes an abandoned object, a slave without a master.

When our sages describe the people of Israel in Egypt as idolaters sunk in forty-nine levels of impurity,[3] they had this spiritual pattern in mind. As long as the Hebrews regarded the Egyptian idolatry as "the abomination of Egypt," it followed that their servitude was strictly a result of coercion; their attitude was marked by at least an aspiration to be freed and redeemed. But when the Jew, too, begins to believe in Egyptian idolatry and considers it a way of life for himself, he no longer has any reason to leave Egypt. To be sure, he is capable of groaning under the hard labor; he is capable of requesting for himself easier work and higher social status. But on the whole, he considers himself and his life as woven of the same Egyptian cloth, not under duress but of his own volition.

We do not know how the Jews in Egypt rationalized their servitude, but we do not have to search far in order to find Jews today who have acted and continue to act the very same way. These Jews idealize servitude, exile, and life among the nations. The ideal of the Jew, to their mind, is to continue being what he is: a servant to the nations and to their values. The Jew's aspiration is to do the nations' bidding. Even the blows and the suffering inflicted upon us by the nations cease to be something that should be complained about. For some Jews, these, too, have become part of the Jewish People's "mission" – to be exiles and sufferers, carrying the burden of other people's lives and work.

When the slave cannot free himself from his servitude because it has ceased to be a disgrace, a burden, or a source of pain for him, when

3. *Zohar Ḥadash, Yitro,* 52a.

he claims that it suits him and that he should remain in this state forever, he thereby changes from a temporary slave into an eternal slave.

For this reason, the redemption is described as "taking one nation from the midst of another;"[4] the people of Israel was entrenched in the midst of the enslaving nation, swallowed up by it and assimilating into it. At the time that the people were redeemed from Egypt, they had almost no desire anymore to leave and be redeemed. For this reason, the process of redemption had to be accompanied not only by the miracles in Egypt, but also by the reeducation of the Jewish people.

The plagues of Egypt became increasingly severe, not only so that the Egyptians would agree to let the Jews leave their country, but so that Pharaoh himself would give the final push to all the hesitators: "He will drive you out of here."[5] The Egyptians themselves had to help everyone who was making various calculations of feasibility, as well as all sunk in the impurity of Egypt, to finally leave their servitude. The Egyptians themselves had to inform these Jews that they were strangers and were not welcome in Egypt, not even as slaves of slaves.

"TO CELEBRATE A FESTIVAL UNTO GOD IN THE WILDERNESS"

The reason that Moses and Aaron presented to Pharaoh for their request to allow the people to leave Egypt was the people's need to celebrate a festival unto God in the wilderness.

At first glance, this appears to be merely an excuse; the people of Israel wanted to leave Egypt, and toward this end, they invented a reason by which to justify themselves to Pharaoh. In fact, however, this element of celebrating a festival unto God is central to the Exodus, for it expresses the essence of going forth from slavery to redemption.

The turnabout from exile to redemption is not made all at once. Between ceasing to be a slave and acquiring freedom, the individual must pass through an intermediate stage in his development, without which he cannot become truly free – he must develop inner qualities of his own. To become not merely runaway slaves but truly free people

4. Deuteronomy 4:34.
5. Exodus 11:1.

who work for their own sake, the people of Israel had to develop their own way of life and essential character.

As Pharaoh himself quickly perceived, the very desire to serve God is a sign of the weakening grip of the servitude, for true slaves have no real gods. The primary duty of the slave is to do his work and serve his master. The moment the slave discovers that there is a Master above all masters, that there is authority and duty higher than all other obligations by which he, too, is bound, he is internally no longer a slave. He may be detained for a certain period of time to perform forced labor, but that labor can no longer be considered total servitude. Rebellion and organized efforts toward achieving the goal of freedom may be delayed for quite a while, but if the desire to go out to celebrate a festival unto God remains, the opportunity will ultimately come.

In order to prevent national revival, Pharaoh tried to break the people's spirit with harsh, purposeless labor. His goal was to reduce them to a state in which they would no longer be able to dream, to desire things beyond the realm of the simplest pleasures. Pharaoh knew that true liberty begins when there is a purpose behind the will to go free beyond avoiding the harsh labor of slavery. Freedom begins when the slaves reject slavery as a system of life, morality, and values obligating the slave.

This was the importance of delineating a purpose to the Exodus – "to celebrate a festival unto God in the wilderness." When there is a genuine purpose and the new way of life that is aspired to is not simply an imitation and continuation of the slavery, but truly different – then the redemption begins.

Liberation, then, depends on acquiring an authentic identity, not on rejecting external labor. The meaning of liberation is accepting an authentic system of values, an authentic scale of goals. One who has no identity of his own and no God of his own is bound to always remain a slave, even if his master is not at this moment standing over him. He can escape his servitude only artificially; ultimately, he will remain a slave to Pharaoh, even if he flees Egypt. The external whip can be broken, but the stamp of the slave within his soul remains.

BONDAGE THAT DID NOT END

In this sense, the bondage of Egypt did not end with the exodus from Egypt. The people of Israel is liable to revert to that bondage while in other exiles and even while on its own land.

As long as the Jewish People in exile retained their authentic spiritual character, their spiritual principles, their internal leadership, and their distinctive way of life, they were not, in this dimension at least, subservient. The Jew in exile was persecuted, humiliated, and despised; he had to admit to being weak and helpless in many areas of life. Nevertheless, his exile was not complete, for he still considered himself endowed with an independent will; his spiritual world was like a substitute for a homeland.

Paradoxically, it was assimilation that made exile complete, for it was then that the Jew lost his own distinctive character. Such a Jew, even when he leaves the physical exile and arrives in his own land, continues carrying the exile with him. He continues to be subservient to the external world – subservient in his way of thought and principles of faith. Although the external world may no longer rule his body, it continues its tyranny over his soul.

Large sectors of the Jewish People act this way. They work and toil, build cities and edifices, found cultures and bring about revolutions, develop sciences and write literature – all for the Pharaoh in each generation. The "taskmasters and officers" at times appear openly, but at times they are internalized, so that there is no longer a need for an officer from without to keep the slave in his slavery. Thus, the Jewish People's servitude continues, as it creates and builds for others, performing *avoda zara* – service that is alien to itself. This is exactly how the nation expresses itself in *Song of Songs*: "They made me keeper of the vineyards, but my own vineyard I did not keep."[6]

One of the Hasidic masters aptly observed that taking the Jews out of the *galut* is easier than taking the *galut* out of the Jews. Externally leaving the *galut* can serve many great ends, but in and of itself, it is not even the "beginning of the redemption." Attempts that have been made in various ways to achieve the liberation of the Jewish People by

6. Song of Songs 1:6.

merely external departure from *galut* are incapable of bringing about true redemption. External departure from exile entails only the migration of slaves from one place to another; there is no liberation, no leaving the house of bondage. The true beginning of the redemption comes when the people reject not only the yoke of Egypt, but also the yoke of Egyptianism.

In order to achieve true redemption and not only an end to exile, it is not enough for the Jewish People to leave "the wilderness of the nations;" it must also reacquire its own essence, its character, spirit, ways of thinking, and ways of life. Only then can it be a nation of free people.

On Seder night, we emphasize this essential point: "Once we were slaves, and now we are free." As we go through the rituals and recite the *Haggada*, as we discuss the written text and what lies beyond it, we must bring ourselves to understand that escape from slavery is not enough; we must also be our true selves, thereby becoming truly free.

The Eating of Matza

THIS MATZA THAT WE EAT

On all the festivals and Sabbaths of the year, an honored place is assigned to the day's meals. In fact, the prominence of eating does not pertain only to special days of the year; rather, even our daily eating – despite its connection to the satisfaction of bodily needs – has a deeper meaning.

This attitude toward eating takes on additional significance in the case of the Seder meal. The Seder is essentially a reenactment of the way the Pesaḥ offering should be eaten, and mitzvot involving eating are thus involved – the mitzva to eat matza and the prohibition against eating *Ḥametz*.

The eating of matza and the abstention from *Ḥametz* are not simply a commemoration of the events that occurred in the exodus from Egypt, but rather represent our actual participation in those events. Many mitzvot are performed in remembrance of the exodus from Egypt, but on Pesaḥ we do more than that – in a certain sense we personally and communally re-experience the process of the Exodus. Eating matza on Pesaḥ, then, constitutes a revitalization of the essence of the Exodus, which in the human soul means rising to a different level and different form of awareness.

The eating of bread of either kind – whether *Ḥametz* or matza –

is connected to human awareness, *da'at*. The Talmud teaches that "the tree of which Adam ate...was wheat, since a child does not know how to call 'father' and 'mother' until he has had a taste of grain."[1] There is an inner connection between wheat and knowledge, between wheat and the essential nature of man as endowed with *da'at* and awareness.

From a cultural-anthropological standpoint as well, bread is classified as specifically human food. Like other animals, man eats meat and fruit. Bread, however, is the unique food of man qua man. When man eats bread, he is connected on a higher level to human civilization, to his own essential nature as an intelligent human being who knows good and evil.

Hasidic works emphasize the Talmud's choice of words: "A child does not know how to call '*father*' until he has had a taste of grain." The child's relationship to his father is not a primary relationship; rather, his primary and natural relationship is to his mother, as she is the first and most immediate object in his consciousness, particularly when he is still nursing. The relationship with a father is not a direct, instinctive-biological relationship, but a cultural one, which develops only after the child passes the stage of basic awareness.

In its early stages, even the relationship with the father is not an intellectual relationship driven by awareness and understanding. The child who says "father" does not understand all the implications and meanings of the term. He does not grasp exactly what a father is or what connection he has with his father. But when the child says "father," although he does not understand the whole significance of the expression, he makes the first jump of consciousness toward a more perfected essential nature, which is not yet his essential nature.

Our initial and basic perceptions are perceived through the physical senses, which are crude. Higher perceptions require a certain intellectual or emotional jump to a nature that transcends the senses. That sort of jump must be made by the infant in order to reach the level on which he will be able to call "father." This process always requires a leap, as it always entails stages that are not reached consciously. The early

1. *Berakhot* 40a.

stage of eating bread for the first time, the call of "father," represents the jump to a different type of consciousness, a different level of awareness.

PORTAL TO A DIFFERENT MODE OF BEING

The festival of Pesaḥ literally means the festival of "leaping," the festival on which we recall and experience the great jump, after which we became capable of calling "Father."

The problem faced by the child who must say "father" for the first time is the heart of the problem faced by the people of Israel upon its departure from Egypt. It is around this problem that Seder night revolves each year, when we are to re-experience the Exodus and bring it to life. This is the profound meaning of the festival of Pesaḥ, on which one must pass over and leap to a new awareness.

When the people of Israel left Egypt as a slave people, they ascended all at once to a level that, from their standpoint, transcended *da'at* and rationale. For the first time, they said, "Father." From above, the Holy One, blessed be He, brought a people that was not yet ready and that did not yet understand to its conclusions, skipping over all the intermediary stages of thought, logic, and insight, until reaching a place where that which cannot be understood meets that which is beyond all understanding.

The people of Israel at the Exodus was still like a child, learning for the first time who and what a Father is, how to say "Father" and how to relate to Him. For such development to take place, what is required is an attitude not built on methodical, intellectual understanding, but one whose point of departure is that man is ready to accept things that are without structured explanation and beyond reason.

The opening of the portal to the new mode of being is represented by the primitive, undeveloped, and incomplete matza. Leavened bread is a product of civilization and requires time for gradual preparation. Kneading, rising of the dough, and baking require permanent quarters and a certain level of development. Matza, by contrast, is basic bread – unrefined wheat that underwent insubstantial change – for it has not yet risen or leavened like regular bread. Nothing unnecessary is added to this bread. It is tasteless, saltless, and has no room for delicate or refined flavors.

Matza, then, is the most basic thing that can be termed "bread," the first food that belongs to the human level. For this reason, matza represents the change that resulted from the exodus from Egypt – historically, as the dawn of the Jewish People, and inwardly-personally, as a stage of man's initial recognition and basic awareness of the divine. This is the stage at which he first says "Father" to his Father in heaven, not as a result of contemplation or intellectual comprehension, but through undeveloped absorption and perception.

The process represented by the eating of matza is the attainment of the ability to accept as conclusions, as axioms, things that are not understandable. This is the ability to recognize that there are things that are not sufficiently understood, yet one can accept them and believe in them nonetheless.

The development of this ability is the first step on the way to any kind of awareness, and on the historical plane, during the Exodus, it was necessary at the beginning of the path to recognition of God at Mount Sinai. But the level of "matza" is necessary in personal development as well. The beginning of every new spiritual path or awareness must be based in a starting point of unalloyed, pure faith, devoid of rationalization and adornment. It is necessary to leap over many emotional and intellectual stages, beyond the bounds of the known world and regular concepts, straight to the conclusions – "The people believed and they heard."[2] When faith precedes the hearing-understanding, it enables the development of understanding and awareness on a different level and of a different scope.

On the night of Pesaḥ, each individual is required to make his own jump and leap, and begin presenting himself to God. Only after this stage of matza is it possible to advance to higher levels of awareness, the eating of regular bread – *Ḥametz.*

FOOD OF FAITH

The eating of matza, representing pure faith, will always be the first stage of the process, but it has meaning in later stages as well. After all, matza was eaten alongside the Pesaḥ offering, but it was baked again the next

2. Exodus 4:31.

morning as well. This second matza teaches us that whatever spiritual level a person is on, even if it is the highest of levels, he must return to the starting point and renew himself, return to the point of the first leap that is represented by the matza – the fundamental point of basic faith.

Even contemporary man must go through such a process and connect to this point in his soul. We live in a civilized world, very clever and developed, and we all consider ourselves so wise and discerning; we think we know everything. Precisely for this reason, we must return, time after time, to the point of simple and basic faith, faith based on not knowing. We must know that there are things we do not understand and will never be able to understand. As a great philosopher said, "The ultimate knowledge is that we cannot know."[3]

This is the meaning of matza as representing direct divine revelation in Egypt and at all times. All of man's greatness, his culture, everything that became puffed up and leavened during the course of the year or over thousands of years, is shattered, flattened, in the face of the revelation of the King of kings, the Holy One, blessed be He. As we learn in the Haggada, the revelation was "not through an angel, not through a seraph, and not through an emissary; rather, the Holy One, blessed be He, He Himself." In such a revelation, there is no room here for error or misunderstanding. When all of reality is opened up and God Himself appears, no matter where man is or on what level he finds himself, he returns again to the basic, primary point, to the point of the matza.

The *Zohar* calls this aspect of matza "the food of faith,"[4] for like faith, the matza is both the beginning and the end of the process. It is the same faith – that of the slaves who for the first time called "Father," and that of those who know the Torah and yet feel that there is something above and beyond understanding. Although the second is faith that begins from a higher stage, the same "not knowing" underlies it as well.

3. *Sefer HaIkarim*, vol. 2, ch. 30 (end).
4. *Zohar*, Exodus 183b.

MATZA IN THE SANCTUARY

Just as the Jewish annual cycle, the cycle of time, requires Pesaḥ, so too does the world. Place also requires such a focus, a focus that empowers new beginnings and forward leaps.

This is the task of the Sanctuary. In the Sanctuary, matza was present all year round. With very few exceptions, *Ḥametz* was not admitted into the Sanctuary. In the face of the holy, man's position is always like that of one who is just beginning. In the Sanctuary, one may not stand with the baggage of the previous day or year; one stands alone, without any addition, like the matza.

Matza symbolizes the return to the beginning and to simplicity. In our worldly lives, we eat bread and cakes, which represent forward movement into the midst of the world, development and complexity. The opposite movement – the eating of matza – represents our ability to return from the complicated world to the simple place. Both on Pesaḥ and in the Sanctuary, we return to the starting point to build anew our basic relationships.

Preserving the starting point is very important, because it serves as the basis on which the larger structure is built. If the start is defective or soiled, everything that subsequently will be built upon it will likewise be defective. For this reason, we must ensure that the matza remains pure and free of admixture, so that it will be able to serve as a basis for further progress. We must watch over it to prevent it from becoming leavened. Similarly, we are taught, "Above all that you guard, watch over your heart."[5] One must guard the heart, the center point, the first kernel of goodness and innocence, just as we safeguard matza to the utmost, so that it should not become leavened, but rather serve as a good beginning and a starting point for renewal.

Each year on Seder night, we re-experience this process. At that time, everyone becomes like a small child, who can ask all the questions anew, in spite of all the knowledge that he has accumulated during the year. On Seder night we – all of us, children and adults – can act like one who does not know and is not wise, and ask the four questions as if we never heard the answer before.

5. Proverbs 4:23.

Pesaḥ is the Spring Festival, when everything begins to blossom and bloom; all of existence undergoes renewal, and with it comes the renewal of man. Nisan – like *nitzan* (a bud) – is the beginning of the blossoming, from which everything springs forth again from the beginning.

The Devotion of Your Youth

The festival of Pesaḥ holds a position of special prominence in our calendar, by which it stands out among all the other festivals and leaves its imprint on all the days of the year. There is almost no Jewish holiday on which the exodus from Egypt is not mentioned; not only the pilgrimage festivals, but also Rosh HaShana and even the Sabbath are "in remembrance of the exodus from Egypt." In this sense, the festival of Pesaḥ extends throughout the course of the year.

At first glance, it would be appear that the exodus from Egypt was far less important than the truly decisive event in the history of the Jewish People – the Giving of the Torah. Of course, the Exodus marked the Jewish People's emergence from bondage to freedom, but the people's essence and character were bestowed upon it only at the Lawgiving.

The Giving of the Torah is the Jewish People's primordial point, whereas the Exodus – like the whole period of exile in Egypt or the lives of the patriarchs in the Land of Israel – belongs to the people's prehistory. The Exodus was merely a preparatory stage before the Lawgiving. Scripture itself expresses this in God's words to Moses: "And when you have taken the people out of Egypt, you shall serve God at this mountain."[1]

Hence, the special emphasis on the exodus from Egypt requires clarification.

A PERSONAL INNER PROCESS

Our sages teach us that "in every generation, one is obligated to regard himself as though he personally went forth from Egypt."[2] This approach provides a key to understanding all of the festivals – we must regard the festivals not just as collective processes of the entire nation, but also as inward phenomena and spiritual events in the lives of each individual. To view the festivals in such a manner, one must deeper meaning within them, significance that is not always apparent in one's initial understanding of the festival.

Thus, when considering the festival of Pesaḥ, one should not perceive only the plain meaning of the festival of freedom. Physical liberation from slavery is not an event that occurs to all people, and so not everyone can identify with it. The festival has a more abstract, spiritual meaning, however, and therefore pertains to everyone in every era.

If we transpose the historical events in the nation's experience onto the personal life of the individual in his divine service – his spiritual journey to the "Promised Land" – we can view the three pilgrimage festivals as landmarks on the journey, which are paralleled in the natural agricultural symbolism of the Spring Festival, the Harvest Festival, and the Festival of Ingathering.

The first stage – the exodus from Egypt – represents a departure from nothingness, from utter want (physical as well as spiritual) to a new destiny, unknown and mysterious. At this time of fateful decision, the person's spiritual legacy amounts to nothing. No real content can be found in this kind of awakening. When a person, after his initial awakening, goes out without content to the arid wilderness of life, he carries with him, at the very most, "bread of affliction."

Only after a while, in the course of this journey that began in

1. Exodus 3:12.
2. Mishna *Pesaḥim* 10:5.

ignorance, does the person arrive at full understanding and insight, at a clear, absolute, and well-defined determination of his purpose and aspiration. Only then is it possible to see the complete picture, the full development of his path and the purposes and goals that lie before him. This is the time of the Lawgiving to the entire nation, when its path as a unique, defined, and separate people is finally determined. In the life of the individual, the time of receiving the Torah is the time of the inner identification with the fully developed path.

The time of receiving the Torah is a stormy time, when one does not feel properly integrated. There is spiritual and intellectual perfection, but no inner peace. Things are forced from above ("He overturned the mountain over them like an inverted cask"[3]); it is difficult to reconcile oneself with all the new assets that one has received, which, to be sure, are close to one's heart, but are still foreign to one's soul.

For this reason, the receiving of the Torah is not infrequently followed by the "making of a calf," an expression of the difficulties entailed in receiving the new assets, a reaction against the new content that seems unfamiliar and does not seem to blend in with the existing reality.

Only after an extended period of time, in which one digests the new assets and adapts himself to them, does one attain a sense of inner wholeness, followed by the ability to gather in the harvest and enjoy it with peace of mind.

Thus, there are three points: decision, understanding, and the happiness of harmonious wholeness. All three are fundamental stations in each individual's personal journey. The first point, however, has such basic importance that one must recall this station in particular again and again.

THE INITIAL EXODUS

Slavery, in addition to being an external phenomenon, is also an inner feeling. When the people of Israel were slaves to Pharaoh in Egypt, they identified with Pharaoh's basic will and with the Egyptian outlook. Their slavery did not mean only that they carried out in practice the Egyptian aspirations; rather, inwardly as well, they were slaves to these aims. They

3. *Avoda Zara* 2b.

were spiritually and emotionally attached to the Egyptian system of life, which they regarded as ideal, even though they were considered worthy only of being its servants.[4] They were slaves, devoid of spiritual content, without aspirations or a path of their own.

All that was left of their true selves was a nebulous feeling of continuity, a feeling of some obscure connection to their ancestors – that somehow they were different. There was still something that preserved the nation's interconnectedness and made the people feel that even while they were slaves in Egypt, they still possessed a certain unity. A certain feeling kept them from assimilating entirely and becoming exactly like the Egyptians who surrounded them and controlled their bodies and souls. At this point, there was no understanding or content attached to this feeling, but it did have a predisposition to receive content.

Then came the call to the people to leave Egypt.

Even when considered from a simple historical standpoint, it is not self-evident that a slave people aspires to go out to freedom. Obviously, every slave wants to be relieved as much as possible from the burden that weighs down on him. However, slavery that has lasted for generations becomes slavery of the spirit and acceptance that the situation cannot be changed. Such slaves do not even know how to relate to human freedom.

Hence, the very desire for freedom, the call to leave Egypt and the people's readiness to do so, themselves constitute an upheaval in the people's soul. The possibility of being free does not even occur to a slave. Such a development, then, is none other than the revelation of the root of freedom in the soul, the awakening of the essential freedom of the human personality.

When the call came to the people to leave Egypt, it came from God, who was not known to them and whom they did not understand. Paths were proposed to them that they could not grasp. Nevertheless, their response was characteristic of this situation, not only on the part

4. This attachment to Egypt was expressed in Israel's aspirations – in their longing for the Egyptian fleshpots – as well as in their deeds – in the sin of the golden calf, for example, which was a specifically Egyptian form of worship.

of the people as a whole, but on the part of each and every individual: "And the people had faith."[5]

A DECISION TRANSCENDING THE INTELLECT

The decision to leave Egypt – to abandon the vague distress of a life without direction for a destiny that is distant and strange – is the very essence of the exodus from Egypt. The people of Israel, without knowledge and without understanding, headed towards the wilderness, which no one knew how to cross or whether it could be crossed at all. Nevertheless, the power of simple faith, the awakening of the initial decision, lit the spark to set out on the journey. Such faith can carry those who adhere to it beyond all dangers and pitfalls.

Although this way of faith is intellectually poor and insignificant, although it lacks profound content, nevertheless, inherent in it is a connection far deeper than any other. The connection of faith is a connection of essential, inner attachment – beyond all understanding – to the sublime essence of God.

This decision, this unexplained faith, contains latent within it everything that will later manifest itself. With this decision, the close connection is established. Although the external revelation appears only later, the essential inner connection appears already at the first moment, in the initial movement of "And the people had faith."

For this reason, the people's immediate and categorical response before receiving the Torah – "We will do and obey"[6] – should come as no surprise, for the essential relationship to the Torah, although concealed, was in place already from the beginning, from the first moment of the decision to follow God. As the prophet Jeremiah says: "I remembered for you the devotion of your youth, your love as a bride – how you followed Me in the wilderness, in a land not sown."[7] The memory of the people's fundamental relationship to God is the memory of the decision to leave Egypt.

The Jewish People in its youth, lacking experience and

5. Exodus 4:31.
6. Ibid. 24:7.
7. Jeremiah 2:2.

understanding, follows God without knowing anything about His essential nature, about the duties that He would impose or about the route they would be expected to take. The people agrees not only to leave Egypt and bondage, but also to follow God in the wilderness, in a land not sown. Despite the insecurity, the people is willing to bear any burden and accept all future obligations that will follow in the wake of this agreement.

The essence of the exodus from Egypt, then, lies in the initial decision, born of faith, to leave one's accustomed order of life and follow God. The explanation and elaboration come afterward, but the essence and main object begin from the moment of the very decision – *that* is the true starting point, which contains everything within it.

This primordial point is found in every man by virtue of his being a man, and that is why the festival of Pesaḥ – the festival of simple faith – attained its central place among the holidays. The month of Nisan is the month of spring, when the natural course is still in its infancy, in the beginning of its growth. It is therefore "the beginning of months; it shall be the first of the months of the year for you."[8]

8. Exodus 12:2.

The Splitting of the Red Sea

The splitting of the Red Sea was a striking historical event, but – like other events in Jewish history – its importance extends far beyond its historical time and place.

Our sages teach that "in every generation, one is obligated to regard himself as though he personally went forth from Egypt."[1] The exodus from Egypt, as well as the other important events that occurred to our ancestors, is endowed with inner, eternal meaning for all Jews in all times. The splitting of the Red Sea, besides being a memory of the past, is an aim and aspiration of every man – each person must cross and split his own personal "Red Sea."

Hasidic literature explains[2] that the parting of the Red Sea represents the parting of the sea's essential nature, as it says in the Midrash: "This teaches us that all the waters … everywhere were divided."[3] In other words, the parting of the Red Sea did not serve only to solve a momentary problem, to enable the people of Israel to cross the sea. Rather, an

1. Mishna *Pesaḥim* 10:5.
2. See *Torah Or* 62b, *Likutei Torah*, *Vayikra* 16d.
3. *Shemot Raba* 21:6.

essential change occurred in the nature of the sea, which turned into dry land.

LIFE IN THE MIDST OF DUALITY

The concepts "sea" and "dry land" represent the two general states of existence. In the *Zohar*, the sea is called the "concealed world,"[4] whereas dry land is called the "revealed world." Dry land represents the reality that is above the surface, visible to the eye; life exists on the face of the earth. By contrast, the sea represents reality that conceals what takes place inside it. The sea is the great mystery; things do not happen on its surface but within it.

People generally act like creatures of dry land, and their consciousness deals with the visible world. The higher, exalted elements of man – all that transcends plain and ordinary consciousness – are represented by the sea. These are the concealed worlds in man.[5] As a rule, we see only the lower end of the exalted things, the "tip of the iceberg" protruding above the surface. Usually, we do not see what is happening within. It is as though man's essence is sunk inside the great space, within the hidden sea, and what is visible to our eyes is but a small part, the thin stratum in which we operate.

This, in practice, is man's main problem. His present existence is always a dry-land existence, and it is this existence that engages his being. All his thoughts are dry-land thoughts, thoughts of a visible world, and he relates to life only via the visible. He is certain that he lives on a giant continent and that there is nothing besides it, but actually he lives on a small island; the visible world of man is like a small point of dry land surrounded on all sides by the sea.

The awareness that there is a hidden component within us, a concealed world that is part of our being, is our key to the mystery within ourselves, and it is this awareness that enables us to reach it. When we

4. *Zohar* I, 18a; *Tikunei Zohar*, Introduction, "*Pataḥ Eliyahu*," 17b; et al.
5. Psychologists speak at length about the "subconscious," the lower part of the soul. That is not what is meant by the "sea." The true conception of the mysterious relates to the "superconscious," the parts of the soul that transcend consciousness. They are the "sea" in man.

do reach it one way or the other, then even though it is not the sphere that is known to us and with which we are familiar, in a certain sense we return home, to our roots.

The parting of the sea – the revelation of the sea and its transformation into dry land – brings about the unification of worlds, so that man sees the complete form of himself and of the world. The ability to experience the parting of the sea and to live like amphibious creatures, in the sea and on dry land, is what distinguishes us as human beings. For such duality exists in man, as well, in the combination of body and soul.

THE SEA IN MAN'S SOUL

In the sea, life takes place on all its levels and depths of existence at once, above and below. For this reason, the sea symbolizes the supernal world, where everything is integrated. The visible world – dry land – is different. There, individual things are separate from one another, and life is lived only in the uppermost and most superficial level of reality. In the sea, life takes place *within* the medium, whereas on dry land, life takes place *upon* the medium.

In man, there is naturally a drive to be an "I," to be separate. Hence, the world in which man lives belongs to "dry land," to plain and visible reality. In a certain sense, man cannot live in an integrated world, for there he has no existence as a separate being. Human beings, as creatures of dry land, have a clear division between above and below, high and low, and their world is differentiated and separated in all its detail.

By contrast, this division does not exist in the sea. In the sea, all worlds are combined and form an integrated reality. We find such a principle in the halakha as well, as our sages say: "One may perform immersion in whatever originates in the water,"[6] and "One may perform immersion in the eye of a fish."[7] In a certain sense, the fish itself is a part of the sea; it flows within the sea and the sea flows within it, and there is no difference between it and the medium in which it lives.

Man, then, exists in an entangled state, which has no complete solution; He exists on land, and it is not within his power to disengage

6. *Zevaḥim* 22a.

7. Rambam, *Hilkhot Mikvaot* 8:11.

from it and enter the sea. On the other hand, a large part of his essence is hidden precisely there, in the integrated world of the "sea."

This may be compared to the birth of an infant. While in its mother's womb, the fetus is essentially "part of the mother;"[8] it is in complete unity with its environment and does not have independent existence. After birth, through which it is exposed to the possibility of living in disunited worlds, it will never be able to return to such an integrated state. From that point on, its relation to everything is from the perspective of a certain state, from the reality of an individual existence. Similarly, man can never attain the fully integrated reality of the sea. All that he can do is to stand on dry land and try to see the depths of the sea from there.

THE UNITY OF OPPOSITES

The process of the sea's parting – "He turned the sea into dry land"[9] – is, in a certain sense, the antithesis of the world's creation.

The process of creation is a process of demystification, where mystery is concealed and only the revealed is seen; the revealed is separated from the hidden and stands as a world unto itself – "the revealed world." In Creation, dry land emerged from the sea[10] and became a separate reality.

By contrast, at the parting of the sea, the sea opened and the land inside it appeared. Man enters into the midst of the sea, and there he sees dry land. This is not a process of the land emerging and separating from the sea, but a process of revealing the land inside the sea. It is a process of revealing the hidden.

In this sense, the parting of the sea is like a reversal of the process of creation. While the process of creation is generally a process of contraction and concealment, the parting of the sea is the reverse process, through which we are cast back into the sea, in whose midst dry land is

8. *Gittin* 23b.
9. Psalms 66:6.
10. "God said, 'Let the waters under the heavens be gathered into one place, that the dry land may appear'" (*Genesis* 1:9).

revealed. The Jewish People walked "into the sea on dry ground;"[11] from that point, it is possible to see the whole depth of reality.

The ability to be in the sea and on dry land simultaneously is a paradox that appears frequently throughout Jewish literature, and our early sages termed it the "unity of opposites."

Whenever our sages wish to refer to this paradox, they use the expression "as difficult as the parting of the Red Sea." For example, our sages say that the pairing of man and woman is as difficult as the parting of the Red Sea.[12] The union of man and woman, who are entirely different, their joining into one reality, is almost impossible; hence, it is compared to the parting of the Red Sea, in which the sea turned into dry land. In marriage, as in the parting of the Red Sea, the union prevails and manifests itself in the face of the disjointed reality.

Man's glimpse into an integrated world is the meaning of the splitting of the Red Sea. It is the unity of opposites. This return, albeit incomplete, is what forms the paradox of "into the sea on dry ground." In this process, all the heavens open, yet man continues to stand on the earth; sea and dry land, heaven and earth intermingle, and the whole mystery is revealed at once. The world, as it were, is split open, and one can view all the layers of reality, creation as a whole spectrum. This explains the well-known saying of our sages: "Maidservants beheld at the sea what even the prophet Ezekiel never saw."[13] For at the parting of the sea, the veil of mystery is torn away and the highest heavens open entirely.

FAITH AT THE PARTING OF THE RED SEA

Although the divine revelation in Egypt during the plague of the firstborn and the revelation at the Giving of the Torah were awesome and profound, there is a difference between them and the revelation at the parting of the sea.

The revelation at the Red Sea was not a revelation in the ordinary sense – revelation of the Other, when the heavens open and man

11. Exodus 14:22.
12. See *Sanhedrin* 22a, *Sota* 2a, et al.
13. See *Mekhilta DeRabbi Yishmael, Beshallah, Masekhta DeShira*, 3; *Mekhilta DeRashbi*, ad loc.

beholds visions of God. The uniqueness of the splitting of the Red Sea was that they beheld all of reality entirely laid open. In such a revelation, man descends into his own reality; he returns to his own *ein sof* (infinity) and rediscovers it. In this sense, the parting of the Red Sea involves not just revelation of profound heavenly things, but primarily revelation of the depths of reality, perception of reality from a different angle. In other words, it is the return to the roots of things, where everything is in a state other than what is generally recognized.

This revelation is the basis of and preparation for the revelation of the Lawgiving, in which the essentially Other is revealed. Before receiving the Torah, we must know what we are capable of. We must know what there is within our own reality, depth within depth.

This is the revelation of the parting of the Red Sea: not the great miracle, but the opening of our own doors, door after door, until, unobstructed, we see freely inward, within our own selves.

Every divine revelation in Scripture elicits faith, but there are several forms and types of faith. Before the exodus from Egypt, "The people believed;"[14] at the parting of the Red Sea, "They believed in God and in His servant Moses;"[15] at the Giving of the Torah, Moses was told, "And then they will believe in you forever."[16]

The people's faith before the Exodus was elementary faith, which may be called simple or primitive faith. At this stage, one neither knows nor understands, yet one believes nonetheless. This is faith in the sense of faithfulness, in the sense of agreement about something.

At the parting of the Red Sea, something different occurred. The faith at this stage is faith born of verification, of apprehending the truth. "They believed in God and in His servant Moses" – they now recognized that everything they had been told, everything they had believed in until now with simple faith, was actually true.

There are things that many people believe in; thus they were told, and thus their ancestors were told. Everyone has known these things for generations, and everyone believes in them with perfect faith. But when

14. Exodus 4:31.
15. Ibid. 14:31.
16. Ibid. 19:9.

a person crosses the Red Sea, he sees their truth for himself; everything is verified, for now he has experienced a personal vision of them.

The central motif in the parting of the Red Sea is "*This* is my God"[17] – "This," as one points with his finger, as opposed to the more removed "That" or "He." As the midrash describes, "Each one of those who emerged from the sea pointed with his finger and exclaimed, 'This is my God and I will glorify Him!'"[18] Infants as well as adults – everyone saw that what formerly was "He," the Other, had now become "This," something close and immanent.

Everything that was "up in the air" was verified by the passage in the midst of the sea and the faith that came as a result. This vision was the required foundation and preparation for the next stage – the receiving of the Torah.

FISH ON DRY LAND

Why is it that after witnessing the splitting of the Red Sea, the people believed "in His servant Moses"? In a certain sense, only at the parting of the Red Sea were the people of Israel truly able to understand Moses our Master.

In Hasidism, some men are described as "fish of the sea that walk on dry land."[19] Some people never leave the sea. They may live among ordinary people "on dry land," but they see the matters of the concealed worlds. Moses our Master was such a man; "she named him Moses, saying, 'I drew him out of the water.'"[20] Moses never went out entirely onto dry land; he lived in the revealed world as though he were in the concealed world.

Since Moses was on such a high level, distinguished from and exalted above other human beings, he lived in a different dimension. He could hardly speak the same language as his people; indeed, he was "heavy of mouth and heavy of tongue."[21] Moses had a basic lack of

17. Ibid. 15:2.
18. *Shemot Raba* 23:15.
19. *Likutei Torah, Bemidbar* 22b
20. Exodus 2:10.
21. Ibid. 4:10.

understanding of ordinary human beings and everything concerning them. When the people demanded of him, "Give us meat to eat," he answered, "Where am I to get meat?"[22] He did not understand how it was possible that people could be so preoccupied with food. Was it necessary to cry over such a matter?

For Moses, the state attained by the people at the parting of the Red Sea – revelation of the concealed – was his ordinary state of being. At the one-time event of the parting of the Red Sea, the entire people reached the level of "fish of the sea that walk on dry land." Now they were better able to understand Moses our Master, a man who lived on dry land in the midst of the sea. Thus, "They believed in God and in His servant Moses."

THE PARTING OF THE RED SEA FOR ALL GENERATIONS

Each one of the holidays forms an engraving in reality. This engraving is not just a memory, the impression made by a past event, but is an actual change in our reality, which as a result is no longer as it once was. To borrow an analogy from another sphere, each holiday creates a genetic mutation within the Jewish People.

At the parting of the Red Sea, we beheld with our own eyes the depth of reality. This vision can perhaps be forgotten superficially, but something of it is engraved within us. Even when we are not conscious of it, it allows us to rely upon it. Thus, as we continue in the path of serving God, as we build edifices of Torah and mitzvot, we have on what to rely. Generations after the great miracle, a Jew can say that he does not remember the event, and he can even deny it. Nevertheless, the point of "This is my God and I will glorify Him" is found in his "genes." No matter how much he does not want it, no matter how much he tries to deny it, he cannot divest himself of this identity, this engraved impression.

We are fish that do not asphyxiate on dry land; this ability has remained with us ever since the parting of the sea. We have our sea, which we sail from end to end and in which we are united with the divine, besides whom there is none else. At the same time, we are called upon to live our lives in this world, with all that entails.

22. Numbers 11:13.

The Jew is called upon, then, to take his "sea" with him wherever he goes on dry land. We go from one exile to the next, and at the same time continue to live within our true reality, which is not dry land, but sea.[23]

23. This is expressed in our prayers as well. A Jew, wherever he may be, prays for the Land of Israel – for the rains of *Eretz Yisrael,* for the holidays in *Eretz Yisrael.* In this sense, he lives the Land of Israel outside the Land. (There is a saying in the name of *Admor HaTzemaḥ Tzedek*: "Make the Land of Israel here.")

The Days of Counting The *Omer*

The Days of the Counting

CUSTOMS OF MOURNING

The Halakha dictates special laws pertaining to the days of counting the *omer* (*Sefirat HaOmer*). Although these laws are marked by differences in custom, their common denominator is that they reflect a form of gloom.

The well-known reason for these manifestations of mourning is that during this time period, the disciples of R. Akiva died:

> R. Akiva had twelve thousand pairs of disciples, from Gevat to Antipatris, and all of them died in one period because they did not treat one another with respect... All of them died between Pesaḥ and *Atzeret* [Shavuot].[1]

Yet, as the sole reason for the customs of mourning during this period, this explanation seems highly anomalous. After all, periods of mourning as long as the days of counting the *omer* were not established even for serious and painful events that affected the general state of the nation. The custom of the Ashkenazim is to observe three weeks of mourning before Tisha B'Av, which is beyond what is dictated by the Talmud – but

1. *Yevamot* 62b.

no more than that. Even for serious tragedies, such as the destruction of Betar and other tragic events,[2] only one day of commemoration was established, whereas here we are dealing with a long mourning period of seven weeks!

Even though the period "between Pesaḥ and *Atzeret*" is mentioned in the Gemara, this does not sufficiently explain why there are differences in custom regarding the mourning period – whether it ends on Lag BaOmer (the 33rd day of the counting) or begins on Rosh Ḥodesh Iyar and lasts until the festival of Shavuot.

In order to understand the reason behind the customs of the counting of the *omer*, we must first clarify a basic point relating to the reasons underlying halakhot in general.

There are some laws and customs whose rationale, as ascribed to them in the literature, is sufficient for the one who observes them. Although they also have an esoteric reason, a person can ignore it, saying that he does not get involved in esoteric matters.

There are other laws, however, whose exoteric rationale is not sufficient, neither halakhically nor conceptually. Sometimes, the rationale that immediately presents itself to the eye of the observer, or the rationale that appears in the literature, is only one of the reasons for the law or custom. It may, in fact, not be the primary rationale, but rather a secondary one. For whatever reason – whether because the matter is esoteric or because of a concern about publicizing the true rationale – it was not considered prudent to explain the reason behind the law or custom, which therefore remained obscure and veiled.

The customs of *Sefirat HaOmer* are just such a case; they are best understood on the basis of their esoteric rationale.

During *Sefirat HaOmer*, we count each day on the way from Pesaḥ to Shavuot, and it appears that the customs observed during these days derive from this process. These customs are not rooted in mourning; they stem from the need to prepare for the festival of Shavuot. During the days of counting, we concentrate on preparing ourselves spiritually, and for lack of time, we do not engage in other distractions, such as getting married or getting a haircut and shaving.

---

2. *Ta'anit* 4:6.

A similar phenomenon may be observed through the comparison of Yom Kippur and Tisha B'Av. On these two days, the laws of fasting are identical; both days are fast days that last from evening to evening, and five abstentions are required. Nonetheless, their natures are clearly different. A well-known saying underscores the distinction between the two fasts: "On Tisha B'Av, who can eat? On Yom Kippur, who wants to eat?" Tisha B'Av is a day of mourning, and its fast stems from that sorrow. By contrast, Yom Kippur is a day of holiness, and its fast stems from the day's exalted standing.

A very similar relationship pertains to *Sefirat HaOmer* and the three weeks before Tisha B'Av. Similar customs are observed during these two periods, but the basic reason for the customs differs in each case. During the three weeks and the nine days of Av, the customs stem from mourning over loss. By contrast, during *Sefirat HaOmer*, the customs stem from the need to focus our energies inward, on our inner life. Hence, although the two periods resemble each other in their customs, their essential natures differ, and one's spiritual relationship to each must differ as well.

BETWEEN PESAḤ AND ATZERET

Pesaḥ and Shavuot share the same inner nature, for Shavuot is what gives meaning to the freedom of Pesaḥ. In and of itself, going out to freedom is meaningless as long as a new independent personality is not formed to invest the freedom with inner content. The connection between these festivals takes on further meaning because of the connection between two events in the agricultural year. The first crop of barley, animal food, is harvested and offered on Pesaḥ, while the crop that is the food of man, wheat, is offered on Shavuot.

The symbolic significance of this dual connection has been interpreted throughout the generations as the relationship between the primary, incomplete festival – the exodus from Egypt, which is essentially the negation of exile – and the level of the people's full development and inner freedom at the Giving of the Torah.

The days in between, the days of *Sefirat HaOmer*, symbolize the "journey in the wilderness," the path of wandering and searching, the bewilderment, thirst, and deprivation that a person experiences from the first stage of liberation until the reception of the inner light.

It is impossible to reach Mount Sinai directly from Egypt. In order to receive the Torah, there must first be a period of inner preparation. God gave the Torah only once, but we are required on the festival of Shavuot to receive the Torah each year anew. Our readiness to receive the Torah, to declare, "We will do and obey," requires preparation, and that is why the receiving of the Torah is delayed for seven weeks.

In the mystical literature, an analogy is drawn between the seven weeks of *Sefirat HaOmer* and the seven clean days in the laws of *Nidda* (the menstruant woman). In the Torah, there are two mitzvot connected with counting: "She shall count to herself,"[3] in the case of *Nidda*, and "You shall count to yourselves"[4] of *Sefirat HaOmer*. Just as the woman must purify herself during these seven days and prepare for the renewed encounter with her husband, the days of *Sefirat HaOmer* are days of self-purification and preparation in anticipation of the Giving of the Torah and the encounter with the Holy One, blessed be He, at Mount Sinai.

RECTIFICATION OF CHARACTER

What is the preparation required for these days? How can one prepare oneself for receiving the Torah?

Aside from *Sefirat HaOmer*, there is another period in the year dedicated to rectification and purification – the Ten Days of *Teshuva*. Yet there is a difference between these two periods.

In the Ten Days of *Teshuva* and the month of Elul, *Teshuva* is required for sins actually committed, and one must strengthen himself as regards future conduct. By contrast, the days of *Sefirat HaOmer* are not days of *Teshuva* from sins; the theme of these days is rectification of the soul, not rectification of deeds. During this period, one is required to examine one's inner nature more than one's outer deeds. It is possible that, in practice, one does all that is required of a person of his caliber, yet there may still be defects that he can find within himself. There are people who, despite their good deeds, have character defects, and *Sefirat HaOmer* is the time to rectify those defects. In order to receive the Torah fully, one must go through a process of self-refinement.

---

3. Leviticus 15:28.
4. Ibid. 23:15.

The Talmud states that our patriarch Abraham fulfilled the entire Torah even before it was given.[5] Some explain that if a person were truly refined – as was our patriarch Abraham – he would fulfill the Torah of his own accord, without having to receive the Torah from above.[6] Rectification of the soul serves as an introduction to receiving the Torah.

The days of *sefira* are days of inner growth, as well as days of self-improvement and war against all character traits that block one's spiritual development. The seven weeks of *sefira* are linked to the seven attributes-*sefirot*: *Ḥesed* (love), *Gevura* (strength), *Tiferet* (beauty), *Netzaḥ* (perpetuity), *Hod* (majesty), *Yesod* (foundation), and *Malkhut* (kingship). The *sefirot* are a kind of guidance for rectification of character, and in each one of the seven weeks we direct our attention to a different element represented by one of these attributes.

This idea is expressed in the "*Ribono Shel Olam*" ("Master of the Universe") prayer, in which we say, each day after the counting:

> By the merit of *Sefirat HaOmer* which I counted today, may whatever I have impaired in the *sefira* of be rectified. May I be purified and sanctified with heavenly holiness, and through this may a beneficent outpouring be effected in all worlds, to refine our lives and spirits [so that they are free] of any dross or defect, purifying us and sanctifying us with Your exalted holiness.

We rectify ourselves inwardly, stage after stage, in order to receive the

5. *Kiddushin* 82a.
6. The story is told that when one of the great *tzaddikim* was still a boy, he was studying tractate *Shabbat* and reached the discussion dealing with a person who loses track of the day of the week and does not know which day is the Sabbath (*Shabbat* 69b). He asked, "How is it possible for a person not to know which day is the Sabbath? Why, one sees it immediately! One can simply go outside and see that now it is Sabbath!" In order to be able to see that "now it is the Sabbath," in order to know on one's own what one must do on the Sabbath, one must possess a refined and pure spirit to such a measure that he will be attentive to all this. However, in most people, there is some distortion that does not allow them to distinguish between good and evil and to naturally do what is good; they must be told what should be done. This distortion is what should be set right during *Sefirat HaOmer*.

Torah. It is possible to receive this gift without any preparation; but without the inner preparation, the Torah's impact on us is not as it could be.

These days of *Sefirat HaOmer* are essentially days of inner struggle; hence, there is a veil of sadness spread over them. This is not mourning, but solemnity. This solemnity accompanies us until we reach the day of conclusion, the festival of Shavuot, on which light shines forth and joy breaks out and the journey reaches its culmination.

Thus, the inner rationale for the customs of *Sefirat HaOmer* is not emphasis on mourning but rather avoidance of distraction. The preparation required during these days neither allows nor leaves one time to engage in other matters. This time is dedicated to purification and to rectification of character, which are preliminary stages that enable one to receive the Torah fully.

The Dream of Independence

There is one childhood memory from when I was about ten that remains alive in my mind as if it occurred yesterday – the vote of the United Nations General Assembly in favor of a Jewish State in Palestine on November 29, 1947. As I was falling asleep, I heard the counting of votes from our neighbors' radio: "...Greece – no...Uruguay – yes..." The following morning, I got up to go to school as usual, and to my surprise I saw that the streets were packed with people rejoicing, dancing.

No one organized it, yet all of Jerusalem was beside itself with joy – joy over something that was not even proper independence, but the dream of independence.[1]

This was a very powerful experience, and I do not recall having seen such rejoicing ever since. This joy was shared by all, despite the fact that even the children knew clearly that a war was sure to ensue. The feeling that from now on, I can somehow decide for myself – that was an extraordinary, unforgettable feeling.

Indeed, with states as with individuals, the knowledge of having

1. The actual Declaration of Independence of the State of Israel was pronounced by David Ben Gurion some six months later, on May 14, 1948, 5 Iyar, 5708.

become independent, of now being on one's own, can be an awesome, even frightening experience. To be responsible for oneself entails an entirely new life, a change that is difficult to absorb. Yet it is not entirely terrifying; it also has its element of joy.

Formally, the State of Israel was established in 1948, but the process of its creation began a few years earlier. In the distress and struggle that characterized the years that preceded Israel's declaration of independence, the *Yishuv* ("settlement") that emerged here was both the source of glory and the root of the problem. Not only a new settlement but also a new kind of a Jew was created here, a new species that undoubtedly wanted to be – and in many ways, indeed was – very different from the Diaspora Jew.

This new Jew clearly parted with the past and created new things, many of which were extremely beautiful. These creations also contained quite a number of questionable elements – but at any rate, there was something new. This "New Jew" was no longer the wretch who is beaten up and remains silent, humbly accepting his suffering. He learned to fight, to stand on his own, to strike back. He also ceased to be a *luftmentsch*, or the *lumpenproletarian* of the entire world. Rather, the New Jew became productive, producing basic products and making a tremendous effort to return to the soil, to strike roots and grow from working the land.

Indeed, one of the characteristics of Jews living in this land – which may seem immaterial, but in fact is deeply significant – is that they are Jews who plant trees. Diaspora Jews – even landowners – do not ordinarily plant trees, not even if they tend the roses in their garden. This phenomenon reflects the inner feeling that life anywhere in the Diaspora is temporary. The soil is, at most, a place of wandering, and there is always the imminent possibility of having to move – either of one's own will, or by force – to another land, to a different exile. Even when people do not think about it consciously, they feel it; they do not feel that they have a permanent soil under their feet. Here in Israel, however, people plant trees not only because they know that they will grow, but also because they feel that they belong to this place and that their children and grandchildren will sit under the shade of these trees.

A new language was created here as well. The revival of the Hebrew language is a unique phenomenon. In Ireland, for instance, the government is devoting its resources to reviving the Gaelic language – which is not extinct, but is used by an ever-decreasing number of people – with no apparent success. Yet Hebrew, which for so many years was not a spoken language at all, has reawakened. To be sure, this new Hebrew is not exactly Biblical, Mishnaic, or Talmudic. It is a new type of Hebrew, slightly impudent and slangy, but also full of vitality. Consciously and unconsciously, intentionally and unintentionally, what was severed for two thousand years is now being reconnected.[2]

Such changes were probably inevitable. My parents' generation not only lived in this country, they also built it; they laid its foundations, fought for it, contracted malaria for its sake. And that generation accepted – sometimes with regret and sometimes without it – that the new generation would forget some, and perhaps more than some, of its past. They assumed that in the course of time, we would have to part with many things, some of them lofty and glorious. But they also hoped that whatever would be created here would make this loss worthwhile.

What actually is happening, however, is that there is an ever-increasing blurring of our selfhood for the sake of imitation. Culturally speaking, we are not even a small USA; we are just a very provincial province of it. We imitate its movies, its manner of speech, its slang, its sins – without, unfortunately, acquiring its virtues as well. There were similar previous situations in our history,[3] and it is happening again in our time.

What is selfhood? How do we become ourselves? Can it be done by returning to the past? I think not. Returning to the past is a dream, an impossibility. One can turn back the hands of the clock, but no one can turn back time. One cannot be the way one's father, grandfather, or great-grandfather were; at most, one can become a reactionary, which is not quite the same thing.

In order to become ourselves, we must "draw from the wells

2. For example, I was astounded to find certain very prevalent Israeli Hebrew colloquialisms in the letters of Bar Kokhba (the leader of the Great Revolt against the Romans, 132–135 CE). Bar Kokhba was not intentionally imitated; in fact, the people who use these phrases have no knowledge of him. It seems that once we returned to this land, we also began, unknowingly, to imbibe from it linguistically as well.
3. See Nehemiah 13:24.

of salvation"[4] and penetrate our own depths. We must identify shells of imitation, the desire to make it in this or that society, and seek out what is real. This means digging for our own soul, finding out where it is. And wherever our soul is, it can still hear the echoes of the Giving of the Torah; it still says *Shema Yisrael,* even when it is no longer familiar with the verse.

A few decades ago, I taught a class on the issue of "Who is a Jew." I said then that a real Jew is one who would choose to sanctify God's name, even die for the choice, rather than worship idols. Indeed, Jewish history is replete with thousands of examples not only of righteous people, but also of simple Jews who died for the sanctification of God's name.

A man in the audience then asked me: This was surely true in the past, but do you think it is still valid? At that point, I did not know what to reply, and the question was left hanging.

The next day, I flew to a kibbutz near Eilat and spoke there. I do not remember exactly what I said, but I do remember that I managed to make my listeners furious. At some point, one man, who could no longer contain himself, got up and screamed: "I am a secular Jew, and so were my father and grandfather. But I am telling you: if someone were to try to force me to worship idols, I would die rather than do it." It was almost like a voice from Heaven; I received the answer some twenty-four hours after having been asked the question from someone who had not even heard it.

The essential core does, then, exist in the wellspring, but we have to get to it and dig it out. It seems that this is what God wants. He wants us – with our problems and complications, with our crooked, stubborn, tortuous souls. And He has given us the possibility of attaining independence – that is, of, reconnecting with ourselves for the sake of our Jewish independence, so that our existence will be based not on "safe borders" or a "safe peace," but on a genuine foundation.

So what is independence? The Hebrew word for "independence," *atzma'ut,* stems from the same root as *etzem,* "self." Being independent means being more myself. Just as the external, political manifestation of independence is not being dominated by others, the inner meaning

4. See Isaiah 12:3.

of the term is not imitating others. Waving a flag and declaring a government are the easy part; being myself is surely a more difficult, more complicated path.

Thus far, the independence of the State of Israel has been largely expressed in external forms – a flag, an army, a national anthem, ambassadors, a government, elections. In essence, however, we have lost parts of our selfhood along the way. What I would really like to wish the State of Israel is that it will attain independence – not necessarily with different borders or a different population, but true independence.

Pesaḥ Sheni – Day of Rectification

In our times, Pesaḥ Sheni, the second opportunity to offer the Pesaḥ offering on the 14th of Iyar,[1] has little practical significance, even where the custom to eat matza on this day is observed. Nevertheless, the remembrance of this date serves to remind us of the day's essential meaning, above and beyond the former practice.

It is said in the name of the *Maharash*, Rabbi Shmuel, the fourth Rebbe of Lubavitch, that "the meaning of Pesaḥ Sheni is that there is no 'lost' situation. It is always possible to correct, to repair the situation. Even someone who was impure, someone who was on a distant journey, even if his deeds were *lakhem*[2] – willful – in spite of everything, it is still possible to rectify everything."[3] Even the Pesaḥ offering – the lack of which is a serious deficiency and whose deliberate neglect entails the penalty of *karet* – has a corrective. Even for this mitzva, one is given a second chance.

One of the major challenges in life is that things happen to a

1. See Numbers 9:6–14.
2. Ibid. 9:10.
3. *HaYom Yom*, 14 Iyar.

person, physically and spiritually, which appear to be irreparable. The meaning to be gleaned from Pesaḥ Sheni is the possibility of a second chance, the possibility of rectifying things that were missed the first time around.

REQUESTING A SECOND OPPORTUNITY

We should add that a special lesson emerges from the manner in which Pesaḥ Sheni came into being:

> There were, however, some men who had come in contact with the dead, and were therefore ritually impure, so that they could not make the Pesaḥ offering on that day. They approached Moses and Aaron…These men said to him [Moses], "We are ritually impure as a result of contact with the dead. But why should we lose out and not be able to offer God's offering at the right time, along with the people of Israel?"[4]

As a rule, questions of only one type were addressed to Moses: clarification of the law of one who gathers wood on the Sabbath,[5] clarification of the penalty of one who blasphemes the name of God,[6] clarification of the law of one who dies leaving no sons but only daughters to inherit him.[7] Underlying all these questions is simply the will to know the law.

Here, however, we have a question of a different type. The questioners come up with something new. They argue, "Why should we lose out?" They decide that it is their right not to be deprived of a mitzva, and they request a second opportunity to fulfill it.

The fact that they were ritually impure as a result of contact with the dead exempted them from the obligation to bring the Pesaḥ offering at the appointed time. They were exempt, but they felt that they were missing this mitzva. Unwilling to forgo its fulfillment, they complained, "Why should we lose out?"

---

4. Numbers 9:6–7.
5. Ibid. 15:32.
6. Leviticus 24:16.
7. Numbers 27:1.

Actually, the rectification offered here transcends ordinary *teshuva*. On the face of it, even *teshuva* does not provide a corrective that makes up for positive mitzvot that one failed to perform. "Of this it says, 'What is crooked cannot be made straight; what is not there cannot be counted.'"[8] If one did not recite the *Shema*, the missed recital cannot be made good, even if one fasts for thirty days.

Teshuva out of love, however, true and complete *teshuva*, also provides rectification for what one failed to do; even this deficiency can be remedied. Such a rectification was what those men sought.

We see, then, that Pesaḥ Sheni signifies not only that there is a second opportunity, but also that it is necessary to desire and request that opportunity in order for it to materialize. This is true in worldly matters as well as in spiritual ones. Sometimes, when a person fails, he would be given a second chance if only he would request it. Even serious matters can be rectified, but one must request this rectification. "Fortunate is he who did not sin. And if one sinned, he should know that there is another opportunity; if only he will desire it, he can return and be forgiven."[9]

THERE IS NO DESPAIR

On the Talmudic principle of "*ye'ush shelo mida'at*" (despair without knowledge),[10] the early masters expounded: "*Ye'ush* (despair) – *shelo mida'at* (stems from ignorance)." If a person does not fall into despair and hopelessness, there is always a way out. Even if, due to the great damage that was caused, the rectification seems remote and impossible, it can still be accomplished. Sometimes, a person thinks that he has gone so far, and declined so badly, that there is no opportunity for him to rise anew – and then, even when the opportunity does come, he does not make use of it. Sometimes, a person can take advantage of the opportunity and return from a place of seemingly no return.

In practice, even someone who was "on a distant journey, *lakhem*," at the time of the Pesaḥ offering – even one who deliberately ate *Ḥametz* and drank beer on Pesaḥ, and was motivated solely by desire – can begin

8. *Ḥagiga* 9a, citing Ecclesiastes 1:15.
9. Based on *Sukka* 53a.
10. See *Bava Metzia* 21b.

a new life; there is a door by which he can reenter. But this opportunity is given only to one who requests it.

The story is told that Elisha ben Abuya – known as *Aḥer* ("Other") because of how far he had fallen – heard a *bat kol*, a heavenly voice, that declared, "Return, backsliding children – except for *Aḥer*." As a result of this experience, he was sure that there was no longer any corrective for him. Even when the opportunity for *teshuva* presented itself to him, even when his disciple R. Meir said to him, "You, too, return," he did not return.[11]

To be sure, according to his level and his deeds, *Aḥer*'s fall was truly monumental. Nevertheless, had he persisted and requested the opportunity, he certainly would have found the way to return and repair the broken vessels: "Just as vessels of gold and of glass, even if broken, can be repaired; so, too, a Torah scholar, even if he has sinned, can be rectified."[12] *Aḥer*, however, thought that there was no corrective for him; he despaired of rectification, and thereby missed his second chance.

The Talmud relates that there was not a prostitute in the world with whom Elazar ben Dordaya did not have relations. In order to return in *teshuva*, he had to reach the conclusion that "the matter depends on me alone. He placed his head between his knees and wept aloud, until his soul departed." And what was his rectification? "A *bat kol* was heard proclaiming, 'Rebbe Elazar b. Dordaya is destined for the life of the World to Come.'"[13]

On this story, R. Yehuda HaNasi said two things: "R. [Yehuda HaNasi] wept and said: One person may acquire eternal life after many years, while another may acquire it in one hour. [He] also said: Not only are penitents accepted, they are even called 'Rebbe!'"[14]

That Elazar ben Dordaya was forgiven is understandable, but why was he called "Rebbe"? An explanation, although perhaps not according to the simple meaning, is that a Rebbe is someone who shows the way to others. Rebbe Elazar ben Dordaya became the Rebbe of a great

11. *Ḥagiga* 15a.
12. Ibid.
13. *Avoda Zara* 17a.
14. Ibid.

many people. He taught that even one who was addicted to sin his entire life can do *teshuva*; even one who is mired in the depths of sin can set things right.

King David, too, exalted the yoke of *teshuva*,[15] but he showed the way to those for whom it was pertinent to begin with. Rebbe Elazar ben Dordaya taught that even one who was caught up in sin all his life can do *teshuva* and be destined for the life of the World to Come.

A further story is told of Yakum of Tzerorot, nephew of R. Yose ben Yoezer of Tzereda. While his uncle was being brought to the gallows for the crime of teaching Torah, Yakum, who was riding on a horse on the Sabbath, questioned divine justice:

> "Look at my horse, on which my master has put me, and look at your 'horse,' on which your Master has put you!" R. Yose answered him, "If this is how [He rewards] those who anger Him, all the more so [does He reward] those who do His Will." Yakum said to his uncle, "Has anyone done His Will more than you have? [And yet look at how you are afflicted!]" R. Yose answered him, "If this is how He afflicts those who do His will, all the more so does He afflict those who anger Him."

R. Yose's words penetrated and burned in Yakum's soul like the venom of a serpent. He went and carried out upon himself the four forms of judicial capital punishment...

> As R. Yose ben Yoezer of Tzereda was dying, he dozed off and saw Yakum's bier flying in the air. R. Yose said, "Through a short spell of *teshuva*, he [Yakum] managed to precede me on the way to Paradise."[16]

Thus, we see that it is possible for everyone to return – not just those who originally were *tzaddikim*, but even people like Rebbe Elazar ben Dordaya and Yakum of Tzerorot.

15. Ibid. 5a
16. *Bereshit Raba* 65:22.

THE NATURE OF THE REMINDER ON PESAḤ SHENI

Pesaḥ Sheni – even though it certainly does not apply in our time – is noteworthy because it serves to remind us of the important principle of "Though he may fall, he is not utterly cast down."[17] One may fall, but one need not remain in a fallen state. In practice, this is the difference between the *tzaddik* and the wicked. "Seven times the *tzaddik* falls and gets up" – the *tzaddik* gets up each time he falls, for in order to fall seven times, one must rise seven times. "But the wicked are brought down by one misfortune"[18] – after even one time, they do not get back up.

The foregoing explains R. Yehuda's statement about the distinction between the righteous and the wicked:

> In the time to come, the Holy One, blessed be He, will bring the evil inclination and slay it in the presence of the righteous and the wicked. To the righteous, it will have the appearance of a high mountain, and to the wicked it will have the appearance of a thread of hair. Both the former and the latter will weep. The righteous will weep, saying, "How were we able to overcome such a high mountain?" The wicked, too, will weep, saying, "How is it that we were unable to conquer this thread of hair?"[19]

A high mountain is built by piling one thread of hair, and then another and another and another. The wicked man encountered the first thread of hair and remained there; the righteous man passed over one thread of hair and then another and another, until over the course of his life, an entire mountain of hairs had piled up. The righteous looks at the mountain and wonders how he could have passed over such a mountain; the wicked takes a look and says, "How is it that I was unable to conquer the thread of hair?"

The important lesson to be learned from Pesaḥ Sheni is that there is a second chance, a second Pesaḥ, and there is no situation in which

17. Psalms 37:24.
18. Proverbs 24:16.
19. *Sukka* 52a.

all hope is lost. Even if it seems to us that all is lost, it is not so; whoever requests another opportunity receives it.

WITH YOU THERE IS FORGIVENESS – THEREFORE YOU ARE FEARED

What we have said explains a difficult verse in Psalms: "With You there is forgiveness, and therefore You are feared."[20] Why is it that God's ability to grant forgiveness produces fear of Him?

When a person knows that there is no forgiveness, there is nothing to do to counteract the sin – it is all over, and he has nothing left to lose. Such a person does not fear anything, because he is already dead; nothing can be done to him. But when a person knows that "with You there is forgiveness," the situation is not lost. Although he may have done something very wrong, everything is not yet permissible, because it is still possible to set things right. God still exists in the world, and there is still a place for the fear of God.[21]

The Pesaḥ offering is not a trivial matter. It entails the penalty of *karet*[22] – and yet even for such a matter, a remedy exists. One must remember this principle always – in the month of Iyar and in the month of Av, in the month of Mar-Ḥeshvan and in the month of Adar. Rectification exists in the world, and one need only request it.

20. Psalms 130:4.
21. Cf. *Vayikra Raba* 30:7.
22. Under the penalty of *karet* (literally, "cutting off"), the offender's life is cut short by Providence. See Numbers 9:13.

Lag BaOmer[1]

In the Land of Israel, Lag BaOmer is a very popular day. The land is filled with bonfires, in preparation for which many children gather wood over the course of several weeks. Lag BaOmer is not a holiday, yet the universal custom is to cease on this day the mourning practices of *Sefirat HaOmer*, and there are numerous and diverse traditions regarding the manner in which this day is celebrated. These range from the Sephardic tradition of holding a public auction of candle-lighting in honor of all the *tzaddikim* the synagogue beadle can recall, to the custom prevalent in Eastern Europe of making bows and arrows for the children, with which they would go out to the forests.

This day is mentioned in various places in Jewish literature, yet to a great extent, its meaning and theme remain a mystery. Sources record that it was on Lag BaOmer that the plague ceased to afflict the disciples of R. Akiva, but there is no real proof for this claim. From other sources and from an obscure tradition, we learn that this day is the yahrzeit of

1. The numerical value of the Hebrew letters ל״ג (whose transliteration is *Lag*) is thirty-three. Thus, Lag BaOmer is the 33rd day of *Sefirat HaOmer*, the counting of the *omer*.

R. Shimon bar Yoḥai, and that all the celebrations are in honor of this occasion.

In the sources, this day is called the "*hillula* day" of R. Shimon bar Yoḥai. The literal meaning of *hillula* is "wedding," and the expression "the *hillula* of R. Shimon bar Yoḥai" that is mentioned in the sources appears there in its literal sense – referring to the celebration made for R. Shimon bar Yoḥai when he got married in his youth. In the case of Lag BaOmer, however, "*hillula* day" is mentioned in connection with the day of R. Shimon's death.

At first glance, of course, the association of the term *hillula* with the day of someone's death seems puzzling. After all, over the generations, a person's yahrzeit was observed by his family and children as a fast day, and certainly not as a day of celebration. Nevertheless, over time, the association of this term with R. Shimon's yahrzeit has become so accepted that the yahrzeits of other *tzaddikim* are also designated by the term *hillula*.

A more profound explanation of the association of the yahrzeit with the *hillula* appears in brief in one of the discourses of our Master and Teacher, R. Schneur Zalman of Liadi:[2] He explains that the main theme of a wedding is the joy of the bride and groom, which stems from the union of two individuals who were destined to each other even before they were born,[3] but who were apart for many years. We might say that before they were born, they were acquainted with each other and had a relationship, but this relationship was severed after they were born. The great joy of the reunion, after years of longing and yearning, is the source of the joy of a wedding.

Similarly, the *tzaddik* who descended to this world had to part from all the souls who were together with him in Gan Eden. As long as he remains in this world, these souls yearn for him. When he departs this world and returns to his original place, these souls hold a celebration and rejoice over the reunion.

---

2. R. Schneur Zalman of Liadi, founder of Chabad. See *Ma'amarei Admor HaZaken* 5562, vol. 2, p. 430.
3. *Moed Katan* 18b.

The implication is that this supernal joy over the reunion is so great that it overcomes the sorrow felt by people in this world over the *tzaddik*'s death. They, too, overcome their sorrow and share in the soul's joy at having reached a happier place. Thus, an ancient text records a eulogy from Talmudic times: "Weep for the mourners, but not for the departed; for he has gone to rest, and we – to lament."[4] All the more so in the case of R. Shimon bar Yoḥai, who at his death requested that people not mourn for him but rather rejoice over the ascent of his soul.

This element of joy that we recall, note, and celebrate even when there are points of sorrow may also be expressed in other aspects of this day. We can theorize that there was a connection between the death of R. Akiva's disciples and the Bar Kokhba revolt, especially since R. Akiva was a great supporter and believer in Bar Kokhba and may even have been the central figure behind this rebellion. That rebellion ended disastrously, and almost all those who were involved in it were killed or died otherwise. Nevertheless, there may be in Lag BaOmer a dim memory of the other side of the rebellion – that of hope and of expectations that were aroused then – and it could be that for this reason the day has several festive customs. Even the bows and arrows are partial memories connected with this aspect.

This explanation fits in well with the figure of R. Shimon bar Yoḥai himself, for among all of R. Akiva's disciples, he was the one who carried on a consistent policy of war against Rome, even if he did not fight them physically.

The practice of lighting bonfires (and perhaps also candles) on Lag BaOmer derives from an ancient custom to light a large bonfire beside R. Shimon bar Yoḥai's grave in Meron, to the accompaniment of singing. In stories from centuries ago, it is told that this bonfire was fed not only with wood, but also with fine clothing and other valuable articles. In this context, the question was raised whether it is forbidden to destroy things, even if one's intention is for the sake of Heaven.

This bonfire is perhaps a remnant of a custom that was observed in First and Second Temple times. When a king died, they would make an

4. Ibid. 25b.

immense bonfire, into which they would also cast articles that belonged to the king.[5] This was an expression of mourning that also contained an element of solemnity, expressing the majesty of kingship. As a result, the greatest expression of dishonor for a dead a king would be that no bonfire was lit for him.[6]

This practice of lighting bonfires for kings continued for many centuries, even when there were no longer any kings. For example:

> When Rabban Gamliel the Elder died, the proselyte Onkelos burned after him more than eighty *minas* [a huge sum]. They asked him, "What was your purpose in doing this?" He replied, "It is written, 'You will die in peace; and with the burnings of your fathers, the former kings that were before you, so will they make a burning for you.'[7] And is not Rabban Gamliel worth more than a hundred useless kings?!"[8]

In every respect, R. Shimon bar Yoḥai had not only the standing of one of the Sages of Israel, but also the royal standing of an exalted personality. This is how he was perceived not only by his disciples, who learned mystical lore from him, but by others as well. In the Talmud, which does not deal specifically with mysticism, R. Shimon bar Yoḥai is mentioned as one who could atone, through his deeds, for all of Israel's sins from the creation of the world to his own time. Since he was such a "king," it is fitting that a great bonfire be lit for him, as they would do in the past for kings. And since he himself regarded his departure from this world as liberation and redemption, others, too, share in his joy.

There are various kinds of Lag BaOmer bonfires. There are bonfires around which songs about Bar Yoḥai are sung, and there are, no doubt, many more bonfires in which potatoes are roasted. The children who light bonfires in Tel Aviv, thereby endangering the public welfare,

---

5. See, for instance, II Chronicles 16:22.
6. See Ibid., 21:19.
7. Jeremiah 34:5.
8. *Semaḥot* 8:6.

are presumably unaware of the reason for the lighting and may not even know anything about R. Shimon bar Yoḥai. But R. Shimon bar Yoḥai was, after all, a complete mystery, and these children, too, unknowingly show him honor.

Jerusalem Day

Love of Jerusalem

CONTACT BETWEEN HEAVEN AND EARTH

The special holiness of Jerusalem stems from its being "the site that God will choose,"[1] the city where God decided to establish His House, the Temple, so that His Presence should dwell there.

This connection between God and the city of Jerusalem is found not just in Heavenly Jerusalem, in the spiritual part of the city, but also in earthly Jerusalem, the city as we know it.

This may be compared to a geological fault. When the earth, which is composed of strata, is fractured as a result of various pressures, one section is displaced and pushed upward in relation to other sections, whereupon it can be seen that the strata are no longer continuous. Upper strata lie next to strata that formerly were much deeper. Similarly, in Jerusalem, instead of the upper and lower worlds being in normal relation, one above the other, they meet. Instead of the heavens being above and the earth below, there is a point at which heaven and earth are on the same plane.

The contact between heaven and earth is expressed in its most radical form in the Temple's holiest place – the Holy of Holies. The Holy

1. Deuteronomy 12:5, et al.

of Holies, as described by our sages, is unlike any other space known to man. "The place of the ark and the cherubim is not included in the measured space"[2] – the ark and cherubim occupy no space in the chamber. On every side, space remains as though nothing were placed in the center.

Transition to the Holy of Holies entails leaving this world and entering a place where the laws of the physical world do not fully apply. The cherubim and the ark do not exist within this world, but in a different dimension of reality, a dimension in which objects and measurements have no application.

In this place, the upper world touches the lower world.

The Holy of Holies is the center of this world. In the Holy of Holies lies the foundation stone, from which the universe was founded.[3] According to the Midrash, this site is the source of the dust from which Adam was formed.[4] This site may be likened to the world's "umbilical cord" – the point of connection to the Creator, the foundation and basis for all that was created in the wake of this single point.

The Holy of Holies marks the central point of contact, which is ringed by the Temple Mount, the entire city, and finally all of the Land of Israel – all concentrated around the single point, around the place where the heavenly world and the earthly world touch.

THE GATEWAY TO HEAVEN

There are various central places throughout the world. There is a place that is the earth's magnetic pole, and another place that is the earth's geographic pole. These places are extraordinary and are marked by unusual phenomena. The compass goes haywire, and day and night are confused. They are exceptions to geography. Jerusalem, too, is such an extraordinary place, as it is a place where this world and the supernal world intermingle.

Jerusalem lies at the margin of the material and the physical, on the edge of the nonphysical world. In *Pirkei Avot*, we are told of the miracles that occurred in the Temple – the sacred flesh never spoiled, no fly

2. *Bava Batra* 99a.
3. *Yoma* 54b.
4. The *Midrash* on Psalms 92.

was ever seen in the slaughterhouse, and though the people stood pressed together, they bowed with ample space. We also learn of miracles that occurred in the city itself – neither serpent nor scorpion caused harm in Jerusalem, and so forth.[5] The contact with the holy brings about a change in the laws of nature even in the outer circle of the entire city.

Besides the supernatural events that occur in Jerusalem, there are also physical places in Jerusalem that are not within the bounds of this world. The Talmud relates that the entrance to Gehenna lies nearby,[6] and that "Azazel," too, is not far from there. In Jerusalem, worlds from different levels meet and coexist, forming a unique and singular city.

Our sages call Jerusalem "the pupil of the eye."[7] The pupil of the eye is an opening in the body through which impressions from the outside reach inside. In fact, the eye is the only part of the body in which the nerve is connected directly to the brain. Outside impressions perceived by other parts of the body are filtered and processed, but in the case of the eye, they enter directly, as they are. Jerusalem is an opening of this kind, a direct passage between the earthly world and the heavenly world. It is the gateway to heaven, a passageway from the physical to the spiritual.

For this reason, we pray in the direction of Jerusalem, as it says in Solomon's prayer: "And they pray to You in the direction of their land which You gave to their forefathers, the city which You have chosen,

5. "Ten miracles were wrought in the Holy Temple: No woman ever miscarried because of the odor of the sacred flesh; the sacred flesh never spoiled; no fly was ever seen in the slaughterhouse; the High Priest never experienced an unclean accident on Yom Kippur; no disqualification was ever found in the *omer*, in the two loaves, or in the showbread; the people stood pressed together, yet bowed with ample space. Never did a serpent or scorpion harm anyone in Jerusalem, nor did any man ever say to his fellow, 'The place is too tight for me to spend the night in Jerusalem'" (*Avot* 5:5).
6. "There are two palms in the Valley of Hinnom, between which smoke rises ... and it is the entrance to Gehenna" (*Sukka* 32b).
7. "If one spits in these times on the Temple Mount, it is as though he spat into the pupil of His eye, as it says (1 Kings 9:3), 'My eyes and My heart will be there always'" (*Berakhot* 62b).

and the House which I have built to Your name."[8] Prayers are directed toward Jerusalem, via which they ascend heavenward.

Because the pupil forms the link between the brain and the external world, it must be guarded to the utmost. Likewise, Jerusalem is the most sensitive place in the world. When someone smites Jerusalem, the eye of the universe, it is as painful and dangerous as a blow to the physical eye. More than what happens anywhere else in the world, things that happen in Jerusalem are liable to have implications for the whole world.

PERFECT IN BEAUTY

The connection to the supernal worlds produces a flow of holiness through the Holy of Holies, Temple, and Temple Mount to the entire city – not just to the exalted things in the city, but to all its physical parts: its houses, its stones, even its thorns, and all who dwell in it, great and small. The stones of Jerusalem are different; its thorns are all of gold.

Jerusalem is "the city perfect in beauty," more beautiful than many beautiful cities in the world. But the city's beauty does not stem from handsome buildings or lovely external design. As a rule, the opposite is true. Jerusalem's beauty, its sun and light and other beautiful things with which it is endowed, stem from its inwardness, from its holiness.

The surplus of Jerusalem's inwardness, the drops that overflow from its holiness, are what make it beautiful and give it grace. The Midrash says that when God finished writing the Torah, He wiped the pen on Moses' hair, and for that reason, "his face was radiant"[9] and it was impossible to look at him. Similarly, the crumbs of holiness, the bits of surplus spirituality in the air, are what make Jerusalem beautiful in the physical world.

It does not matter whether the architecture of Jerusalem is extraordinarily beautiful or not. When one looks at the city as a whole, there is nothing more beautiful than it. When something is truly beautiful, its flaws do not detract from its great beauty; on the contrary, they give it added grace. Thus, even the things that are not beautiful about

---

8. I Kings 8:48.
9. Exodus 34:29.

it join in forming Jerusalem; every part, every corner, and every crumb are there in order to add beauty.

Jerusalem's beauty slowly spreads to its various neighborhoods. Indeed, it takes some time until a new neighborhood is absorbed into Jerusalem and becomes part of it; its inhabitants must also with time turn into Jerusalemites. Just as when a person enters a perfume shop, perfume adheres to him whether he likes it or not, the Jerusalemite nature sticks to its inhabitants. To be sure, this process may sometimes take a generation, but ultimately everything is absorbed into Jerusalem, and this adds to its essential physical perfection.

JERUSALEM DAY

The importance of Jerusalem Day far exceeds the commemoration of the day on which the city was liberated from foreign rule. This day's eminence is found in that it is celebrated in honor of this unique city, "a rose of Sharon, a lily of the valleys."[10] It is a day that does not relate specifically to the destruction or rebuilding of Jerusalem, to its distress or to its beauty. Rather, it is day of thanksgiving and joy over the city's very existence, joy over the fact that we have merited to have in our world a point of connection with the supernal world.

The holiday over Jerusalem is a new holiday; in former generations, we were not privileged to celebrate it. We did know that it is possible to offer praise and rejoice over Jerusalem even before it is rebuilt completely, that it is possible to give thanks for the fact that, despite the humiliations and after all the degradations, Jerusalem cannot be deprived of its uniqueness. We were unaware that we could give praise for the fact that even when Jerusalem is degraded, its essential nature cannot be concealed. Jerusalem can be exiled and disdained, but it is still a royal city, like the palm. Even when it is in the depths of Sheol, it is still the source of blessing.

The prophet Isaiah prophesied: "Rejoice with Jerusalem and be glad for her, all you who lover her! Join in her jubilation, all you who mourned over her."[11] One should mourn over Jerusalem, but one should

10. Song of Songs 2:1.
11. Isaiah 66:10.

also be among those who love her. One should love not only her holy places, but also the city in its own right, as it is, with its neighborhoods and its cats, its fences and stones, the lunatics and the loafers who are all part of it.

One must love Jerusalem not just because it is home, but because there is no other place like it. For all these reasons, we hold a celebration in honor of Jerusalem – earthly Jerusalem and heavenly Jerusalem.

Jerusalem Day, Nowadays

At its inception, Jerusalem Day was a glorious day. This feeling was to a great extent bound up with the Six Day War and its outcome, which for a while produced an exalted feeling of release from dread and anxiety to liberation, well-being, and greatness.

Over the years, however, the aura of the day has dimmed. This process is the result of an objective and subjective change in the attitude toward the Six Day War and its results, for it became clear that the war, and hence also Jerusalem Day, had not heralded the beginning of a new and better world as had then been hoped.

In reality, many of the apparent results of that war are only partly connected with it, and are inflated and magnified – both positively and negatively – only because people do not properly remember the situation that existed beforehand. Many of these "results," both good and bad, appear to us today as watershed events, but actually already existed before the war: the conquest, the settlements, the military government. Thus, the facts have not changed. Those who object to the settlements in Judea and Samaria would also object to the establishment of new settlements in the Negev, because they encroach upon the Beduin.

Even in its more limited meaning, Jerusalem Day does not

celebrate "a city joined together."[1] The divisions and rifts that existed in the city beforehand remain in place; perhaps they have even intensified. Even today, when it is not divided by concrete walls and barbed wire fences, Jerusalem remains, in practice, three cities that exist side by side: Jewish-secular, Jewish-religious, and Arab. It could be that these groups avoid excessive friction only because they wish to remain distinct, each one unto itself.

To be sure, Jews can now go the *Kotel*, the Western Wall. But even this did not produce essential changes, neither in those who come to visit the *Kotel* regularly nor in those who do not come to it at all.

Nonetheless, there is a need for Jerusalem Day nowadays, especially if it is detached from the context of the war and focused primarily on Jerusalem itself.

Jerusalem is not just another city, small or large, in the State of Israel; nor is it merely the capital city, in practice or in title. Jerusalem is a symbol, part of the basic fabric of Jewish life in the last few thousand years. Jerusalem is special in this way not only to the Jewish People but, to a great extent, also to other peoples – for in Jerusalem there are sites holy to Christianity and, to a certain extent, to Islam as well.

But this, too, is not what determines its special standing; Jerusalem's inner essence and meaning go far beyond what it contains as a city. Jerusalem is an image of the Land of Israel, with all its historical and emotional connotations. It is a city with a very strong presence, with which some people fall in love and which others cannot bear.

However, historical memories and open or concealed sentiments are insufficient. Even something profound and significant cannot be preserved unless it is sustained and cultivated; what is not cultivated tends to shrivel and erode, for time and habit erode everything.

Hence, in order to intensify and strengthen the meaningfulness of Jerusalem, we should connect with all the layers of its content, not just of the present, but also of the hundreds and thousands of years of the past.

Jerusalem Day does not require flags, many or few, nor will it grow in stature from them. It could become more meaningful if people would sing the songs of Jerusalem, tell the stories of Jerusalem, and if

1. Psalms 122:3

the day's broadcasts relating to Jerusalem would not be devoted to the current, peripheral issues. No less important, more people must come to visit the city.

For the connection with Jerusalem is more than commemoration of this or that date in recent history. Rather, it is primarily the effort to know Jerusalem as she is or as she was, as a reality and as a legend.

Shavuot

The Formation of Jewish Singularity

THE TORAH – BASIS OF SINGULARITY

The day of the Giving of the Torah is indisputably the most important date in all of Jewish history. Although the Jewish calendar is full of momentous dates – days of remembrance of redemption and salvation, days of mourning over destruction and downfall – all these dates are dwarfed in comparison to this central event.

We have experienced many national turning points, events of extreme importance to our destiny. The exodus from Egypt marked the beginning of the Jewish People's emergence as a nation; Joshua's conquest of the Land supplied the nation with a homeland; the establishment of the Kingdom of David and the building of the Temple created a governmental structure and permanent center for the Jewish People. Nevertheless, the day of the Giving of the Torah is more distinctive and exalted than all these days and events.

To fully understand the significance of the event, we must first examine several of its aspects.

First, the Giving of the Torah is a singular event; it distinguishes the whole essence of the Jewish People and constitutes a characterizing point for the whole course of its existence. Other events, although important to our history, are not, in and of themselves, unique to us alone. Many peoples wandered until reaching the place of their permanent settlement; many nations established a state and kingdom, and even lost them.[1] Those important and central events in Jewish history thus have their parallels in the histories of other nations. Although that does not detract from the importance of those events, it does detract from them their singularity.

This is not the case regarding the revelation at Sinai and the receiving of the Torah. This event is singular and without parallel in the history of any other nation, whether in recorded history or in folk tales. The singularity lies not only in the very acceptance of a new faith and way of life, but in the unique manner in which all the members of our people accepted this way of life.

The Giving of the Torah is a singular event primarily because of the event's influence on the Jewish People's essential nature. Due to the content and character of the Giving of the Torah, it alone formed the singularity of the Jewish People for all time.

Clearly, there is an element of distinctiveness in the very fact that the Jewish People at its inception left the house of bondage, but this distinctiveness could not have taken on its full significance without the acceptance of the Torah, which inscribed the exodus from Egypt as an enduring memory within the collective Jewish memory.

Neither the existence in the past of a Jewish state, nor the creation of classical Jewish literature, nor the Jewish People's lengthy exile could have taken on their unique dimensions without the Giving of the Torah. The Giving of the Torah not only invested our entire historical system with meaning, but also made it possible for each event to contribute to the character, human type, and spiritual creativity unique to our people. Following acceptance of the Torah, everything that happens to the Jewish People automatically takes on unique significance, which not infrequently increases and heightens our distinctiveness. From the Giving of the Torah onward, everything that happens to us – for good or for bad – necessarily is done and happens in a unique manner, in a Jewish manner.

1. Only a very few, however, were exiled from their place and then returned to reestablish their state. This, then, can also be regarded as part of Jewish singularity.

AN IRREVERSIBLE EVENT

Another aspect of the unique significance of the Giving of the Torah lies in the fact that it represents an irreversible process in our history.

In the course of history, the Jewish People has experienced many ascents and descents, often counteracting one another. Opposite the conquest of the Land, there is the catastrophe of exile from it; opposite the building of the Temple, there is its destruction; and opposite the exile and the suffering, there are periods of return to the Land and its rebuilding.

In other words, even the most momentous events are, by their very nature, reversible. There is no situation or state of being that does not have its antithesis, an event that is likely to cancel its effect and change its value.

The Giving of the Torah, however, is different; it is an event from which there is no turning back. The change in essence and status brought about by the Giving of the Torah is such that the Jewish People cannot back out of it even if they so desire.

Ever since the Jewish People's transformation at the revelation at Sinai into "a kingdom of priests and a holy nation,"[2] it can no longer become something else. To be sure, it is possible that individuals among the Jewish people, large parts of the people, or even the entire nation will at times not want to fulfill the Sinaitic commitment. This non-fulfillment, however, does not negate the unique nature of the Jewish People; it is merely an attempt not to live up to it, not to persist in it. It is possible that the Sinaitic covenant will not be upheld at one time or another, but it cannot be abrogated or changed.

There have been attempts to nullify this covenant ever since Sinai, and not only in recent centuries. But these attempts – "when you say, 'We will become like the nations, like the families of the lands'"[3] have never succeeded. Ever since the acceptance of the Torah, the Jewish People has had its own special path, which it cannot leave. Any attempt to do so leads to one of two results – either the people (or part of it) recommits itself to the covenant again and yet again, or else the segment

2. Exodus 19:6.
3. Ezekiel 20:32.

of the people that is not interested in the covenant separates from the Jewish People entirely.

The latter result was what happened to the Ten Tribes, who abandoned the way of the Torah and ultimately were eliminated from the Jewish People. The dilemma of whether to make the choice to follow them – the choice to return or to disappear entirely – has been and continues to be faced in many other situations in our history. For the change in essence effected by the Giving of the Torah is permanent. There is no possibility of returning the Torah to its Giver while continuing to be the "Jewish People."

THE TEN COMMANDMENTS

The importance of the Giving of the Torah is further illustrated through the revelation of the Ten Commandments that took place at the time. These commandments would seem to be the message of the great spectacle, yet ancient and contemporary Jewish thinkers have already debated what precisely their uniqueness is. After all, the Ten Commandments do not seem to include any special or novel content beyond the general conception of "natural religion." Apart from the special aspect inherent in the mitzva of the Sabbath, there is nothing in the Ten Commandments that transcends the bounds of the most universal morality. As one of the great thinkers put it: Did God have to descend upon Mount Sinai with thunder and lightning and a mighty shofar blast in order to inform us of the mitzva of "Do not steal"?

The answer to this question lies not in the content of the Decalogue, but in its context. The content of these ten commandments takes on unique meaning only when they are part of the Ten Commandments, only as part of the "great spectacle."

There are two decisive elements in the Ten Commandments that turn the event of their revelation into the great, irreversible turning point. These two elements express one central idea in different ways: The Giving of the Torah constitutes the point of connection through which Jewish life – even when it is externally identical to other phenomena, actions, and ways of behavior – forms an enduring bond between God and the people.

KINGDOM OF PRIESTS

The first aspect of the Ten Commandments is their covenantal role. Beyond what the commandments actually say about various acts of commission and omission, faith and commitment, they epitomize the covenant and the concept of a life of holiness.

The Decalogue represents, first and foremost, the special inner bond within the Jewish People, which becomes "God's people." Instead of becoming a nation like all other nations, the Jewish People becomes a special unit: "You shall be My special treasure among all the peoples."[4]

This chosenness is not based on race, blood, or homeland, but rather on our unique role – "You shall be to Me a kingdom of priests and a holy nation."[5] The Jewish People agrees not to be just one more nation, for it can no longer be defined as one of the world's seventy nations.

The Jewish People may possess all the markings of any other nation – homeland, language, culture – but these alone do not define it. Precisely for this reason, even when the Jewish People appears to have lost these defining elements – when it has been living in exile from its homeland for hundreds or thousands of years, when it no longer has a single spoken language or an independent national-economic structure, and when the world's experts on nationality even deny its existence as a nation – even then, it remains alive. Because our covenant defined that we are not like any other nation, we do not cease being unique – namely, being "a kingdom of priests and a holy nation."

As a collective entity, the Jewish People struggles a great deal with itself regarding the extent to which this characterization is realized in practice. At all times, however, the promise, the covenant, and the uniqueness continue to exist and to operate.

This is the significance of the entire Sinaitic covenant, and it is expressed in its strongest form in the formula of the Decalogue's first commandment. This commandment, which presents the principle of God's unity, is not worded in the universal-human sense, but in the particular-Jewish sense. It does not identify God as "Creator of heaven

---

4. Exodus 19:5.
5. Ibid. 19:6.

and earth," but rather, "I am God your Lord, Who brought you out of the land of Egypt."[6]

Needless to say, the exodus from Egypt does not nullify God's relationship with the world. After all, He is "King of the universe" and "His name is great among the nations."[7] The exodus from Egypt actually strengthens this relationship, as it demonstrated God's ultimate kingship and power over all existence. Nonetheless, the Exodus represents the relationship between the people of Israel and the God of Israel in particular. The revelation of the Ten Commandments thus emphasizes that unique covenantal bond.

THE ABSOLUTE COMMAND

The second aspect of the Giving of the Torah manifested in the Ten Commandments is the removal of life's ideals and supreme values from the realm of the neutral to the realm of serving the Creator.

From a practical standpoint, it makes no difference which system establishes the prohibition of adultery or stealing; it is forbidden regardless. Yet there is a tremendous difference between the command "Do not commit murder" whose purpose is to regulate the normal life of society, society which cannot afford murder, and the "Do not commit murder" of the Ten Commandments. The prohibition of murder in the criminal law of every nation is a social contract, a cultural convention. "Do not commit murder" of the Ten Commandments, by contrast, is an absolute command, a command directly linked to "I am God" which appears in parallel on the first Tablet. Unlike practical morality, the commands of the Torah ought to be followed because they are expressions of holiness, of connection with the divine.

The Torah's distinctiveness lies in its removing the neutral dimension from Jewish reality. The good deed is not the deed whose benefit is determined by its practical, social, or educational value. Torah is more than a system of laws and regulations, conventions and customs. Torah endows all these with a new dimension – the dimension of the

6. Ibid. 20:2.
7. See Malachi 1:11.

sublime, of the connection that is higher than the high, reaching to the First Source.

The laws and regulations of society are all in the "horizontal" dimension; they relate to interpersonal relationships, to the array of contacts and relations between man and his fellow, and even between man and his morality. The Torah's system of laws, in contrast, is a "vertical" system, relating to the relationship between man and God, between the people and the First Source of life.

Hence, the distinction of the Ten Commandments lies not in the novelty of their content, but in the fundamental change that they create in the meaning of everything. From this point on, the good deed is a mitzva, the bad deed is a sin, and the laws and ways of life are Torah.

The Word He Ordained for a Thousand Generations

THE PREPARATION

The Talmud and the Midrash interpret the verse "the Word He ordained for a thousand generations"[1] as referring to God's intention and will to give the Torah a thousand generations after Creation. In reality, God gave it much earlier, after only twenty-six generations. The generations that originally were meant to live before the Giving of the Torah were shriveled and shrunk, as it were, and so did not come into existence in the world.

This Midrash requires explanation. First, what need was there for such a long wait, a thousand generations, from Creation to the Giving of the Torah? What was supposed to have transpired during those generations? Second, if indeed there was a need for a thousand generations of mankind before the Giving of the Torah, why did God forgo those generations? Why was the world not given the time required before the receiving of the Torah?

Apparently, the intended thousand generations before the Giving

1. Psalms 105:8; *Ḥagiga* 13b, Rashi ad loc., *Bereshit Raba* 28:4 et al.

of the Torah were to be a thousand generations of preparation. Giving the Torah from above is a complicated and complex act, which requires special conditions. For human beings to be able to receive the Torah, they must undergo a long process of inner development from generation to generation, a process at the end of which they will have attained a suitable level of refinement and sensitivity. The unfolding of such a process, like the flowering of culture in general, requires a great deal of time. Only after a thousand generations can the world reach a level of development that is sufficient to enable receiving the Torah.

The decision to give the Torah so much sooner than expected entailed forgoing many generations of preparation. God's "afterthought" was that there was actually no need for those generations. God chose to cut the preparations short and forgo the world development and perfection necessary for the reception of the Torah.

This divine decision not to wait for the ideal time is evidenced as well by the character of those who received the Torah – the people of the wilderness generation. Logically, the Torah should have been given only to those who were worthy of receiving it – people who, from the standpoint of their character, intellect, and spiritual life, were already on a level suitable for the reception of the Torah. Instead, those who actually received the Torah were a slave people who never had the time to develop a culture of their own. Indeed, the complaints of the people of Israel in the wilderness reveal their essential nature at the time – they longed only for physical comfort, and had no connection to the extensive spiritual and cultural life that existed in Egypt.

God brought a people of simple folk out of Egypt, and almost without a pause gave them the Torah. Only fifty days separated the Exodus and the Giving of the Torah, and during this short time, the people experienced hardships and journeys. They had no opportunity to compose themselves in preparation for the Giving of the Torah. At first glance, then, it seems that the Torah was not given to people who were worthy of receiving it; rather, it was given in haste, without waiting for the appropriate time or for a generation worthy of it.

Thus, the question presents itself even more strongly. Why was the Torah given precisely at this stage, when there was no one who could receive it properly? It seems that the skipping of generations and the shortening of preparations are essential to God's way of giving the Torah.

BREAKING THE PROGRESSION

At the root of this policy is the paradox of giving the Torah in its perfection. The gulf between mankind and the Torah in its most perfect form, in its full significance and truth, is a gulf that is not at all simple to bridge. Certain elements can be attained with great effort, but there are aspects that will always remain unreachable. The distance between man and God is infinite; even after a thousand generations, when the vessels would be purer and mankind would have a more refined understanding, that distance would remain the same. Man will always remain on one side of reality, and God on the other, unknown side.

To give the Torah, God, as it were, had to descend into the world, into our reality. Such a descent entails breaking the laws of nature. The Giving of the Torah is not an event that can take place progressively and gradually, because it is essentially a leap from one side of being to the other side.

Because there is a need for a leap transcending all degrees, the need for preparation in the form of ascent to a higher level of spiritual perfection loses its importance. The state and character of the receiver are insignificant in the face of the great revelation and the shattering of reality taking place at the Giving of the Torah.

The reaction of the people of Israel to the Giving of the Torah reflects this point. On the one hand, the Talmud relates that God "overturned the mountain over them like an inverted cask;"[2] the people are portrayed as though they accepted the Torah under duress. On the other hand, their response to Moses's words is categorical: "We will do and obey."[3] In our prayers, we reiterate, "And His kingship they accepted upon themselves *willingly*" – not under coercion.

One of the solutions to this apparent contradiction is that the "the mountain overturned over them" was a direct result of God's revelation,

2. *Shabbat* 88a.

3. Exodus 24:7.

which automatically rules out freedom of choice. In most situations, man has autonomy; he retains his human freedom, and therefore can decide. But when God reveals Himself to man, man has absolutely no choice.

For the people of Israel at the revelation at Sinai, there was no difference at all between "He overturned the mountain over them like an inverted cask" and "His kingship they accepted upon themselves willingly." They may have accepted the Torah willingly, but this willingness was born of constraint. They were not coerced by a threat, but by the reality. When a person has only one choice, the issue of free choice as opposed to coercion is merely theoretical. God put the people of Israel into a situation where human free choice was inclined to one side; there was no longer a possibility of real choice.

By its very nature, receiving the Torah is contingent upon God imposing Himself on the recipient, and the receiver's considerations are therefore no longer of any significance. Similarly, the encounter with the *Ein Sof* (the Infinite Being) dwarfs the people's preparations in anticipation of the event, whether they are elaborate or not.

For this reason, the people of Israel could receive the Torah irrespective of their level. Indeed, there would never be a truly suitable time for receiving the Torah, and so any time was eligible for it.

A DAY WITHOUT COUNTING

A similar pattern of interruption and transition to a different time continuum is found in connection with counting of the *omer* (*Sefirat HaOmer*), which concludes with the festival of the Giving of the Torah.

The Torah commands, "You shall count to yourselves seven complete weeks after the day following the [Pesaḥ] holiday... Until the day after the seventh week, you shall count fifty days..."[4] However, in spite of the Torah's commandment to count fifty days, we do not fulfill it that way; we count seven weeks – forty-nine days. The fiftieth day is the festival of Shavuot itself, and it is not counted in *Sefirat HaOmer*.

The transition from the days of *Sefirat HaOmer* to Shavuot is a

4. Leviticus 23:15.

leap from one level to another. The Maharal, in discussing this transition, focuses on the number forty-nine versus fifty.[5]

Although the distance between these two numbers is slight, they actually represent two different kinds of numbers. The number forty-nine is composed of a system based on multiples of seven, whereas the number fifty cannot be arrived at through that system, but rather through a system based on the number ten. Thus, between the two consecutive numbers, there is a transition from one numerical system to another. In the terminology of the Maharal, it is a transition from numbers patterned on nature to numbers of an entirely different kind.

The unnatural and unsuccessive transition from forty-nine to fifty signifies that even after all the counting, day after day and week after week, the counting does not reach completion. It reaches the number closest to fifty, but the fiftieth day itself is not counted. This day does not follow from those that precede it, but rather arrives as a gift from above. The final, culminating point of the counting depends not on us but on God; only He can bring us to the fiftieth day.

A person can reach the point where he stands ready, but he cannot reach beyond that point. The giving of the gift, the execution of the leap, is a point that lies beyond us. Forty-nine is the limit that can be reached, but the culminating point itself, the final day, does not pertain to the counting from below.

God's decision to skip generations and the commandment of counting the *omer* represent two sides of the same coin. Time, whether shrunken or leaped over, is under the exclusive and absolute control of the Holy One, blessed be He. He determines it, He counts it, and He brings us to the Giving of the Torah.

THE NECESSITY OF MAKING A LEAP

Because it is never possible to be completely prepared for the Giving of the Torah, had God postponed it until people were worthy, the delay would have been endless.

To reach the Giving of the Torah, to arrive at the fiftieth day, is not a matter of simply counting an additional day. The fiftieth day is an

5. *Tiferet Yisrael* 25.

entirely different spiritual dimension, and its significance is that no matter how prepared a person can be, he is never truly prepared.

Similarly, even a thousand generations are not enough for mankind to produce a generation worthy of receiving the Torah. For all that man makes himself a vessel, he is never a perfect vessel. Hence, there is no reason for such a length of time, and it deserves to be cut short.

This transition to the Giving of the Torah may be compared to what Maimonides writes regarding the spiritual preparation required to attain prophecy.[6] He explains that after one fulfills all the prerequisites for becoming a prophet, it is then possible that prophecy will rest upon him. Nevertheless, it is also possible that after all the preparations that he makes, he still will not attain prophecy. There could be a person who has all the abilities, qualifications, virtues, and special qualities of a prophet – and yet does not become a prophet. A person can reach only as far as the limit of his capability; beyond that, there is a point that only God can cross, and that point is a completely different spiritual dimension. In the end, prophecy is a gift from above.

ACQUIRING TORAH

We can glean deeper insight into the meaning of interrupting the natural process of preparation through consideration of the forty-eight ways the Torah is "acquired," which are listed in *Pirkei Avot*.[7]

The Mishna appears to mix the modes of conduct required for acquiring knowledge of the Torah (attendance on scholars, moderation in sleep, etc.) and the virtues of the Torah student, which result from study (loving God, loving people, etc.). This mixture is not unintentional and is not a scribal error. The qualities through which the Torah is acquired cannot be perfected independently. In order to develop these qualities, Torah study itself is required. The ways of acquiring the Torah are the instrument, the receptacle for Torah, and also the result of Torah study.

To offer an analogy, a snail does not first build its shell and then

6. *Hilkhot Yesodei HaTorah* 7:1.
7. *Avot* 6:6.

move in to live inside it. Rather, the two things occur simultaneously – the snail grows, and its shell grows along with it.

Similarly, the instruments of Torah grow along with it, as the ways of acquiring Torah and the virtues of Torah coincide. Just as each one of the ways of acquiring Torah is a necessary instrument in order to attain Torah, a person must possess Torah in order to be able to attain each of these virtues.

The fact that the ways of acquiring Torah and the virtues that result from Torah coincide teaches us that there is no preliminary stage before the receiving of the Torah. The sole instrument of receiving the Torah is the simplest and most self-evident instrument – the willingness to accept it.

WE WILL DO AND OBEY

The great secret of receiving the Torah is the ability to listen without setting preconditions that impair the reception of the Torah's wisdom, feeling, and inner dimensions. To the receive the Torah, the people must assert, "All that God has spoken we will do and obey."[8]

Just as willingness and ability to receive make the reception of the Torah possible as a whole, the same applies to its individual laws.

The Midrash relates that before the Giving of the Torah, God offered it to all the nations. God showed the Torah to the Ishmaelites, and they asked, "What is written in it?" He said to them, "You shall not steal," and they did not want to accept it. God showed the Torah to the Edomites, and they, too, asked, "What is written in it?" He said to them, "You shall not murder," and they refused to accept it. Presumably, thus it was with every nation. By contrast, the people of Israel did not ask what was written in it; rather, they accepted the Torah however it may be.[9] This difference between Israel and the nations is an essential difference.

The main impediment to the giving of the Torah to the nations was not the fact that it contains a paragraph that did not find favor with them. What is more serious is man's attempt to dictate in advance the

8. Exodus 24:7.

9. *Sifrei, VeZot HaBerakha*, 343, cf. *Avoda Zara* 2b.

nature of the Torah. When from the outset man is willing to accept the Torah only regarding certain points, he cannot truly receive it.

The Torah is not someone's private Torah, but rather God's Torah, and therefore it – like God – is infinite. A human being never has the authority to limit the Torah to areas, to proportions, and within bounds that he determines. If he does so, it is no longer God's Torah, but merely the imprinting of his own image on those parts of the Torah that happen to accord with his personal views. God's Torah cannot be realized in such a fashion.

There is no way to prepare for receiving the Torah other than cultivating the sheer willingness to accept whatever it may entail. When man does not limit the Torah and does not qualify it according to his own yardstick, his own taste, and his own understanding – then the Torah can be given and properly received.

Freedom on the Tablets

FIRST FRUITS OF THE WHEAT HARVEST

Each of the three pilgrimage festivals has a dual meaning; they are nature festivals and historical holidays. Pesaḥ is the Spring Festival and also the festival of the Exodus; Shavuot is the season of the Giving of our Torah and also the day of "the first fruits of the wheat harvest;"[1] and Sukkot – the Festival of Ingathering – is also a remembrance of the *sukkot* in which our ancestors dwelled during the period of wandering after the exodus from Egypt.

This dual meaning of the festivals always appears in Scripture as one essence, without distinction between the aspects of the festival's content. Indeed, the relation between the two meanings, the two aspects of the pilgrimage festivals, is not merely external or accidental; it is an expression of a unified conception of reality. Hence, we must understand each aspect of the festival in light of the other aspect, and thereby perceive a complete picture of the festival's essence.

In Jewish sources, Shavuot is designated by several names. On the one hand, it is the "season of the giving of our Torah;" on the other hand, it is the "festival of the first fruits," because on this day the first

1. Exodus 34.22.

fruits of the wheat harvest are brought to the Temple. Yet the primary name of the festival is Shavuot (Weeks), signifying that this festival is the culmination of Pesaḥ; seven weeks after Pesaḥ, we celebrate Shavuot. To use a later, Rabbinic term, Shavuot is the day of *Atzeret*, the final festive day that was fit to fall immediately after Pesaḥ.

Pesaḥ and Shavuot complement each other in terms of content. They both celebrate the first fruits of the harvest – the barley crop on Pesaḥ and the wheat harvest on Shavuot. After the hard work and the dangers of the agricultural year, we can finally take pleasure in the year's crops.

Thus, the essence and basic content of these two festivals is the same. They are festivals of thanksgiving for our having merited to see the results of the preparations and labors of the preceding period.

Moreover, the two festivals are one continuum, beginning with Pesaḥ and ending with Shavuot, with a certain ascending line.

On the Spring Festival, when we celebrate the first crop of barley, the joy is not yet complete, for barley is not human food – "barley and straw [are] for the horses and swift steeds."[2] Bread made of barely is edible, but it is the bread of the poorest of the poor, eaten only in times of famine and distress. The bread that people eat, even black bread, is made of wheat. Thus, it is understandable that even when the barley crop turns out well, there is still a waiting period of seven weeks. During this time, there is still room for much worry and anticipation, until the ripening of the main crop – the wheat. There can only be complete joy on the *Atzeret* of Pesaḥ, the festival of Shavuot.

FREEDOM – FOR WHAT PURPOSE?

Along with their natural, land-bound significance, both of these festivals have general and historical significance. Pesaḥ is primarily a remembrance of the Exodus, the festival of freedom, whereas Shavuot is the day of the Giving of the Torah.

Even in their historical and spiritual sense, however, Pesaḥ and Shavuot must be regarded not as separate festivals, but as one contin-

2. I Kings 5:8.

uum. In this sense, as well, they are festivals of beginning, festivals that express the experience of the dawn of the Jewish People.

Pesaḥ defines the people almost exclusively in the negative. The Exodus was the negation of assimilation, the negation of the Egyptian exile, and the negation of the Jew's identity as one type of Egyptian.

Shavuot, in contrast, is the time of accepting the Torah, the positive definition of the Jewish People. Shavuot marks the establishment of the people's authentic character, the determination of its life's purpose and the direction in which it is heading.

If freedom were merely a negative concept – namely, the absence of slavery – then the release from slavery would, in and of itself, secure freedom. However, freedom also has positive content, which is not realized merely by removing the injustice. Servitude is a condition in which a person (or nation) does not do what he wants to do but what others tell him to do. Freedom, in contrast, is a state in which a person can do what he wants to do, lead his own life. Toward this end, however, he must have his own aspirations, his own life content. A freed slave who lacks such content is not, in fact, truly free.

This point pertains not just to human beings or to particular interpretations of the concept of freedom; rather, it is the basic definition of freedom. Freedom without an independent will has no content or essence, and therefore no existence.

This principle applies to every individual and every living creature, not only to the complex patterns of the nation's spiritual life. Animals born and raised in captivity that escape their cages do not know how to live in freedom. They have no inner drive for an independent life and are thus incapable of living in a free world without masters and caretakers. When in their cages, they appear to be striving to get out, acting out of vague instinct. But when they do attain this freedom, they do not actually want it. Generally, they return after a short time to the comforts of the pen and its routine, to the caretaker who looks after them – even if he works them hard.

If this is true of animals, it is certainly true of human beings. To be free means to have a personality of one's own, a life goal of one's own, a goal that is worth striving for despite all the difficulties.

This idea is expressed succinctly in a famous saying of our sages.

On the words "*ḥarut al haluḥot*"[3] (which means "engraved on the Tablets"), our sages expound: "Do not read '*ḥarut*' (engraved) but '*ḥerut*' (freedom), for no man is free unless he engages in Torah study."[4]

The paradox inherent in this saying is the paradox of freedom itself. One who does not occupy himself with Torah, one who does not have Torah, does not have a life of his own. The fact that at this moment the yoke of external enslavement is not upon him makes no difference. For what will he do with this freedom when there is nothing he really wants for himself? Hence, naturally and inevitably, he enslaves himself once more to whoever is willing to be his master and tell him what to do and how to act.

CULMINATION OF THE REDEMPTION

The Giving of the Torah, then, is the conclusion of the process of casting off the yoke of enslavement. On Pesaḥ, freedom is attained only in the negative sense. The festival of Shavuot, of the Giving of the Torah, is required in order to acquire true freedom, to impart positive, authentic content to the Jewish People.

There is no life in an abstract, disembodied existence. Hence, the physical redemption must come first. There must be a Jewish People willing to accept the teachings of Judaism, and there must therefore be an Exodus. However, the exodus from Egypt was only the initial message of freedom, the spring season; Pesaḥ is only a festival of "*minḥat seorim*" (a meal-offering of barley). It is insufficient for the nation to remain in a state characterized by a crop of animal food; it is insufficient if their freedom is merely the negation of others – the urgency of "the people had fled"[5] – without any content of its own.

It is no wonder, then, that there is a veil of sadness and apprehension spread over the seven weeks of *Sefirat HaOmer*. At first, national liberation generates great excitement. The joy of liberation and the removal of the physical burden and all its accompanying symptoms induce the feeling that everything has already been attained. Later, however, other

3. Exodus 32:16.
4. *Avot* 6:2.
5. Exodus 14:5.

days begin to come – these are necessarily days of misfortune and calamity, but days in which one begins to feel that freedom is not the solution to all the problems. Freedom affords possibilities, but then almost immediately the feeling of "*Sefirat HaOmer*" sets in. Today is the first, the second, the third day of the *omer*; this year is the first, the second, the third year since independence; but these alone do not suffice. It is impossible to be contented for many years merely with produce that is fit for horses. The human being, too, demands his portion.

Hence, along with this post-freedom counting, another count must begin, a counting of anticipation, of preparation for receiving the Torah. For only with the receiving of the Torah do the festivals of beginning end. When the people receives the Torah and accepts it as the guide to its life path, it can then set out on its way.

FOUNDATION STONE OF THE PEOPLE

Attaining freedom by accepting the Torah, by "accepting the yoke of God's kingship," is not a simple or self-evident matter. A penetrating question arises, which was probably also asked by those who came out of Egypt and which continues to be asked even today: Why can other peoples, large and small, live their lives simply, without Torah? And why must the people of Israel in particular be exceptional in order to exist?

The answer is rooted in the anomaly of the Jewish People, an anomaly that has existed not only since its exile, but since its inception as a people – ever since the Exodus. This peculiarity is expressed in the words of the prophet: "Who has heard of anything like this? Who has witnessed such events? Can a land pass through travail in a single day? Is a nation born all at once? Yet Zion travailed and at once bore her children!"[6]

As a rule, the formation of a people is a slow process which takes centuries, during which a common existence little by little binds the individuals into a larger unit until it finally attains self-identity. This was not the case with the Jewish People, which was "born all at once," in a one-time process. Since the beginning of its existence, its unity and unique national character have not simply stemmed from the fact that "we are

6. Isaiah 66:8.

here." The development of the Jewish People is not "natural," like that of all the nations. Hence, it cannot satisfy itself with mere existence in order to secure its being as one nation.

The Jewish People emerged as a nation on the basis of a unifying idea, and in all generations the nation's continued existence is connected with that idea. R. Sa'adia Gaon taught: "Our nation, the people of Israel, is a nation only by virtue of its laws,"[7] and this statement remained meaningful even in generations when the majority of the people did not adhere to the Torah. The Torah has remained the foundation of our people's life because ties of identity always draw upon a common past, and this common past is inscribed with the unifying seal of the Torah.

Thus, the Jewish People requires a kind of freedom deeper than that of other nations. The Messianic times are defined in the halakha as entailing the removal of foreign oppression – physical freedom – but this can be meaningful only against the background of a previous meaningful Torah existence. It is not possible to lead a true Torah life under foreign rule. Without Torah, however, the removal of oppression does not constitute real independence; it is only the preliminary step toward full freedom. The Festival of Redemption awaits its completion by the Giving of the Torah.

7. *The Book of Beliefs and Opinions* 3:7.

The Significance of the Giving of the Torah

After the momentous revelations of the exodus from Egypt and the parting of the Red Sea, after the preparation of journeying in the wilderness amidst various trials until Israel became "as one man and with one heart,"[1] the time came for the Giving of the Torah. After the thunder and the lightning and the blast of the shofar, God revealed Himself to His people face to face, pronouncing the Ten Commandments to the entire people.

Here, we are greatly surprised: What was the purpose of all the grand preparation, this whole sublime revelation? Was it to reveal to the world what is said in the Ten Commandments? At first glance, it would seem that these commandments – belief in God, honoring father and mother, "You shall not murder, You shall not commit adultery"[2] – are the foundations of human morality in every time and place, and can be arrived at through the investigation and inquiry of the human intellect. What, then, is the innovation of this revelation? Wherein lies its preeminence?

1. Rashi, Exodus 19:2, s.v. *vayiḥan sham*
2. Exodus 20:13.

This question regarding the essence of the Giving of the Torah can also be approached from another angle. The Talmud teaches that our patriarch Abraham fulfilled the entire Torah even before it was given,[3] as it says, "And he kept My charge, My commandments, My statutes, and My laws."[4] The patriarchs grasped the Torah, with its detailed content, even before the revelation at Sinai. What, then, was added in the revelation at Sinai? What was the essential change that was brought about at the Giving of the Torah and in the period after it, over and above previous generations and the pre-Sinaitic world?

THE ASPIRATION FOR GOD'S NEARNESS

Every Jew contains within himself a "part of God from on high,"[5] a divine spark of light that is the inner point, the deepest and most hidden core of his spiritual life. To be sure, man does not always merit to know the divine nature of his own soul; he cannot always see behind the curtains that conceal the divine essence that calls him. Nevertheless, this core is always present.

Since this inner point of man, his soul's "holy of holies," is divine, man – consciously or unconsciously – aspires to godliness.

In various ways, man becomes aware that his desire and will is to have a relationship with God. Some people reach this awareness through contemplation and profound reflection on themselves and the world. Others are brought to it by events in their lives and their personal experiences. In some cases, a person who was far from Judaism and from thoughts of divinity all his life suddenly discovers – at a time of personal crisis, when he must decide finally where he belongs – the great strength of this inner core of life.

The contemplation and study that bring a person to religious consciousness, to the desire to draw near to God, are similarly not of one kind. Some people come to it through contemplation of God's greatness as revealed in the world He created, through recognition and contemplation of God's works and His overflowing light and goodness.

3. *Kiddushin* 82a.
4. Genesis 26:5.
5. Job 31:2; see *Tanya*, ch. 2.

They attain an inner state of excitement and enthusiasm, which leads to fuller consciousness of the will to draw near to God. Others come to it through reflection on Jewish destiny and on the Jewish People's special nature, through appreciation of God's mercy on us, which has accompanied us constantly ever since the Exodus.

There is yet another way – a person may attain the desire for God through himself, through contemplation of his own life and being. "From my flesh I behold God"[6] – through my very life and emotions I realize that God is behind them. This is the thought underlying the concept "For He is your life"[7] – the true heartfelt awareness that God is the essence of life, and that He is the source of life, not only of the whole world but also of my very being. This feeling corresponds to the *Zohar*'s[8] interpretation of man's call to God, "My soul, I yearn for You in the night:"[9] You, Who are truly my soul, my being, the true source of my life – You I desire, for You I long in the night, in the darkness and concealment of existence. All these thoughts awaken and reveal the desire to reach God, to draw near to Him, to be always with Him.

STRIVING TOWARD A SPIRITUAL WORLD

When man's aspiration to draw near to divinity reaches the stage of awareness and knowledge, it motivates him to set out on a path of searching and trial in the quest to draw near to God. For even when a person's aspiration to be close to divinity is clear to him, and even when he sets for himself the search for divinity as a life goal, not everything becomes clear. He is then faced with the momentous question asked by all God-seekers, from the Heavenly hosts to earthly man: "Where is the place of His glory?"[10]

The first feeling, the first movement of one who searches for and seeks God, is self-elevation – an attempt to transcend the limitations and bounds posed by corporeality and advance toward the abstract, the

6. Job 19:26.
7. Deuteronomy 30:20.
8. *Zohar* III, 67a.
9. Isaiah 26:9.
10. "*Kedusha*" of the *Musaf* Prayer of Sabbaths and Festivals.

spiritual, that which transcends the senses. The seeker thinks that once he frees himself of the many physical desires that surround his life, he will automatically become closer to God. The body, material things, physical desires and instincts – all these seems to be the main impediments. More subtly, he feels that the very fact that he is bound to the desires and aspirations of his ego is what interferes with and prevents his true attachment to God.

As a result, the God-seeker turns to spirituality. He tries to deepen his feeling for divinity, to attain love of God and the feeling of devotion and intimate spiritual connection.

Needless to say, it is possible to attain heights where one becomes oblivious to himself amidst the awakening of this abounding love, amidst a storm of longing to draw near to God, when the world is forgotten, when one renounces one's desires and passions in order to be closer to God.

Thus far is the reach of the first movement, the initial direction of the will to reach divinity. At this point, however, comes the time for reflection and criticism. The question arises: Is this perception, this awakening and emotional excitement, truly connected with and conducive to closeness to divinity?

LIMITED PERCEPTION

Upon deeper reflection, we discover that everything we know and everything we are capable of comprehending regarding divinity does not add up to any understanding whatsoever. Everything that we are more or less able to "feel from our flesh," to experience – the light that flows down and gives life to our world and to the myriads of spiritual worlds beyond us – all this is but a tiny spark, reflected light that has already gone through countless contractions. In the language of the Kabbala, this is called "*malkhut shebemalkhut shebe'asiya*" – the lowest level.

God Himself – the One for whom we yearn – is high and exalted, far above and beyond any perception or conception, unfathomable to the mind. Not only is the human intellect unable to grasp divinity, but the very comprehension of the intellect on any level is unable grasp Him, unable to make any kind of contact with Him. The Holy One, blessed be He, is "holy" – that is to say, separate, removed, and exalted above everything. He is the Infinite Being.

Hence, all human attempts to attain closeness to God through the effort of man himself are, by their very nature, doomed to failure. For how can man, who is essentially a limited and finite being, transcend the bounds of his existence? How can man, even at the pinnacle of spiritual exaltation, come in contact with what is inaccessible, the Holy and Separate One? All the experiences reflective of man's uplift in love and fear of God, his keeping far from the material world and its attainments, still do not bring man close to God.

Man thinks that divinity is found in the spiritual realm. Hence, he makes an effort to renounce material life and divest from the physical. He aims for nullification of the natural instincts. In reality, however, God is high and exalted above everything; even the highest spirituality – just like the lowest corporeality – is as naught compared to His infinite greatness.

Thus, even if man ascends to the highest levels attainable to him (and man is capable, potentially, of reaching levels higher than angels and seraphs), he remains far and removed from God. The infinite gulf that necessarily separates man from God – the gap between a limited creature who, despite his majesty, always remains bounded and the separate and infinite Being – cannot be bridged by man. In spite of all his efforts in his human way, man can never be truly close, nor even "closer," to God.

Thus, the way to God seems impassable. No human being, whoever he may be, can overcome all the obstacles, all the limitations of man – an essentially limited creature – and actually reach divinity, the transcendent Being. The desire and will of the "part of God from on high" within us is to ascend to God, but there is no way we can do this on our own.

CONNECTION TO HEAVEN

This is the significance and the role of the Giving of the Torah. Since we human beings cannot, through our own efforts, reach divinity, God Himself, in His infinite love and goodness brings Himself down to us in order to fulfill the original intention of Creation.

God's revelation to us – the Giving of the Torah at Mount Sinai – does not constitute only practical guidance regarding how we are to act and behave. God's descent at the Giving of the Torah is the enclothing of His will in the Torah and mitzvot. It is the revelation of the way in which we actually unite with God – by fulfilling His mitzvot. Thus, the mitzva becomes more than just the fulfillment of a command, a *tzav*; it contains within it deeper and more essential content. Mitzva derives from *tzavta* – to be together, together with God.

God "descended on Mount Sinai;" He lowered His essence, which transcends every category and definition, precisely into the categories and boundaries, the limits and confines, of the Torah that He gave us. Since the Torah is the expression of God's wisdom and supreme will, this revelation is much more than the reception of "Torah *from* Heaven." The Giving of the Torah brings down to human beings, to the human level of intelligence, the highest thing, the Torah – which *is* Heaven.

Hence, there is a fundamental, intrinsic difference between the mitzva as it appears externally, as it is grasped and understood by the intellect, and the inner nature of the mitzva as a way of connecting with God. The command "You shall not murder" of human morality is a profound law, an exalted level of human understanding. But even when "You shall not murder" is understood in the subtlest and most spiritual sense (motivated by neither personal interest nor the desire to establish and stabilize human society), it ultimately remains a human conception, limited by man's nature and essential character. It is a human pinnacle, which does not transcend the human realm. By contrast, when revealed at Sinai in the Ten Commandments, "You shall not murder" is a divine command, part of a context in which the Other, the Transcendent One, enters into a relationship with us.

This command is the limited instrument for attaining the unlimited, the finite tool for attaining the infinite. The world before the Giving of the Torah is a world where man tries to reach God, and yet in spite of all the efforts remains distant from Him. From the Giving of the Torah onward, the way is opened to reach divinity. God Himself descends and reveals Himself in the Torah, disclosing the way, telling us how it is possible for man to overcome the obstacles of his very humanity and to draw near and cleave to divinity.

Receiving the Torah

The giving of the Torah" and "the receiving of the Torah" would seem to be self-evident concepts, giving and the receiving being two sides of the same act from different perspectives. For this reason, we use these two terms interchangeably.

Closer examination, however, reveals that in truth there is an essential difference between the two expressions. The giving of the Torah and the receiving of the Torah are two poles of reality that, while interrelated, are not at all identical. Each of these concepts expresses a whole world of ideas, of being, with its own particular historical actuality.

To be sure, there is no giving without a certain component of receiving, and there can be no receiving without some prior giving. Nevertheless, the gulf separating the two is easily distinguishable.

The difference between receiving Torah and giving Torah is expressed in two dimensions: in the manner of the act and in the time of the occurrence. In kabbalistic terminology, the giving of the Torah is a movement from above downward, whereas the receiving is a movement from below reaching upward. In the dimension of time, the giving of the Torah is essentially a one-time act, whereas the receiving of the Torah is a multifaceted process of many stages.

CONNECTION BETWEEN GOD AND MAN

The Torah's general meaning, the meaning that encompasses the whole essence of the Torah, is found in each one of the Torah's details. For in the most general sense, the Torah is a connection and a bridge between the divine essence and man.

This description of the Torah is classically expressed in the statement, "Three are interconnected: Israel, the Torah, and the Holy One, blessed be He."[1] The people of Israel are connected to the Torah, and the Torah is connected to God. This connection between heaven and earth, between above and below, is the meaning of the Torah.

For this connection to be meaningful, it is by its very nature composed of two necessary elements. On the one hand, the will on the part of the giver of the Torah to give Torah – that is to say, to form a meaningful connection with man – is required. On the other hand, the will of the receiver of the Torah to accept the Torah, to bind himself to the Creator, is necessary as well.

The mutuality of the connection appears in the sources in an analogy between the Giving of the Torah and a wedding. This analogy strongly emphasizes the dual connection that lies at the heart of the matter, for if one of the parties in marriage does not consent to the connection, it is not a relationship of drawing closer but an entirely different act. Thus, the two-way connection – movement from above downward and from below upward – transpires in the midst of the Giving of the Torah on Mount Sinai, in the drawing close from both directions simultaneously.

A BRIDGE OVER AN INFINITE GULF

A fundamental point in Jewish thought is the understanding of the gulf that separates God from the world. Scripture speaks of God as the Creator of the world and as One who watches over its existence and being; at the same time, however, there is the recognition of the infinite distance between the created and the Creator. In a certain sense, this feeling – which casts doubt on the existence of any connection or contact between God above and man below – is the heart of the religious experience.

1. *Zohar* III, 73a.

The central message contained in the Giving of the Torah and in the Ten Commandments is the answer to this question, for this is the central subject dealt with in the verses describing the Giving of the Torah: "It is true that God our Lord has just shown us His majesty and greatness, and we have heard His voice out of the fire. Today we have seen that when God speaks to man, he can still survive."[2] The focus is not on the actual words spoken by God, but on the very possibility of His revelation to man, on the very fact that He entrusts man with a mission and that He considers it important to form this relationship with man. Indeed, this, in a word, is the entire Torah; all the rest is merely commentary and expansion, explanation and guidance.

Thus, the Giving of the Torah is primarily the formation of the connection, the bridging of the gulf – an act that man himself cannot accomplish, but only the Creator. The importance of this event lies in the very act of giving, the formation of the connection from above downward. This is a unique event, unlike any other event in which instructions or laws were given or new truths revealed.

RECEIVING THE TORAH – AGREEMENT AND INTERNALIZATION

The Giving of the Torah is thus an event in which the divine is the decisive factor and which is anchored in the basic connection and relationship of the divine to the world. The receiving of the Torah is of a different nature; it is human, familiar and understandable to us.

Nonetheless, there is a paradox involved in this dual process. The Giving of the Torah, with all its fundamental and theological importance, has meaning only when accompanied by the complementary act – the receiving of the Torah. For the Torah – which means instruction, guidance, charting a direction – has meaning only when there is someone who receives it, someone who takes it to guide him and show him his path.

Our sages emphasize the other side of the Giving of the Torah – the Jewish People's willingness to accept it – in their bold interpretation

2. Deuteronomy 5:21.

of the verse, "You are My witnesses … and I am God."[3] They interpret as follows: "When you are My witnesses, I am God; when you are not My witnesses, then I, as it were, am not God."[4] Because the Jewish People are willing to accept the Torah and to receive the message, the revelation of it – the encounter between God and Man – can take place.

The concept of receiving the Torah has dual meaning. First, it entails fundamental acceptance – willingness to obey the Torah. Second, it entails beginning to absorb and to understand what has been given.

Man's initial willingness to accept the Torah is vital to this giving-receiving connection, but the process of absorbing, integrating, and identifying with the content is also not indispensable. Indeed, the Scriptural account clearly establishes that the willingness to accept the Torah preceded even the Giving of the Torah: "All the people answered as one and said: 'All that God has spoken we will do.'"[5]

It is also possible to understand in this way the meaning of the words that became the watchword of Israel's experience at Sinai: "All that God has spoken we will do and we will hear."[6] Preceding "we will hear" with "we will do" is equivalent to preceding the process of absorbing and understanding with the willingness to obey.

This distinction between "we will do" and "we will hear" is the same as the aforementioned distinction between the two aspects of receiving the Torah – a distinction whose historical significance expressed itself in practice. Moses, upon taking leave of the people forty years later, referred to this when he said, "But until this day, God did not give you a heart to know or eyes to see or ears to hear."[7] Indeed, only many generations later could it be said that the people of Israel had developed a heart able to know the Torah, for receiving in the sense of internalizing takes much longer.

3. Isaiah 43:12.
4. *Sifrei*, Deuteronomy 346.
5. Exodus 19:8.
6. Ibid. 24:7.
7. Deuteronomy 29:3.

RECEIVING THE TORAH – WHENEVER WE WISH

The Kotzker Rebbe defined this duality of giving and receiving as follows: The festival of Shavuot is called the "Season of the *Giving* of our Torah" because on that day the Torah was given to Israel. But as for the *receiving* of the Torah – each individual receives it according to his way, when he is ready to receive it.

The Giving of the Torah as an act of forming a connection between the Creator and His creatures is a one-time event – not only because it happened only once, but also because the disclosure that man is indeed capable of receiving things from the Infinite requires no further proof. When the event is recalled, this suffices for it to remain meaningful. Hence, there is a mitzva to remember the day of the Giving of the Torah, to remember the event itself: "But take heed and watch yourself carefully, so that you do not forget the things that your eyes saw… the day you stood before God your Lord at Ḥorev."[8] The memory of the event is its main content.

An analogy may be drawn from Norbert Wiener's quip about the secret of the atom bomb: The greatest secret about this bomb was revealed to the entire world on the day of the explosion – namely, that it is possible.[9] Similarly, the great secret and revelation in the Giving of the Torah lie in the very fact that the Holy One, blessed be He, is interested in giving the Torah, that He is interested in human beings and in the human individual to such an extent that it is His will to give him guidance regarding how he can attain closeness to Him.

For this reason, the Giving of the Torah is essentially a one-time act, unique in human history. The event itself is the revelation of the content of the Giving of the Torah, and is sufficient in and of itself.

While the Giving of the Torah is the one-time flashpoint in history, the receiving of the Torah is an exceedingly lengthy process. This is not a mere witticism, but rather a thread that runs throughout the Holy Scriptures. All of Scripture is none other than a detailed account of the difficulties, the ups and the downs, on the way to receiving the Torah,

8. Ibid. 4:9–10.
9. Norbert Wiener is regarded as the originator of cybernetics.

on the one hand, and an account of the deviations and straying from the receiving of the Torah after the incident of the golden calf, on the other.

The sages interpret the statement in *Megillat Esther,* "The Jews confirmed and accepted:"[10] In the time of religious persecution, the Jews confirmed what they had already accepted upon themselves at the revelation at Sinai.[11] The implication is that only in the time of the Second Temple could it be said for the first time that the Jewish People as a whole had accepted the Torah as an obligatory way of life.

More than a thousand years elapsed, then, between the giving of the Torah and the receiving of the Torah. This lengthy period attests that, unlike the Giving of the Torah, the receiving of the Torah was not a one-time event. The receiving of the Torah was a long process of many stages, and many years and hardships were required in order to actualize it.

Even to this day, receiving the Torah remains an "open question." It is not simply a matter of the spiritual and intellectual capacities of one generation or another. As long as human beings possess free will, the problem of accepting the Torah will be posed anew in every generation. This decision, even in the original sense of "We will do and we will hear," and certainly as regards the acceptance of the practical details, remains the provenance of each and every individual. The receiving of the Torah, though it is an event of basic and fundamental importance, continues to take place in a never-ending process.

THE ROAD TO COMPLETE ACCEPTANCE IS LONG

As a historical fact, the receiving of the Torah lasted a long time. As a personal-individual experience, it continues to this very day. The Giving of the Torah cannot be fully compared to the receiving of the Torah. The Giver of the Torah, being omnipotent, can give it at any point in time, whereas the receiver, as a human being, is bound to the limits of time. The receiving of the Torah can last for many generations – but is this inescapable?

Of necessity, the receiving of the Torah cannot be accomplished in its totality, all at once. Certainly, it is possible for there to be a one-

10. Esther 9:27.
11. *Shabbat* 88a.

time act of reception ("We will do and we will hear"), but only in the sense of acceptance, not in the sense of absorption and understanding.

Indeed, the receiving of the Torah by the people of Israel has been a difficult absorption process throughout the generations. As long as the issue is only one of external form (such as the carrying out of specific acts), the commandments present no special difficulty, and where there is willingness to undertake them, they are easily absorbed. However, receiving the Torah entails more than just formal-external mimicry of certain actions. Moreover, these external forms are liable to assume a negative meaning because within the receiver's consciousness and within the societal structure, they have assumed a different meaning. For example, regarding the divine service of offerings, in order for there to be not only basic reception and acceptance but also absorption and internalization, the receiver must study and develop until he reaches the level at which he can, to some degree, absorb what has been given to him. The more multifaceted this process is, the more detailed it is, the more it demands the receptivity of the heart and the understanding of the mind, the lengthier and more complex it must be.

The process of receiving the Torah has thus been continuing from the incident of the golden calf until the present day. It is a process of training the receiver to genuinely absorb what has been given to him, and this is not a simple or straightforward learning process. It is delayed not only when there is an attempt at rejection, but also when there is inadequate or premature acceptance – that is to say, without the proper foundation. Then, too, new problems and distortions arise. Only thousands of years, countless good intentions, and incessant preparation on the part of all the individuals can ensure that the Torah, given at Sinai, will be truly received.

The festival of Shavuot remains, then, a day of remembrance and commemoration of the majestic and on-time event – the "Season of the Giving of our Torah." So, too, we recall that at that event, "His kingship they accepted upon themselves willingly." However, the receiving of the Torah did not come to an end then. The Torah continues to be received in our time as in those days.

Torah of Life

From the standpoint of its position on the Jewish calendar, the festival of Shavuot is a day of culmination – *Atzeret* – for the festival of Pesaḥ. The festival of freedom reaches its climax and culmination in the festival of the Giving of the Torah, and the Giving of the Torah is the fulfillment of the hope and wish generated by the festival of freedom.

The unique meaning of the Torah is largely obscured because of the meaning of the term "*torah*" in current usage, as in "*torat hayaḥasut*" (the theory of relativity) or "*torat habishul*" (the art of cooking). Such usage deprives the Torah of one of its basic points – the fact that it is unique and self-defining. The term rightfully has only one usage – for the Torah alone.

Whoever regards the Torah as the law book of a particular religious system distorts Judaism and, thereby, the proper understanding of the Torah's essential nature.

A religion is a conceptual and practical framework whose purpose is to regulate part of life – the part of life that has to do with serving God. Judaism, however, as expressed in the Torah, cannot be limited within such a partial framework. Its whole essence is in viewing all of life as a comprehensive system, encompassing all the ways and details of the Jewish People's life in a special pattern.

Hence, the Torah includes not only elements of worship ("between man and God") and regulation of society ("between man and his fellow man"), but also history and poetry, moral guidance and words of prophecy, categorical pronouncements and words of perplexity and doubt. Moreover, all these components do not appear as distinct parts that join together, but as one, undivided essence.

To discern this special nature, one need not read through the entire Torah. Even a representative segment, such as the Ten Commandments, contains many of these components.

In this respect, the Torah is structured like life itself. Life, too, is not composed of separate compartments, each with its own character and nature. Torah is like man, who is not composed of separate areas dealing only with certain relations and aspects. Man and his life are always a mixture of everything together, of the whole world in all its elements. To meet certain needs, man constructs partitions with which he demarcates separate areas within himself, but this demarcation is technical and artificial. In truth, there is no part of himself that is not nourished and that does not draw sustenance, to a greater or lesser extent, from all the other parts of his being.

The Torah is part of true being; hence, it, too, is not compartmentalized. *Parashat Kedoshim* (which is like a reflection of the Ten Commandments) proceeds directly from honoring parents to the laws of offerings, from gifts to the poor to "Love your neighbor as yourself,"[1] from the prohibitions of revenge and of bearing a grudge to the prohibition of wearing *sha'atnez*.[2]

This is why it is "Torah" – teaching; it teaches and establishes a way of life for the people. The totality of life is found in and directed by the Torah. These two elements together – the Jewish People and the Torah – form what is called "Judaism."

To place the Torah into the framework of religion (whether this

1. Leviticus 19:18.
2. *Sha'atnez*: The Torah prohibition against the wearing of fabric that contains both wool and linen.

is done by those who reject it or by those who uphold it) is to ruin it; it is to reject it as Torah and to turn it into something completely different – into simply one of the world's religions and faiths. Conceiving of the Torah as religion is tantamount to confining it within a limited area and, what is more, divesting it of life entirely. If a Jew is "religious," he thereby denies the true meaning of Torah. For the Torah demands of him to be a *Yehudi* – to give his whole life a special character, whereby everything is Torah.

The whole meaning of the Giving of the Torah after the exodus from Egypt was to complete the formation of the people, its structure and character, in all the details and parts of its being. Forming the character of the people is the very essence of the revelation at Sinai. This, then, is the culmination of the process that began on the festival of Pesaḥ and concludes on Shavuot – the Jewish People's emergence from Egyptian bondage and transformation into a free people.

Gimel (3rd) Tammuz

The Hillula Day of Gimel (3rd) Tammuz

JOY MIXED WITH SORROW

The Lubavitcher Rebbe passed away on *gimel* (3rd) Tammuz, which is termed his "*hillula* day" on the basis of the holy *Zohar*'s designation for the yahrzeit of R. Shimon bar Yoḥai,[1] which thereafter became the designation for the yahrzeits of all the *tzaddikim*.

The great spiritual level of the *tzaddikim* is connected with the fact that the Angel of Death has no power over them; rather, it is God Himself who takes their souls, as it says: "But God will redeem my soul from the power of Sheol; for He will take me. Selah."[2]

Thus, when Maimonides writes of the death of Moses our Master, he formulates the matter in a unique way: "And what befell him was death, for us… but life, for him, considering the level to which he ascended."[3] He does not say that Moses died, for such a thing does not pertain to people like Moses our Master. The *tzaddik* did leave this world, but this

---

1. See *Zohar* (*Idra Zuta*) *Ha'azinu* 296b, 291a; *Vayḥi* 218a; also see above, the essay on Lag BaOmer.
2. Psalms 49:16.
3. Introduction to his *Commentary on the Mishna*.

is a completely different level, involving "death by a kiss" – man's soul "kisses" God. The small fire meets the large fire and is included in it.

On the *hillula* day, the *tzaddik* merits to reach the conclusion of his task, and his soul is exalted even more. Hence, in this respect the *hillula* day is a day of joy.

Yet, in the midst of this joy, there is the pain over the fact that the *tzaddik* has left us. And there is no contradiction here. The *tzaddik* himself completed his task in this world, and he certainly is now in a better place. We, however, feel the absence and vacuum. Of this, it says in the *Zohar*: "Joy is fastened in my heart on one side, while weeping is fastened in my heart on the other side."[4]

Joy is usually only possible after the period of sorrow over the *tzaddik*'s departure has passed, when it is possible to move on. As the pain of loss due to the *tzaddik*'s departure from the world subsides and we are able to console ourselves, it becomes easier to rejoice on the day of his *hillula*.

When we assemble on the *hillula* days of the former *Admorim* – the 24th of Tevet and the 9th of Kislev – we know that the *tzaddik* is exalted to a higher level in the supernal world, and so we rejoice in the joy of the elevation of his soul. But when we still feel the loss even after much time has passed since his departure, it is difficult to rejoice on the *hillula* day. Sometimes, the sense of absence is so acute that it does not recede, not even after a year or two years. Even after several years have passed, we still have the sense that the loss is great, and the problem of the absence intensifies.

What must we do in the present situation? How is it possible to fill the void that was created upon the Rebbe's departure?

Before addressing this, however, we must understand the relationship between the *tzaddik* and the world.

THE TZADDIK DOES NOT LEAVE

The *Zohar* teaches: "The *tzaddik,* even though he has departed from this world, is found in all worlds even more than during his lifetime."[5] In other

4. *Zohar* III, 75a.
5. Ibid. III, 71b.

words, after the *tzaddik*'s passing, he is found in all worlds – including this world – more than he was during his lifetime.

In the *Tanya*,[6] this is explained straightforwardly: The *tzaddik*'s life in this world is bound to the physical body, which limits the soul through the limitations of time and place and through the faculties and concepts of the body. However, after his departure from this world, the *tzaddik* is in a different state – he belongs to the lofty heights of the soul, unbound by the limits of time and place and unconfined to the body. This is another form of existence, of life in a world that is different and higher than the one with which we are familiar. Hence, after his departure, the *tzaddik* can be in this world more than he was during his lifetime.

Even if the *tzaddik* is released from the bonds of the body after his passing, why should he be interested in a continued connection with the physical matters of this world when he could occupy himself solely with the spiritual matters of the Garden of Eden? Why would a soul that, considering its high level, could engage in matters of the supernal worlds prefer to deal with matters of this world?

Actually, the same question could have been asked about the Rebbe's involvement in worldly affairs during his lifetime. It is well-known that a large part of the Rebbe's daily schedule was devoted to worldly issues and to the small problems of individuals. Why would an eminent person of his stature deal with all the problems and difficulties faced by all sorts of people? Why did the Rebbe go to the trouble of dealing with matters of marginal importance, at times even with trivialities? Many would ask for advice in trifling matters, and the Rebbe would always answer them. Why would an person of the Rebbe's stature feel obliged to invest his time in such matters, some of which were real nonsense? In what way is this beneficial to him?

The answer is that this is a central part of the *tzaddik*'s work, and even the main purpose of his soul's descent into this world. In kabbalistic literature, it is written that most souls that descend to this world are souls that have already been here, souls that must come on an additional *gilgul* (transmigration) in order to rectify what was omitted the last time. In every generation, however, there are souls that descend to

6. *Igeret HaKodesh* 27.

this world for a different reason. These are the souls of the *tzaddikim*, which do not require rectification, but rather descend to this world in order to rectify other souls.

Tzaddikim descend to this world "voluntarily." In this world, there are souls that require support, and the *tzaddik* – out of his love for God – agrees to leave his important pursuits in the higher realms and descend to help these people. Like those who volunteer to treat the sick and disabled out of compassion for suffering souls, so does the *tzaddik* on his descent into this world.

The truth is that the *tzaddik* suffers from having to deal with such difficult matters; nevertheless, he does so in order to participate in God's works. "God has washed away the filth of the daughters of Zion"[7] – just as the father of an infant, out of his great love for the child, washes away his filth and cleans him (even though a stranger would not relish the assignment of treating the soiled infant), so does God for Israel. And the *tzaddikim*, who are in the image of their Maker, are willing to do the same. Cleaning the filth is not an especially agreeable act, but it, too, is part of life.

The Rebbe fulfills the role of the father, who not only nourishes and cleans the infant, but also smiles at him and makes funny faces for him to amuse him. When the Rebbe sees that it is imperative to make the other person smile, he does this, too.

Even after the *tzaddik* reaches the supernal world, he continues to engage in matters of this world, despite the fact that it is much more difficult for him to do so there. For during his lifetime, he was still connected, to some degree, to matters of this world, and he better understood the needs of this world.

Once, in a time of great distress, the *tzaddik* Rebbe Mordekhai of Chernobyl gave a dying man an assignment: He gave him a note of request to be given to his father – the *tzaddik* Rebbe Naḥum of Chernobyl, who had departed from the world many years before – asking him to act to bring about the annulment of the decree. After some time, the man, who had passed away, appeared to Rebbe Mordekhai in a dream. He told him that it had been very difficult for him to reach his

7. Isaiah 4:4.

father's chamber, as Rebbe Naḥum had ascended to a very high chamber. Finally, however, when he succeeded in reaching Rebbe Naḥum's chamber and told him, "I have a note for you from your son," the *tzaddik* Rebbe Naḥum asked him, "What is a son?"

In this physical world, there are fathers and sons; but in the supernal worlds, no such relationship exists. When the *tzaddik* resides in the supernal worlds, he sees things from a completely different perspective. To reside on a high level in the supernal worlds and to continue dealing with problems of people living in this world is a complex undertaking on the *tzaddik*'s part.

DIFFERENT WORLDS, DIFFERENT IDEAS

It is sometimes difficult for us to imagine the extent to which our great problems in this world are remote from the world of the *tzaddik*.

Take, for example, a small boy who asks his father to participate with him in a game of collecting colorful papers. For the boy, this game is the basis of the world's existence. In his eyes, the fate of the collection of papers in his possession is the sole source of joy or sorrow. If the father wants to be a good father, he must empathize with the boy's feelings, enter his imaginary world of ideas, try to understand the rules of the game, and be an integral part of the experience. Although to the father it is nothing but a useless game, he takes the trouble to fully understand his young son.

There are many adults who play the game of collecting colorful paper called banknotes. One who has many such banknotes is happy and in good spirits due to his good fortune and goodly lot, whereas one who does not have them feels that he is most unfortunate. In the eyes of these people, all of life revolves around the number of banknotes in one's possession – even if others try to prove to them the foolishness of such an attitude.

The *tzaddik* – who is on an exceedingly high level even while he is in this world – relates to the collection of banknotes just as we relate to children who collect colorful papers. He is willing to involve himself in such matters, even though they are clearly pointless.

This is the difficult nature of the *tzaddik*'s job – he must not only be with the people who live in this world, but also be able to think in their terms, to feel their sorrows and to rejoice in their joys. This is difficult for the *tzaddik* even when he is living in this world, and sevenfold more difficult after his departure. When he is no longer connected to physical concepts, it is especially difficult for him to stay in touch with those who dwell in a physical world.

The story is told of one of the *tzaddikim* who, after his departure, was asked to pray for the annulment of a decree that was hanging over someone. The *tzaddik* said: "From the place where I am now, I do not see any decree. When one is on high, one sees only the good aspect of the matter. Even if I understand that, in the place where you are, you feel that this is an evil decree and that one must pray for its annulment, nevertheless, since I am on high, I cannot help but love everything that happens to someone dwelling below."

If the *tzaddik* is interested in continuing to look after those who live in this world even after his departure, he must refrain from using the concepts of the world of truth (the next world), but, rather, use the terms of the world of falsehood and imagination (this world), in which the earthly creatures feel that they are in distress.

When a *tzaddik* dies, we feel as though we have lost our "shepherd," but we know that he does not really take leave of this world; he still volunteers to be involved with us, according to our own conceptions, despite the difficulty entailed as he becomes further and further elevated. To be sure, this is not a complete solution, but it does offer us some consolation – we are not entirely neglected and forsaken. He was with us, is with us, and will continue to be with us in the future as well.

HEAD OF THE JEWISH PEOPLE

On the one hand, we can take some consolation in that the Rebbe does not abandon us; on the other hand, the Rebbe left a void that no one can fill. The more important and central the *tzaddik*'s place was during his lifetime, the greater is the vacuum left after his departure. The intensity of the sense of the *tzaddik*'s absence is in correlation to the intensity of the sense of his presence beforehand.

The function of the head is to direct the limbs of the body. The body does not carry out actions automatically. By themselves, the feet do not know whether to turn left or right; as a rule, they do not even know that a turn is to be made at all. The head has eyes, and it sees the turn; it knows where to turn and directs the feet accordingly. The function of the head is thus, first and foremost, to set a direction. The head does not have to take steps, but it has to decide where we are going.

The natural state is that the body follows the clear instructions that it receives from the head. The feet do not understand the reason for the instructions that the head gives, but it is crucial that there be a direct system of communication from the head to all the limbs of the body and that the limbs act in accordance with the head's instructions.

The Rebbe was the "head of the Jewish people"[8] in this generation, and now, after his departure, we lack the clear guidance that we used to get from our head. In our present state, even though all the other limbs remain in place, we lack direct guidance. When the feet continue striding without receiving direct guidance from the head – this is a serious drawback.

To correct this drawback, each and every one of us – all of us, as one body – must accept the personal responsibility of acting according to the Rebbe's past instructions to us. Until now, we could rely on the Rebbe as the force that connects and unites us. Now, perhaps more than ever, separation and fragmentation are liable to develop. Hence, precisely in the present situation, each individual bears on his shoulders greater and heavier responsibility. Every one of the body's limbs must find on its own the way to openly connect with the rest of the limbs, to feel that we are all part of one body striving for the same goal.

DO ALL THAT IS WITHIN YOUR POWER

Once, Hassidim thought that the head acts for them, and thereby all the problems are solved. However, it is insufficient for the head alone to act. The head requires a vast nervous system that relays its orders to all parts of the body.

When the Rebbe said, "I have done my part; do all that is within your power," he was saying that in order to bring about the coming of the Messiah, active cooperation on the part of others is required. It is not

8. The acronym of the words "head of the Jewish people" – *Rosh Bnei Israel* – is the word *Rebbe*.

sufficient merely to urge the Rebbe to do what he can; if the hands do not cooperate, even the strongest head in the world cannot lift anything.

At present, when there is a disconnection between the head and the body, our obligation is all the greater to carry out what devolves upon us. To be sure, we cannot function like a head, but we must fulfill our role as feet and carry out the instructions that were issued by the head.

The Rebbe is with us now, even more than during his lifetime, for his message has become much more personally demanding. Until now, it was possible to rely on the head's responsibility, but now there is no one on whom to cast this responsibility except on ourselves. It is our responsibility.

The Rebbe did not always give people specific instructions for every step of the way. The Rebbe sent many people to various places, one after the other, and to all of them he said the same thing: Do all that you can, and most importantly – you should know that this is your personal responsibility. None of the Rebbe's emissaries received from him a list of guidelines and instructions detailing what should be done at every stage. They received from him a few "glowing coals" and the general instruction: You must do all that is within your power.

The Rebbe sought to take away from people their peace of mind, the thought that one may continue to be complacent and not do anything – the thought that "one can sleep peacefully, because the Rebbe is still awake." Precisely now, the Rebbe's instruction is with us even more. The Rebbe says to each and every one of us: "Now, let us see you do something." This places a much greater demand on everyone and requires much greater staying power.

The Rebbe will continue to pray that we should succeed in our service of God, but in practice we have to go and do things by ourselves. Precisely on this day, we are all obligated to do what is within our power, out of the sense that we have no choice. We are compelled to act, for nowadays the easy solutions that used to exist are no longer available.

Instead of saying, "There is no one giving instructions" as an excuse for not acting, one should know that now everyone must get up and begin to do something. There is much to be done, and one person alone cannot do everything. The goal is to transform the world and prepare it for the coming of the Messiah, and every ordinary individual can do small things on the way to realizing this goal. We all must lend a hand to one another, so that we will merit to prepare the world for the coming of the Messiah, speedily in our days.

The Legacy of the Lubavitcher Rebbe – Do Not Evade Your Duty!

THE HOSTS OF GOD

The Torah calls the people of Israel "the hosts of God,"[1] a designation used often by the Lubavitcher Rebbe. Jews of all kinds and in all generations are included in God's army.

The term "army" teaches us about the nature of this system. Like every army in the world, God's army includes not only fighters, but also idle soldiers, non-combatant soldiers who perform other duties, and a great many evaders and deserters. The common denominator of all of them is that they are all army property; they all belong there. No matter how they behave and no matter what they do or do not do, they are all considered part of one army.

Ever since the exodus from Egypt, HaShem's hosts have been on a journey. At first, it was a journey in a small wilderness – the wilderness of Sinai – and later the journey became longer and more complicated,

1. Exodus 12:41.

amidst the "wilderness of the nations."[2] That journey has lasted for over two thousand years.

The struggle in the "wilderness of the nations" is not a struggle against specific human enemies, but a war against the space devoid of sanctity, which the Jewish People is to conquer and restore to God's sphere of influence.

The journeying in this wilderness resembles the way our ancestors journeyed in the wilderness of Sinai. Then, the cloud destroyed all the snakes and scorpions in their path, the small troubles and insignificant physical enemies. The military formation, protected by the cloud, prevented the wild creatures from attacking, and all that Israel had to do was simply to march forward.

This is God's military camp, before which He marches. HaShem's army, which proceeds like an organized and orderly combat unit, sets out to conquer reality, the world. Thus, the Jewish People advances and stops, protects itself and wages war against the "desolate howling wasteland,"[3] against the forces of evil and impurity.

CURSED IS HE WHO DOES NOT UPHOLD

God's army has an objective, whose attainment requires total commitment. The Torah renders harsh judgment against one who does not work to achieve this objective: "Cursed is he who does not uphold and keep the words of this Torah."[4] Indeed, when that curse was recited, the Jewish People responded, "Amen," accepting upon themselves this responsibility.

"Upholding the words of the Torah" does not mean just fulfilling the mitzvot in practice. It is more central than that – one must uphold the Torah so that it has real standing as the focal point of reality. Whoever does not do this is cursed in the presence of all of Israel: "Cursed is the one who will not uphold the words of this Torah." We became obligated in this duty when the people of Israel entered the Land.

Although in our time we have merited to return to the Land and

2. Ezekiel 20:35.
3. Deuteronomy 32:10.
4. Ibid. 27:26.

resettle in it, we do not appear to be actually fulfilling our obligation. This is the collective responsibility of all of Israel and of each individual Jew, and he is told so in the clearest, simplest, and strongest language possible; it cannot be stated more categorically than "cursed."

This responsibility devolves on all those who left Egypt and belong to God's hosts, who left in order to fight the battles of HaShem, to go out and uphold the words of this Torah. The war on behalf of God's revelation in the world continues. As God's army, the war against those forces that fight against His revelation is our war. Things do not happen by themselves.

Today, God's army is no longer very organized, and we do not see God's hosts fighting for His sake. We must reorganize and set out together, especially now, when we are journeying in a much larger and more difficult wilderness. Every snake in our wilderness now has a television camera, every scorpion has a microphone, and all sorts of reptiles have pens in their hands. All these are the teachers, educators, and guides of most of the world. Nevertheless, as God's army, we must sally forth into the midst of this world and fight the battles of HaShem.

EMERGENCY ORDER

The Rebbe constantly spoke about our obligation to once again look like God's army – we must not continue to crawl about, with everyone going off by himself, without knowing whereto or wherefore. His goal in education was to give every Jew a "kick in the pants," to wake him up, to get him moving, so that he should advance and not remain in place. If that does not work, he taught, stronger measures may be used.

For more than forty years, the Rebbe worked day and night, tirelessly and incessantly, without a minute's break, to wake people up and get them going, to motivate them and instill in them the awareness that they are God's army, that they have a common objective. They must understand that all the evaders and deserters, all those who act as though they were dead – all these must be brought back and incorporated into this army, which must begin advancing again as one camp.

To be a soldier in this army is not a simple matter. In the army, someone who cries at every step is forced to run, laden with equipment, more kilometers than he thought he could walk his whole life. A soldier is ordered to take apart his weapon, reassemble it, and oil it, over and over, until he does it to perfection. Even if he does not want to do it, even if he is too tired and exhausted and wants to fall asleep already, nevertheless, he knows that he will continue, for that is what he must do. As in every army, the drills do not always seem to be vital or useful, but the point of it all is to get a person to move, to train, to run.

This task does not fall on others, but on us and on all those who are with us. These are the words of Moses our Master, which still apply and are always relevant: "It was not with our ancestors that God made this covenant, but with us, the living, every one of us who is here today."[5] The repetitious language is purposeful – no one should mistakenly think that Scripture is talking about someone else. Scripture is not talking about others, about the neighbors, about the dead, or about the *tzaddikim*. Scripture is talking about us – all of us who are alive today. God made this covenant with us – despite our problems, our troubles, our crookedness – and it applies to us today. "God our Lord established a covenant with us at Ḥorev." There is no getting around it; the covenant is "with us, every one of us who is here today."

TO BRING THE DAYS OF THE MESSIAH

It is said that on the day of its departure from this world, the soul elevates itself, ascent after ascent. Hence, the Rebbe's cause, his call and his aspiration – all these still stand and even grow stronger every year.

What the Rebbe wanted can be explained in ordinary words or in grand words. In ordinary words, he wanted to transform the world; in grand words, he wanted to bring the Messiah. These words do not differ from each other in essence, but only in style.

In this respect, the Rebbe did not ultimately succeed in accomplishing what he wanted to, for the world has not yet been redeemed. The Rebbe wanted to accomplish much more than launching additional campaigns for the spread of Judaism. To be sure, it was important to him that another child say "*Modeh ani*" and another Jew put on *tefillin*, but

5. Ibid. 5:3.

that was not the objective or the ultimate goal. To influence someone to pray, to influence someone to grow a beard – these are truly good things, but they all still fall short of the main objective: to transform the entire world and, first and foremost, the Jewish world.

Tisha B'Av

Remembering Jerusalem

UNIVERSAL LOSS

On the night of Tisha B'Av, when the Jewish People devotes itself again to mourning for all that it has lost during its long exile, after everyone is seated on the ground and before the *kinot* (lamentations) are recited, there is a custom that the prayer leader rises and proclaims to the congregation, "Today marks such-and-such many years since the destruction of our Sanctuary." The essence of the mourning over the great catastrophe, over the years of exile and all that they have entailed, returns to the focal point of this mourning – to the destruction of the Temple and city of Jerusalem.

The destruction of Jerusalem and the Temple is more than the destruction of our historical capital and our most sacred site. It is not merely a memory of a tragic event that occurred long ago. Rather, it is a blow to the vital center of the Jewish People.

Moreover, the whole world is stricken and cannot return to its normal and rectified state until the city of Jerusalem and the Temple are rebuilt, for Jerusalem is the center point of the world's existence.

The Midrash describes Jerusalem's essential place in the world:

> Abba Ḥanan said in the name of Samuel the Small: This world is like a person's eyeball. The white of the eye is the ocean

> surrounding the world; the iris is the inhabited world; the pupil of the eye is Jerusalem; and the face [the reflection of the observer] in the pupil is the Holy Temple. May it be rebuilt speedily in our days.[1]

Harm done to Jerusalem is therefore harm done to the apple of the world's eye; the light of existence is diminished and obscured when the pupil of the eye is damaged.

The whole world consciously or unconsciously feels Jerusalem's destruction. As our sages say, "Since the day that the Temple was destroyed, there has been no day without its curse... and the curse of each day is greater than that of the one before it."[2] "Since the day that the Temple was destroyed," we are taught, "the sky has not appeared in its full purity, as it says: 'I clothe the skies in darkness and make their raiment sackcloth.'"[3] The mourning over Jerusalem is universal; it is a tragedy from which the whole universe suffers.

Even God Himself participates in the mourning of Jerusalem. One of the sages relates what he heard in a ruin in Jerusalem: "I heard a heavenly voice cooing like a dove and saying, 'Woe to the sons because of whose sins I destroyed My House, burned My Sanctuary, and exiled them among the nations.'" The sage was then told that God says, "What is there for the father who has exiled his sons, and woe to the sons who have been exiled from their father's table."[4] Thus, "Since the day that the Temple was destroyed, God has had no laughter."[5]

The destruction of Jerusalem is for us the ruin of all of existence, and ever since, a curtain of sadness and darkness has covered the face of reality. The mourning over Jerusalem is more than a one-time memorial of a once-a-year day of mourning. All of Jewish life is continually suffused with mourning in remembrance of the *ḥurban* (destruction).

1. *Derekh Eretz Zuta* 9, end.
2. *Sota* 48a, 49a.
3. *Berakhot* 59a citing Isaiah 50:3.
4. Ibid. 3a
5. *Avoda Zara* 3b.

For us, the sharply worded verses, "If I forget you, O Jerusalem, let my right hand forget its skill; let my tongue adhere to my palate if I fail to remember you, if I do not raise Jerusalem above my highest joy"[6] are not mere oratory; they are a living reality, practical and actual guidance on the path of life, in remembering Jerusalem at all times.

The memory of Jerusalem casts a shadow of eternal gloom on the Jewish people. "One may not fill his mouth with laughter in this world"[7] until the coming of the redemption, when "our mouths will be filled with laughter, our tongues with songs of joy."[8] Until then, everything is enveloped in sadness. Ever since the destruction of the Temple, all profane music and singing have been prohibited.

This sorrow and loss should be recalled at all times, even in joyous moments. When the table is set to host guests for a meal, something should be left incomplete in remembrance of the *ḥurban*. When a house is built, it must not be completed entirely; part is left unplastered, in remembrance of the *ḥurban*. The memory of Jerusalem should be raised at the forefront of every joyous occasion. Even amidst the joy of a wedding, ashes are placed on the groom's head; even under the *ḥuppa* (marriage canopy), before all the celebrants, a glass is broken. For it is impossible for us to rejoice fully as long as Jerusalem lies in ruins.

Thus, the mourning over Jerusalem has continued for nearly two thousand years, like a thread of tears running through our lives.

THE CITY OF GOD

The passing of so much time has not erased from our consciousness the memory of Jerusalem; on the contrary, it has expanded and deepened this memory.

Jerusalem has become synonymous with the entire Land of Israel. For generations, every Jew who came from the Land of Israel was called simply "a *Yerushalmi* (Jerusalemite)." Although the Talmud of The Land of Israel was authored and compiled in Tiberias and Caesarea, it has

6. Psalms 137:5–6.
7. *Berakhot* 31a.
8. Psalms 126:2.

remained for the generations of our people the "Jerusalem Talmud" – the *Talmud Yerushalmi*. So, too, in all Jewish sources, the term "the city" without specification refers to Jerusalem, "the city of God."

Through conceptualization, Jerusalem and Zion became more than place-names, more than a city or spiritual center. Jerusalem became the symbol of the *Shekhina* (Divine Presence), the point of *Malkhut* (Kingship), the point of contact and connection at which the Infinite touches the finite, at which time and place touch that which transcends time and place. Jerusalem, as the point of *Malkhut*, is the point at which the silver cord of divine influence is connected to the reality of the world.

Lekha Dodi – R. Shlomo Alkabetz's mystically attuned song of longing, which has become an inseparable part of the *Kabbalat*

service in all Jewish communities – is essentially a song about Jerusalem. The song weaves together all of the world's yearnings and all of Israel's longings for redemption with the essential point – Jerusalem. During the exile, Jerusalem became the image of the Jewish People in the Diaspora, the symbol of the *Shekhina* in exile, of the entire world in its suffering and distress. The destroyed city, abandoned by its children, awaits its redemption, and its rebuilding is the symbol of the Jewish People's resurgence and the renewal of the ancient covenant with it and with the entire world.

Spiritual, symbolic Jerusalem has not made us lose sight of the geographic, this-worldly city of Jerusalem. Throughout all the generations, even in the darkest years of oppression and persecution when no Jew was permitted to dwell in it, this city has been the Jewish People's center and capital. There is no other all-embracing Jewish center besides Jerusalem.

The Halakha's institutions lack full authority until the Jewish People's lawmakers once again sit in the midst of the city of Jerusalem. Only in the unique and irreplaceable city of Jerusalem will the Halakha's laws and regulations reassume their full authority.

FACING JERUSALEM

In the meantime, all turn toward Jerusalem. All the synagogues throughout the world, in all their various shapes and styles, face one direction:

toward Jerusalem. And wherever a Jew may be, when he stands up to pray, he turns his face to the place to which all Jews turn – to Jerusalem.

Many Jewish customs express the yearning and longing for Jerusalem. At the end of the Passover Seder, when we experience the joy of freedom and the joy of family unity more than on any other holiday, we conclude with the wish: "Next year in Jerusalem."

In many places, the practice was that in every marriage agreement, they would write that the wedding will take place, with God's help, on such-and-such a date in Jerusalem, and they would add that if by then redemption has still not come, the wedding will take place in another specified place. This practice expressed, in its innocence, the hope and the ideal that the place where one ought to be is none other than the city of Jerusalem.

The aspiration of every Jew is to be in Jerusalem, to live in its midst. Indeed, according to the halakha, *aliya* to the Land of Israel – and within the Land of Israel, to Jerusalem – overrides all other considerations. Even a slave can compel his master to either move with him to the Land of Israel or to release him.[9]

Although in most generations, this *aliya* was not actually possible, the hope was ever present.

ON HIGH AND DOWN BELOW

Jerusalem is a twofold city – "like a city joined together."[10] Jerusalem below, earthly Jerusalem, which is now in ruins, is parallel to Jerusalem on high, in which there is a glorious Divine Temple, where all the majesty of the supernal world is found. This celestial Jerusalem hovers over earthly Jerusalem. Moreover, celestial Jerusalem depends on and springs from earthly Jerusalem: "The Holy One, blessed be He, said: 'I will not enter Jerusalem on high until I enter Jerusalem down below.'"[11]

These two cities, which face each other, do not reach their

9. *Ketubot* 110a–b.
10. Psalms 122:3.
11. *Ta'anit* 5a.

completion until the people of Israel returns to its one and only capital to reencounter the reality beyond: "Jerusalem built up, like the sister city to which it is joined. For there the tribes ascended, the tribes of God, a testimony for Israel, to give thanks to the name of God."[12]

12. Psalms 122:3–4.

Remembering the Holocaust on Tisha B'Av

FAST DAYS COMMEMORATING THE ḤURBAN

At the time of the establishment of the State of Israel, and even more so after the Six Day War, voices were raised in public calling for the cancellation – or downgrading – of the fast days commemorating the destruction of the Temple and all that it entailed.

In a certain sense, these calls were rooted in the ancient Jewish tradition which regards these days of fasting and remembrance not simply as days commemorating specific historical events, but also as indicators of the state of the nation in general. The Talmud states that the observance of these days depends on current events: When there is war in the world, these days are fast days, but when there is no war, the matter is decided by custom. When there is peace in the world, these days are actually days of joy and gladness.[1]

When the euphoria in the aftermath of the Six Day War subsided, such calls sounded less convincing. Still, a profoundly problematic aspect of the fast days, and especially of Tisha B'Av, was brought to light. To what extent does this day of fasting and remembrance still have meaning for us?

1. See Zechariah, ch. 7; *Rosh HaShana* 18b.

THE DULLING OF THE SENSE OF MOURNING

All mourning – even the deepest sorrow – tends, with time, to be forgotten. With the increasing passage of time, people learn to reconcile themselves to the sorrow and the loss.

This is equally true of both the private mourning of individuals and the communal mourning over the Temple. So many years have gone by since the destruction of the Temple that the sense of its absence has eroded. Nowadays, heartache over the destruction of the Temple is found only in one whose soul is attached, even today, to the Temple in its built state. Only one who "lives" the Temple and the anticipation of its rebuilding and restoration can feel in our time the pain of its absence.

This problem – the weakening of the evocative power of the various remembrance days – is not new. *Megillat Ta'anit*, "The Scroll of Fasting," which was compiled at the end of the Second Temple period, contains a list of festive days commemorating events of salvation for Israel and victories of the kingdom of Israel during this period. This scroll officially ceased to be authoritative because in later generations it lost its power to evoke national memory. The course of time and a host of new troubles and woes erased the memory of the former events and increasingly diminished the significance of the days commemorating them.

Those remembrance days that remained in effect through the ages endured not because of the magnitude of the events, nor even because of the enactment of one halakhic authority or the other, but because the days took on a broader and deeper message that remained meaningful in every generation.

REMEMBERING THE HOLOCAUST

During the six years of the Holocaust, all the tragedies of the *ḥurban*, in all their terrible ferocity, reappeared upon the very body of the Jewish People – the humiliation, the torture, and the cruel destruction of the whole Jewish world in Europe, and above all, systematic and total extermination unparalleled in all of history.

The Jews were once again put in the terrifying isolation of a scapegoat, a target for the seething hatred of an entire world – the fathomless cruelty of the world and its indifference. All the ancient images, all the lamentations of generations gone by, once again became a living reality.

Once again, we sensed Jewish distinctness and all the pain that it entails, the *ḥurban* in all its significance.

All of this cries out to us to be remembered and not forgotten – if not every day of the year, at least on the day designated for this purpose. And there is no day on the Jewish calendar that can express all of this like Tisha B'Av, the remembrance day of national mourning, which, in all its customs and in its whole essence, has become like a day of private mourning.

Remembering the Holocaust on Tisha B'Av would likely arouse and intensify the feeling of mourning on this day among our contemporaries by lending relevance to the mourning over Jewish suffering in all generations. In addition, the Holocaust would be linked with a day that will continue to be observed in the Jewish future. Thereby, the memory of the Holocaust would be linked with the day of mourning for *all* the tragedies experienced by the Jewish People throughout history. And perhaps the flashes and glimpses of the redemption that are inherent in Tisha B'Av would be able to cast a clearer light on the Holocaust.

How Much Longer Is it Possible to Suffer?

A DAY DESTINED FOR TROUBLE

Many troubles occurred on Tisha B'Av: the destruction of the first and second Temples, the destruction of Beitar and, in later generations, the expulsion of the Jews from Spain, the expulsion of the Jews from England, and the outbreak of World War I.

However, the accumulation of tragic events is not the only cause of our intense mourning on Tisha B'Av. The day has become a focal point through which *all* of Israel's troubles throughout the generations have been concentrated and remembered. The day not only commemorates events that occurred on Tisha B'Av itself, but also includes every episode of general mourning that has befallen the Jewish People.

Tisha B'Av has ceased to be a remembrance day for a specific event and has become an all-inclusive symbol – a remembrance day for Israel's troubles throughout all the generations and throughout the world.

That is why the *kinot* of Tisha B'Av commemorate all the tragedies suffered by our people ever since we were exiled from our land: *kinot* lamenting the destruction of Jerusalem as well as *kinot* commemorating the Crusades, the public burning of the Torah, Israel's exiles in eastern lands, and the evil decrees against them. The destruction of the Temple, the subject of the day of Tisha B'Av, has become an all-inclusive symbol of the destruction of the House of Israel and of the *Shekhina*'s exile in all its forms.

THE EXILE OF THE SHEKHINA

Ever since the *ḥurban,* the Jewish People – the people that represents God in His world – has been in an abnormal condition, without independence. This state is termed the "exile of the *Shekhina*."

The meaning of independence is the ability to stand on one's own, without having to act according to the wishes of others. The prophet says, "I will weep by myself *mipnei gava*,"[1] and our sages expound: "What is the meaning of '*mipnei gava*'? Because of Israel's pride (*ga'ava*), which was taken from them and given to strangers."[2] The essence of the exile is the loss of Israel's pride – the ability to stand and exist on our own.

Exile is a condition in which one is more passive than active – like a slave who, in fear of the rod, does everything he is commanded to do. In all generations since the *ḥurban,* the Jewish People has been swept along by events, pulled and swayed by the powers around it.

In the *tokheḥa,* the section of reproof in the Torah, the following curse appears: "He will be the head and you the tail."[3] This is not only a curse, but a humiliation, describing when nationally and individually, we become the tail, while others seize the head position. When God's people become a tail in the protracted exile, it is an awful expression of the exile of the *Shekhina.*

Even now, when we are "a free people in our own land,"[4] we have not become more independent and less subjugated. Independence is more than the ability to have an army, a flag, a government, an anthem. The Jewish People has acquired an inner submissiveness; we have lost the power to stand on our own and to offer resistance. The inner submissiveness of servitude is deeply ingrained in us, and even when we are afforded the possibility of acting independently – even when we have no masters – we still act like slaves.

1. Jeremiah 13:17.
2. See *Ta'anit* 5b.
3. Deuteronomy 28:44.
4. As it says in Israel's national anthem, *HaTikva.*

TACIT CONSENT

We bear and tolerate the pain of the *Shekhina*'s exile in silence, and that is why the redemption is slow in coming. If we were conscious of the enormity of the pain and felt it as though it were our own, we would likely try to do something about rectifying the situation. Instead, Tisha B'Av usually amounts to nothing more than twenty-five unpleasant hours of fasting, which pass and vanish without changing a thing.

Over the course of the entire year, a person may think about sadness, but on Tisha B'Av, one should concern himself more deeply with it in order to decide, once and for all, that this condition must not continue.

The painful situation in Egypt – "They made life bitter for them with harsh labor"[5] – was actually the beginning of the redemption, for it made the people understand that they could no longer tolerate the slavery – "and they then cried out, and their cry rose up to God."[6] The people had gradually grown accustomed to the slavery in Egypt, and they had in effect resigned themselves to being slaves. Only after the Egyptians became increasingly cruel and made their lives so bitter, only after they could suffer no more and cried out – only then did God answer them and take them out of Egypt. As long as they had not cried out, they had in effect consented to the bondage. It was not possible to redeem them before they arrived at the inner realization that this was not their place.

The feeling of pain on Tisha B'Av must be so intense that it cannot be tolerated any longer; it must be so strong that a drastic change in the present reality must inevitably be made. The more painful our experience of Tisha B'Av, the stronger its reminder that the problem is not external, but rather requires inner rectification.

If, as a result of reading the *kinot*, a person decides that this condition must not continue, for it is too grave to be allowed to continue – if, by refraining from eating, his will to be rid of Tisha B'Av once and for all is strengthened – this is already the beginning of the rectification.

We do not want to have to return to the predicament of being ruled by "a king whose decrees are as harsh as Haman's" so that we should

5. Exodus 1:14.
6. Ibid. 2:23.

cry out.[7] Our national ability for endurance of suffering is apparently tremendous, and who knows what troubles we would have to bear until we finally cry out! In the flow of routine, we have grown used to *kinot*, troubles, and casualties – but we can still make the effort to awaken, to sober up from the stupor of our endless suffering. There is still a chance to rouse ourselves before we are struck with more troubles meant to force us to say, "I will go and return to my first husband."[8]

We can bring about the rectification of this situation through profound contemplation and by feeling anew the pain, all the troubles of communities and individuals, for in this way we can arrive at a reawakening.

Until this fast day is cancelled – and God willing, this will happen soon – we must recognize that there is much pain in the world. This pain should be considered closely, so that we not consent to it, so that we decidedly say "no" to subservience, and so that we may be redeemed.

---

7. "If they do not repent… the Holy One, blessed be He, appoints them a king whose decrees are as harsh as Haman's, and as a result Israel repents. Thus God restores them to the right path" (*Sanhedrin* 97b).
8. Hosea 2:9.

Lamentations: The Book of Eikha

RESTRAINT

According to tradition, the author of Eikha (Lamentations) was the prophet Jeremiah.[1] The author's identity is actually less significant than its indication of the time in which the book was composed – this is not a work that was written many years after the events, but rather a direct response to Israel's disasters in the years preceding the Temple's destruction and immediately afterward. The words were written soon after the occurrence of these disasters; they are not the product of retrospection from a distance, from a historical perspective and a state of emotional detachment from the events.

Precisely for this reason, this book stands out in one feature – its great restraint. The events that formed the background of the book were dreadful, from the atrocities of the war to the disasters that followed one after the other – loss of independence, destruction of the centers of life, destruction of the Temple, exile. Yet none of these is described in detail, or even in broad scope.

Of course, each one of these tragedies is noted in Eikha. There is no attempt to mask or blur what happened. Some matters are mentioned

1. *Bava Batra* 15a. There is a Scriptural allusion to this tradition; see II Chronicles 35:25.

in only a few verses, but those verses are unequalled in their sharpness of expression, and a few short words encapsulates the full magnitude of the tragedy.

Nevertheless, on the whole, this book does not attempt to depict the horror and the disaster in a way that would illustrate and dramatize the events fully. The lack of elaboration seems to blunt rather than fan the emotional reaction. This sense of restraint is augmented by the stylized form – all the verses are written in a uniform rhythm and meter, and almost all of them are arranged acrostically (that is, they begin with the successive letters of the *aleph-bet*).

The reason for the restraint is apparently rooted in the fact that the book is a book of lamentations, and not a historical account. This is so precisely because it was written so close to the occurrence of the events; the general disaster and the multitude of individual horrors were known to everyone very plainly, and any attempt to express them in any complete form would have caused unbearable pain. The Book of Eikha was not needed to move the hearts to weeping, for weeping was already present, and in excess. The strict literary style – the meter, the acrostic arrangement, and so forth – was designed to confine and contain the pain so that it could be expressed at all. Were it not for this framework, the emotional outburst would have been boundless. If the lamentations had not been regulated, they would never have ended.

This restraint, however, does not detract from the power of Eikha. To a certain extent, the literary style even adds a special power of expression and an element of greater effect to the book.

Because the book contains no detailed accounts of atrocities, but only short and fragmentary phrases, the reader supplies the rest from his own imagination. The empty space between the fragmentary lines of the sketch is filled in – in a sharper manner – by the reader himself. The scarcity of exclamations and words of grief compels the reader and the listener to develop their own reactions to the things they absorb. In this respect, Eikha is merely a preamble, an introduction to the real weeping – that of the listener. Because the cry is not broadcast out loud, because it is so restrained and regulated, it can be heard better.

AN IMPOSSIBLE DREAM

Three of this book's chapters begin with the question "*Eikha*" – "How?" Indeed, our sources refer to it rightfully as *Megillat Eikha*, not only because it is the opening word of the book, but also because it is one of its keywords.

In the book, there is mourning, there is sorrow, there is weeping, and there is crying out – but beyond all these, there is a series of questions that articulate much pain, but no reproach.

These questions are authentic questions, although they sometimes appear to be merely rhetorical, for they are penetrating questions attempting to attain understanding – and thereby a solution. Although they generally remain unanswered in the book itself, they represent a genuine search for the causes of our troubles, a desire to understand their meaning and even to find a solution and a way out of the predicament.

When the sorrow and the pain become in some way a part of one's consciousness – when the facts of a gloomy reality become something that the mind can bear and comprehend – the implication is that the great shock of the catastrophe has passed. However troubled and threatening the reality may be, when it becomes something to which one can relate and respond in a rational way, it becomes tolerable.

There is a stage, however, in which the present and its troubles are not only painful, but essentially incomprehensible, like an illogical nightmare, of whose actual existence one cannot be convinced by any facts.

The question, "*Eikha*," expresses the essence of this feeling. It does not seek to know the mechanism of the catastrophe – how did it happen and on account of what? Eikha does not attempt to clarify the causes of the events through military, political, or historical analysis, or even through a moral explanation. *Eikha* is rather an existential question regarding the present: How can such a situation be possible? How can it be that a whole world order was destroyed? How could it have been replaced by a different reality which, despite all of its actuality, is basically incomprehensible? The very framing of the matter in such a form creates the sense of loss and pain.

Indeed, the fact that the lamentations are recited again every year and that the question *Eikha* is again articulated means that we have not resigned and reconciled ourselves to the present state of existence.

When the psalmist speaks of Zion's captivity, declaring that "When God returns the captivity of Zion, we will be as in a dream,"[2] the dream of which he speaks is not the redemption but, on the contrary, the exile itself. The exile is perceived as a prolonged nightmare from which the Jewish People will finally awaken, to find itself once again in an authentic and logical state of existence. But so long as this does not happen, the lamenter faces the present reality and wonders: *Eikha*?

GOD IS JUST

Some of the questions in the book are not addressed to anyone in particular, for they serve only to express shock and the inability to reconcile oneself with the existing situation.

Other questions, however, clearly do have a specific address; they are questions that the lamenter directs to God about what happened and what will happen in the future. In this respect, the lamentations are not merely expressions of painful memories of distress and pain; rather, they are an outpouring of the heart, the lamenter's personal conversation with God.

God's presence is prominent in each and every passage of Eikha, whether He is addressed directly or mentioned expressly in the third person. The human enemies of the Jewish People are mentioned in the book, along with their cruel and wicked actions and their rejoicing over our calamity, but they are perceived as peripheral, sometimes merely as material instruments. Everything that they do, they do only by the power of God. It is He who strikes, wounds, and slaughters.

Indeed, many horrible things are attributed to God in *Megillat Eikha* – "He bent His bow like an enemy, poised His right hand like a foe;"[3] "You slew them on the day of Your wrath, slaughtered them without pity."[4] Yet it is devoid of protest against God. The Book of Lamentations contains none of the embitterment towards God found in Job or even in Jeremiah.

A central reason for this is that in Eikha, there is a deep inner

2. Psalms 126:1.
3. Lamentations 2:4.
4. Ibid. 2:21.

awareness that these punishments are not an injustice. Job, who protests about the evil and pain in the world, strongly emphasizes the injustice in the calamity that strikes good and evil people alike. In *Megillat Eikha*, there is no such complaint. The horror exists, the calamity is almost unbearable – but there is no injustice. Despite the fact, however, that the sins of the past are not hidden or concealed (although the book does not deal with them much), Eikha is not a book of *tzidduk hadin*, acknowledging the justness of God's actions; there is no statement, such as is found in Job, that "God has given, and God has taken away; blessed be the name of God."[5] There is recognition that the punishment is just, that it is deserved by those who received it, but this does not muffle the cry of pain, the outcry of "Look, God, and see to whom you have done this!"[6]

The overall mood of Lamentations is connected not only with faith and with acceptance of God's judgment, but also with the lamenter's deep and intimate relationship with God. God is not only Almighty and transcendent; one can weep – one even has the right to weep – before Him. Our relationship with God amidst pain and suffering is not as towards "the Judge of all the earth," "the King of the universe," but as towards "the merciful Father." The blows He delivers are not blows of wickedness – there is good reason for the suffering that He causes – but the fact that the judgment is just does not nullify the pain.

The fact that a child accepts his suffering without rebelling against the father who inflicted it does not mean he does not suffer. But the child knows that he may weep; he knows that he can rest his head on his Father's shoulder and tell Him about his pain.

More than the lamenter addresses the members of his people – contemporaries and future generations – he addresses God Himself. This is neither a plea nor a complaint, but rather the outpouring of the heart – a weeping in which the lamenter knows that his Father, who administered the blows, suffers the pain together with him. As the

5. Job 1:21.
6. Lamentations 2:20.

prophet says, "So I will wait patiently for God, who is hiding His face from the House of Jacob, and I will hope in Him."[7]

When our sages poetically and figuratively depict how God Himself weeps over the destruction of the Temple, how He Himself experiences the suffering and pain of the stricken, these are merely more graphic descriptions of the feeling that pervades *Megillat Eikha*.

THE SUFFERING OF A PEOPLE

The more general and abstract aspects of *Megillat Eikha* are largely found precisely in the chapter that speaks for the most part in the first person.

The third chapter ("I am the man"[8]) of the book is, at first glance, the lament of an individual who speaks of his personal suffering. The earliest commentators ascribed it to the prophet Jeremiah himself. However, although a large part of the chapter is indeed written in the first person, this unique lament is not the private lament of an individual. The person who speaks here in the first person does not speak of his own personal tragedies and pains, but rather on behalf of the entire nation. The suffering he describes is that of the people, for which he merely serves as a spokesman.

In the context of this lament, even statements relating particularly to the life of the prophet ("I have become a laughingstock to all my people"[9]) take on a general significance, transcending the life of the prophet. This chapter, more than the others, presents not only the suffering and the outcry over the pain and humiliation, but also abstract reflections on the suffering and tribulations in their totality.

As in the other chapters of Eikha, in this chapter, one hears a note of patient acceptance of suffering ("It is good for a man that he bear the yoke in his youth"[10]). It is explicitly stated that the evil that comes to pass in the world is not injustice, and the hope that the evil will not last eternally is expressed clearly ("For God does not forsake

7. Isaiah 8:17.
8. Lamentations 3:1.
9. Ibid. 3:14.
10. Ibid. 3:27.

forever"[11]). In this chapter, as in the others, we express our conviction that our enemies and those who hate us will eventually be punished, even unto their total destruction.

These ideas appear in the other chapters of Lamentations, as well, either expressly or by allusion. In this chapter, however, we find an idea that is not found in such clarity anywhere else in the book – the idea that the evil in the world, even that which appears to be a punishment from Heaven, is actually a necessary and almost automatic consequence of man's sins. "It is not from the mouth of the Most High that evil and good proceed. Of what shall a living man complain, a strong man because of his sins?"[12]

CRISIS, ISOLATION, AND HUMILIATION

The themes of the lamentations in *Megillat Eikha* are not arranged in chronological or topical order. As we noted, the lamentations do not contain a historical narrative recounting the chain of events, and the detailed accounts therefore do not appear in a specific order.

Nevertheless, there are central themes in the different chapters. In the first and second chapters, the discussion is about the destruction in general; in the fourth chapter, the subject is primarily the siege and the horrors of starvation, while the fifth chapter focuses more on the situation after the conquest of the city and the exile of its inhabitants.

Beyond the details, the descriptions that sharply and clearly depict the horror, the book as a whole focuses on the state of the nation after the downfall and destruction. In that regard, there are three interrelated motifs: the crisis, the isolation, and the humiliation.

The crisis lies in the fall itself, in the transition of Jerusalem from an inhabited city full of life, a center possessed of strength and security, to almost total destruction. The contrast between the former condition – the strong and beautiful city – and that of a conquered and destroyed place comes up time and time again.

The poignancy of the contrast was heightened by the belief held by the people of Judah and Jerusalem (as described in the books of

11. Ibid. 3:31.
12. Ibid. 3:38–39.

Jeremiah and Ezekiel) that the great city could not possibly be completely destroyed. This assumption was based on long historical experience; for Jerusalem had remained standing ever since the time of David, even when other cities of Israel were completely destroyed. This belief expressed reliance on the sanctity of the city and the Temple, the belief that it could not be that God would let His city and His Sanctuary be destroyed.

The lamenter of Lamentations is the same prophet who prophesied about the destruction. Nevertheless, even for Jeremiah, there was a gap between the rational knowledge of impending *ḥurban* and the deep-seated feeling that it could not actually occur.

After the fall comes the sense of isolation. This isolation is national and political, in that superpowers as well as allies lose interest in the defeated nation, but it also relates to individuals. As a result of the destruction, we are surrounded by enemies on all sides, and there is no one on whom we can depend and rely.

Then comes the humiliation – the humiliation of one who is exiled, disgraced in the eyes of all who see him ("You have made us filth and refuse in the midst of the nations"[13]), as well as the collective national humiliation, the loss of the entire nation's honor.

PERHAPS THERE IS HOPE

Lamentations extensively expresses the suffering and the pain of the fall, the isolation, and the humiliation, but it also contains hope. This hope is articulated expressly in some verses – "Your iniquity, daughter of Zion, is expiated; He will exile you no longer;"[14] "Restore us to You, O God, and we will be restored; renew our days as of old!"[15] – but it is also inherent in the lamentations themselves. Hope is found in the painful outcry to God.

The very act of turning to God contains within it the basic source of the consolation. The calamity is not the result of the actions of a blind and meaningless force; it is a punishment. And however difficult and

13. Ibid. 3:45.
14. Ibid. 4:22.
15. Ibid. 5:21.

unbearable this punishment may be, it relates to God's special providence vis-à-vis the people. As long as there is complete trust in God and in His power, there is always possibility for renewal. As long as there is faith in God's justice, there is always hope.

The Ḥurban[1] *– Removal of God's Presence*

THE TEMPLE – THE MOST IMPORTANT THING OF ALL

The focal point and starting point of the mourning on Tisha B'Av – which constitutes the symbol of all that happened afterward – is the destruction of the Temple. The destruction of the Temple is not just a detail in the chronicle of our suffering; it is the key and defining element of all of Israel's troubles. It is what removes the isolated misfortunes – persecutions, exiles, slaughters, and humiliations – from the status of historical episodes and gives them meaning within a wider context.

For the Jewish People, the Temple was the only place for complete and perfect worship. It was the center for all the Children of Israel, no matter where they were dispersed. Above all, it was the sanctified place, the only one of its kind recognized by Judaism.

We can grasp the extent of the Temple's importance and centrality by examining the list of the mitzvot. Of the 613 mitzvot counted by the sages, less than half have been applicable (and some only partially) since the *ḥurban*! The greater part of the edifice of Judaism – not only matters directly connected with the Temple and its modes of worship, but

1. "Destruction."

a whole complex of mitzvot, practices, prohibitions, and customs connected with the Temple – was suddenly erased as a result of the *ḥurban*.

This picture, this change of the halakhic perspective, gives us some notion of what happened to the essence of Judaism with the destruction of the Temple.

The Temple is the Jewish People's life center, and its absence is a basic defect in the people's image. Even the Torah centers, which were to become increasingly important after the *ḥurban*, were essentially connected to the Temple as long as it stood. The Torah commands that the sole place from which binding Law goes forth is the Temple,[2] which was therefore the seat of the *Sanhedrin*.[3] None of the institutions of government or manifestations of the spirit that arose in Jewish history ever replicated the centrality that the Temple possessed.

Thus, the destruction of the Temple deprived the Jewish People of its central axis, the point around which the religious and national life of the people had been arranged and focused, to which all the manifestations of life had been attuned.

The exile of the *Shekhina* and the removal of God's Presence from Israel's midst are not simply metaphysical facts; they are significant events in the most concrete, historical dimension. When the Temple does not exist, the direction is lost, and with it the meaning of the flow of life.

THE BEGINNING OF THE EXILE

When the Temple was standing and the whole people knew that "God dwells in Zion,"[4] this gave the people's life not only a center but also direction, a beginning and an end in the structures of life. This was true even when there were large numbers of Jews living in the Diaspora and the material and political situation of the Jews living in Israel was far from ideal. As long as the Temple was standing, the Jews outside the

2. "Since this decision comes from the place that God will choose, you must do as they tell you, carefully following all their instructions to you" (Deuteronomy 17:10). See Rambam, *Hilkhot Mamrim* 3:8.
3. The Sanhedrin was a court of seventy-one sages, which was the supreme court and legislature of Jewish Law.
4. Joel 4:21.

Land were merely "scattered and dispersed," people who happened to be in a foreign land.

The loss of national independence did not greatly change the people's situation, for the Jewish People had enjoyed complete independence in its land for only short periods in history. What truly brought change was the destruction of the Temple. The *ḥurban,* destruction, introduced the concept of *galut,* exile; it marked the beginning of the sense of orphanhood. The Diaspora communities – the lands of dispersion that had always had one center of life toward which everything was directed – were orphaned by the Temple's destruction. The troubles of Jews everywhere are no longer incidental misfortunes like those occurring in the history of any other nation. No longer are the Jews subject to merely temporary pressure, suffering that will naturally come to an end. Rather, the people are exiled, truly subject to "the yoke of the nations" in all lands, including the Land of Israel.

The inner meaning of the Temple is the dwelling of God's Presence in the world in general and amidst the Jewish People in particular. Thus, the meaning of the Temple's destruction is the removal of God's Presence from Israel's midst. Israel's suffering throughout the period of the exile is simply an external expression of that same process of *ḥurban,* the repeated wounding of a people that lost its sacred center of life. Hence, all the troubles and disasters that befell Israel are essentially attributed to the destruction of the Temple. For in all of them is found the deep pain, the essential loss, of the removal of God's Presence – the suffering of a people that no longer fulfills its role as a united community, but as fragmented parts subject to despoilment and exposed to every abuse.

RETURN OF GOD'S PRESENCE TO ITS PLACE

The Midrash relates that on the day of Tisha B'Av, at the very time of the *ḥurban,* the Messiah was born.[5] The destruction of the Temple symbolizes the removal of God's Presence from Israel's midst, and the essence of the redemption is in the advent of the Messiah and the return of God's Presence to its place. Rectification of the various individual elements that were destroyed is insufficient. Even our return to our land,

5. Jerusalem Talmud, *Berakhot* 2:4.

the restoration of our political independence, and the rebuilding of the Temple itself cannot rectify all that was damaged and wiped out in the course of the generations. Only complete redemption on a level higher than ever before experienced – redemption that will be brought only by the Messiah – can fully rectify all that was destroyed.

To justify all that happened during the *galut* – the suffering and the orphanhood, the humiliation and the tribulations – it does not suffice to merely restore the situation to its former condition. The redemption must be more than that; it must raise us to such heights that it will be possible to regard the entire past as "descent for the sake of ascent."[6]

Such redemption alone – redemption that can elevate itself above two thousand years of suffering, drawing from it guidance as to how to bring about a more exalted mode of life – would be the proper rectification of the *ḥurban*.

6. Based on *Makkot* 7b.

Elul and Teshuva

Reckoning and Rectification

ESSENTIAL RECKONING

The concept of "self-reckoning," soul-searching, is as ancient as Jewish culture itself. Even if the forms of expression, the formulations, and the issues of self-reckoning change from generation to generation and from era to era, the essence of the matter remains a constant in Jewish life.

Our sages call self-reckoning "a reckoning of this world,"[1] and thereby define one of its central components. Self-reckoning is an accounting of an entire world – an accounting of broad generalities and principles.

This reckoning tends to be itemized in small sums, and sometimes even mere pennies. Nevertheless, the fundamental reckoning is all-encompassing and all-embracing. Even when self-reckoning begins or ends with small matters, it always springs from a sense of the overall importance of those things. If the subjects of the reckoning are very grand but this sense of importance is lacking, they have no bearing despite their apparent value.

1. "'Come to Ḥeshbon' (Numbers 21:27) – Come let us make an accounting of this world, weighing a mitzva's cost against its reward, and a sin's gain against its loss" (*Bava Batra* 78b).

In other words, from the standpoint of the reckoner, self-reckoning is always essential, fundamental, and principled.

THE STANDARD OF JEWISH CULTURE

It is obviously impossible to make an accounting of oneself, or of the world, unless one assumes that there indeed exists an overall reckoning. Without a system of principles by which to set the standard, measurement and evaluation are meaningless.

An accounting can only be made on the basis of fundamental assumptions that include standards and principles of reckoning. This standard does not necessarily have to be religious or even moral, but it must be acceptable to the reckoner as a standard by which to measure things. If there is no standard or means of measurement, there can also be no accounting or reckoning.

Thus, self-accounting can be accomplished only against the background of a culture that has basic values and standards. A lack of basic values – or a relativism regarding them – deprives society and its individuals of the basis on which such an accounting might be made.

Moreover, for a self-accounting to truly be a reckoning in which the individual (or the community) is judged within himself (or itself), this standard must be internalized and integrated and not remain merely an external component of life.

To be sure, even a society whose principles are exclusively behavioral and external can take stock of itself and its relations with other societies, but this self-evaluation is of a completely different kind. For a society of external values, there is never an opportunity for true spiritual introspection, because it has no criteria against which to measure itself and nothing to serve as a true standard of self-judgment.

Jewish culture, in contrast, is fundamentally a value-based culture, a culture that believes in intrinsic good and evil, a culture in which "thou shalt" and "thou shalt not" are not merely social conventions and external rules of behavior. Naturally, then, Judaism possesses the background against which self-accounting of the community (the entire world or the entire people of Israel) and the individual may and must take place.

THE TORAH'S REQUIREMENT OF SELF-ACCOUNTING

In Scripture generally, and in the Torah in particular, self-accounting is primarily a "macro-accounting" – an accounting of the people and even of the entire world. This follows from the scope and overall meaning of the books of Scripture, whose primary concern is to address the Jewish People as a whole and in which the individual is not a lone person, but part of a larger community.

It is not surprising, then, that in the first Scriptural example of what may be termed "self-accounting," the concern is with a reckoning of the entire world, and this evaluation is made, as it were, by God Himself: "God saw that man's wickedness was immense… God regretted that He had made man on earth, and His heart was saddened. And God said, 'I will blot out humanity that I created from the face of the earth… for I regret that I created them.'"[2]

In spite of the theological and substantive problems presented by this passage, it is a classic example of self-accounting, a general reckoning in which the reckoner assesses his actions and decides to act in accordance with the conclusions reached during that assessment. Self-accounting must similarly reach some kind of conclusion, whether positive or negative.

In this first instance of self-accounting – which results in the Flood – all the important elements are present: a consideration and probe of the matter, the conclusion that the evaluation of the situation is not positive, regret, and the resulting practical implications.

However, it is not necessary to derive the Torah's requirement of self-accounting only from God's reckoning, for it is readily apparent in many different sections of the Torah, especially in the stern admonitions of Leviticus[3] and Deuteronomy.[4]

Throughout history, the call for self-accounting was an integral part of the course of a Jew's life. For many generations, the established preachers in the towns (the *maggidim*) and the various itinerant preachers would repeatedly preach repentance and soul-searching. A great

2. Genesis 6:5–7.
3. Leviticus 26:3–46.
4. Deuteronomy 28–30.

deal of time was devoted to the subject in the course of the year – and certainly during the period from the beginning of the month of Elul until after Yom Kippur. In addition, it was customary in many places to observe the eve of every new month as a "minor Yom Kippur," a day of repentance and atonement. The "account and reckoning" that every man must present before the Creator and the self-accounting that everyone must make with himself were the central themes of these days. Many people devoted hours, at least during these days, to studying *musar* literature, which deals with the problems of man's soul and the ways of repairing it.

This was the soul-searching of ordinary Jews, who throughout the rest of the year were preoccupied with making a livelihood and with the various other concerns of daily life.

Needless to say, soul-searching played a larger role – and even became a central issue – in those circles and groups that dedicated themselves to a life of great spiritual intensity, such as the kabbalists, the Hasidim, the Musarists, and sometimes even simple folk. For such people, soul-searching was a daily pursuit and a matter of daily reflection; whether they were Torah scholars or not, they devoted some time to it each day.

DISTRESS THAT LEADS TO RECKONING

Although many individuals engage in soul-searching constantly, the community as a whole would make a true reckoning only under exceptional circumstances. Usually, these were times of trouble and distress, whether because of some imminent danger dreaded by all or because of a past event that left a deep and disturbing impression.

This phenomenon is conspicuous in the Torah's sections of stern admonition,[5] and it is boldly underscored in the narratives of the historical books of the Bible and the explicit calls of the latter prophets. When the nation does not act as it should – and, moreover, when the nation's thought process appears to be impervious to reproof – there is nothing like tribulation and disaster to bring the nation to its senses, to encourage soul-searching.

5. Ibid.

In the Torah, this picture is exceedingly clear. There is a constant call to reconsider, a demand to reflect on a daily basis: "Realize it today and reflect on it in your heart."[6] Yet the Torah presents as well a more pessimistic and perhaps more realistic view: "When all these things have befallen you – the blessing and the curse which I have set before you – and you reflect on them among all the nations where the Lord, your God, has banished you, and you return to God…"[7] Similar passages appear at the conclusion of passages of admonition throughout Scripture. The implication is that it is the tribulation, the disaster and the downfall, that elicit soul-searching and self-reckoning.

This truth appears frequently in the words of the prophets, both throughout the historiosophical system of Judges, where this idea strings together all of the book's events, as well as in the words of the latter prophets. From a historical standpoint, it has proven itself time and again. Catastrophe is the great stimulus that leads to the self-accounting of both the individual and the community.

DISASTER CREATES LEISURE

It is not lack of time that leads to avoidance of self-evaluation, but lack of leisure. Soul-searching can sometimes be complex, requiring much time and profound attention, but this is not always the case; self-accounting can be swift and brief. Several scholars have observed that the higher the level of individuals (or nations) – the better they truly are – the harder it is to make a self-accounting. When things are plain and obvious, there is no need for very extensive searching or for great profundity in order to discover what is amiss, at least superficially.

Every disaster, by its very nature, causes a break in the routine of life. Such a break gives one the leisure in which to contemplate things and make a reckoning. Routine prevents a person from reexamining his situation. People grow accustomed to everything – not only to good things, but also to the non-ideal. Our sages have taught us: "If a person commits a sin and repeats it, it becomes to him as though it were permissible."[8]

6. Deuteronomy 4:39.
7. Ibid. 30:1–2ff.
8. *Yoma* 86b.

Even if a person knows that he commits a sin, nevertheless, when he repeats the same sin several times, it, too, becomes part of his routine, and he no longer pays attention to it as something requiring correction.

The effect of disaster is shock, confusion that seizes the individual and the community in times of trouble. This shock jolts man out of his rut, enabling him to look at things anew, to reexamine his life.

Thus, it is only when things cannot be denied, at the moment of truth, that one is forced to admit that he did not act as he should have.

ERRORS IN FUNDAMENTAL ASSUMPTIONS

The assumption that error is possible and that one needs to reexamine the status quo is the very basis of all true soul-searching.

All people make some sort of accounting even amidst the routine of daily life, but when the reckoning is made in the midst of the action, without pausing or leaving room for change, then even if the reckoning itself is accurate and precise, it may be fundamentally flawed. The final sum may be accurate, but what was considered a credit may actually be debt, and what was entered in the books as profit may actually be loss. Errors of this sort, which are not merely arithmetical, are not discovered by a routine accounting process. As long as things continue to be assessed on the basis of the same fundamental assumptions with which one began, the errors in the account will remain – until some disaster occurs to reveal the defect.

People do not usually make mistakes over "petty cash," the adding up of the pennies of the daily round. A reasonable degree of accuracy is maintained, and even if the accounting is fundamentally flawed, small mistakes are generally quickly recognized and rectified. A fundamental error, however, produces a structure built on unsturdy elements. Soul-searching obligates us to look afresh at the whole picture, including aspects that seem to be whole, good, and beautiful.

A certain *tzaddik* is reported to have said, "When I think of repentance, I do not deal primarily with the sins that I committed, for in their case I know that they are sins. Rather, my primary concern is to review the mitzvot that I performed, for in their case there is room for scrutiny and concern."

RECTIFICATION OF ERRORS AT THEIR ROOT

Soul-searching, then, is much more than a simple accounting of profit and loss. Regardless of the kind of problem it deals with – moral, economic, or political – it is an overall reckoning, one that includes a presupposition of the possibility of a major, fundamental mistake.

There is a well-known fable about animals who decide to repent because their sins have brought disaster upon them. The wolf and the tiger confess that they prey on other creatures, and they are vindicated. After all, it is in their nature as predators to hunt and kill. All the animals confess their sins in turn, and all of them, for one reason or another, are exonerated. Finally, the sheep admits that she once ate the straw lining of her master's boots; here, at last, is obviously the true cause of their suffering. All the animals fall upon the wicked sheep and devour it, and everything is in order again.

On the surface, the main point of this fable is to condemn the hypocrisy of people who ignore the sins of the strong and harp on those of the weak. Beyond this, however, there is a more basic and profound message. The animals conducted an accounting that assumes that the general situation may remain as it is. The wolf may keep on hunting, and the tiger may continue preying upon others. If this is the fundamental assumption, then the sin singled out for correction will always be trivial and no real change will be forthcoming.

True soul-searching is based on quite a different premise, one that assumes that the matters that we take for granted, the status quo and the general consensus, are the very things that require re-examination and reassessment.

In the Bible, this is expressed as follows: "They will then confess their sins and the sins of their fathers."[9] The same idea in a slightly different formula is contained in the introductory formula of the confession in the daily prayer book: "But we and our fathers have sinned." The inclusion of our fathers in the confession is not accidental. It represents an attempt not only to examine things on the level of the immediate present, the here and now, but to penetrate to the roots of the matter.

An ancient error does not become more beautiful by virtue of its

9. Leviticus 26:40.

being ancient. On the contrary, its ancientness makes it more difficult for us to reveal.

The old excuse, "That's how things have always been done," or the no less common variation, "Everyone does it," is no justification for error and sin. The story is told of a man who, standing before a Rabbi, defends himself with the excuse, "But everyone does it," to which the Rabbi retorts, "Hell is big enough for everyone."

THE DIFFICULTY WITH COMMUNAL SOUL-SEARCHING

The foregoing relates to soul-searching at the individual level, but it is even more true at the communal level. Much more is required when it is a whole nation that needs to do the soul-searching; the difficulties and the effort required are infinitely greater.

In a group, soul-searching is discouraged; each member of the community receives communal sanction for his way of life, insofar as it conforms to accepted norms. An individual's deviation from the norm usually meets with society's opposition, but errors and deviations common to society as a whole are only reinforced by the environment.

Furthermore, the effort that enables soul-searching requires the interruption and halting of ongoing processes. The inertia of a large community, and certainly of an entire nation, is far greater than that of an individual, and a great deal of strength is therefore required in order to introduce change.

When an entire nation is headed for disaster, each individual member is not only unaware of what is happening – as everyone around him is in the same condition – but is also swept along by the general movement. At the national level, in order to reach a point at which the individual will realize that he has erred, there is a need for a more intense and drastic shock.

THE FAILURE OF THE "EYES OF THE COMMUNITY"

There is another aspect to the problem presented by a whole nation. The individual has his own thoughts and ideas, but these are not necessarily those of the nation as a whole. Moreover, the course of a nation is not the sum of the wishes of the individuals who make up that nation, just as the body's conduct is not the sum of the nervous impulses of all its limbs and organs. The body's overall conduct is determined by a few organs, each with a specially defined function. Similarly, within every nation there is a particular class that decides and determines, a group that sets the pace, direction, and tone. Sometimes this class or group is very able and broadly representative, and sometimes it is not. It is this leadership, both political and spiritual, that determines the course of a nation, for better or for worse.

In the Bible, the leaders are called "the eyes of the community."[10] The assumption is that the nation's leaders are to be, first and foremost, the "receivers" of coming events, instruments for orientation and control, for sensing danger and anticipating positive developments long before they become manifest. A nation whose eyes are not beautiful is one whose whole body requires examination,[11] because a failure of "the eyes of the community" almost always causes the failure of the entire entity. This is true even when the nation is a lot finer and better than its leadership.

Our sages used a folk saying to explain how great disasters might befall a nation: "When the shepherd is angry with the flock, he blinds the eyes of the leading ewe"[12] – and woe to the nation whose leaders are blind.

This holds true always, for even in times of peace and prosperity it is necessary to assess the situation, to warn of dangers to come, to see what lies far off. But it is especially critical in times that call for soul-searching, when there is a need for a fundamental reexamination of our lives, when the very roots of existing reality must be explored. When a review of the most fundamental values is called for – not simply an accounting of the immediate present, based on existing assumptions – it is essential that the eyes of the community see far ahead, with penetrating insight.

Long ago, a prophet was defined as a "watchman for the House

10. Numbers 15:24.
11. Based on *Ta'anit* 24a: "Oshaya, the youngest member of the group, taught them: 'Then it shall be, if from the eyes of the community it shall be committed in error' (Numbers 15:24). This may be compared to a bride who is in her father's home. As long as her eyes are beautiful, her entire body does not require an examination. If her eyes are tearful, her entire body requires an examination."
12. *Bava Kamma* 52a.

of Israel,"[13] one who sees from afar; he was called simply "the seer."[14] To make a reckoning, a nation needs a watchman and seer. It needs leaders who will carry out the function of the head – the ability to feel and the power to think.

13. Ezekiel 3:17.
14. I Samuel, 9:9.

Ḥai (18th) Elul[1]

VITALIZING ELUL

The month of Elul is a time to review the year that has passed and to prepare for the new year, and it is therefore devoted to returning "in *teshuva*" and to strengthening one's connection with God. In order to accomplish the goal of becoming a God-fearing individual, many people think that it is necessary to be less friendly, to go about with a serious expression on one's face, and to be full of melancholy and solemnity. Obviously, then, an Elul devoted to repentance and to intensified fear of God will, in its entirety, take on such a complexion.

God, however, does not desire worship arising from melancholy. The prophet Malachi admonishes Israel for worshiping God out of heaviness and gloom: "We have walked about in gloom because of the Lord of Hosts."[2] The Holy One, blessed be He, is a living God, the Source of life and a King who delights in life. These days in which we return to Him should thus be days of vibrancy and joy.

The day of *Ḥai* Elul – the birthday of the Ba'al Shem Tov and of

1. The Hebrew word *ḥai* (חי), whose numerial value is eighteen, means "alive," "living," and is related to *ḥayyim* (חיים), the Hebrew term for "life."
2. Malachi 3:14.

the *Alter Rebbe,* R. Schneur Zalman of Liadi, author of the *Tanya* and founder of the Chabad movement – serves to remind us, first and foremost, that Elul is a month of life. It reminds us that this is a month in which we should feel the intimacy of "*Ani leDodi veDodi li,*" "I am my Beloved's, and my Beloved is mine,"[3] intimacy in which there is much joy, love, and awakening. *Ḥai* Elul reminds us that that life-producing hope should spring from this period.

A HUMAN IMAGE

The prevalent method of *teshuva* is to begin from the details, to delve into them, and to intensify one's efforts in carrying them out. Thus, we examine the transgressions we have committed and the degree to which we have carefully observed the various sections of the halakha, and we commit to improving ourselves in these areas.

There would seem to be nothing wrong with such an approach. By paying careful attention to the *Shulḥan Arukh,* by comparing our behavior to what is outlined in the Code of Jewish Law, one clarifies what is permitted and what is forbidden, thereby defining the boundaries of one's life.

But that is the not the main object. Above and beyond all the clarifications regarding the small details of what is forbidden and what is permitted, there is a more important question. Indeed, if we neglect this question – if we fail to address it or take it seriously – we have in fact neglected the most essential part of *teshuva*. Even if a person fulfills every last chapter and paragraph in the *Shulḥan Arukh* and has a beard, side locks, and long *tzitzit,* it is still possible that he has a basic shortcoming that precludes him from being considered a human being; he may be nothing but a "Jewish demon."[4] Keeping all the laws will turn him, perhaps, into a Jew, but it will not yet be possible to call him a person.

The main distinction between someone who is a human being and one who is not is that a human being has a goal to which he aspires; the totality of deeds and mitzvot that he performs has an overall objective. A horse remains a horse even if *tefillin* are put on it daily, and it does not

3. Song of Songs 6:3. The first letters of these four Hebrew words spell out "Elul."
4. Based on *Zohar, Raya Meheimna, Parashat Pinḥas.*

even become a holy horse because of them. A person, too, can put on *tefillin*, keep mitzvot, study Torah, and do many more such things in the course of his life, yet there will still not be much of a difference between him and a horse. The difference between a human being and an animal lies in the goal, not in the acts involving life's details.

A human being must have a goal and a direction; therein lies his uniqueness. To be a human being, one must make the effort of seriously deciding upon a direction, a goal that one wishes to reach.

The month of Elul is a fitting time for this objective. In the month of Elul, we can make important decisions that will not only improve our daily actions, but change and transform the whole course of our lives into that of a human being. In Elul, it is not necessary to preoccupy oneself with details; rather, one should think deeply about an overall redetermination of one's goal in life.

A WORTHY LIFE

Ḥai Elul is, as already noted, the birthday of the *Alter Rebbe,* author of the *Tanya,* and of the Ba'al Shem Tov. The preeminence of these *tzaddikim* did not stem from their success in certain endeavors or from their achievements, but from something far greater.

Some people can be said to have led noble and productive lives; they wrote several books, furthered several important causes, and achieved a few things. There are others, however, whose personalities represent much more than this, for whom these attainments are merely extras. The essence of their lives lies not in what they accomplished or failed to accomplish, but in their very nature and their very existence. When someone's life itself is holiness, we celebrate his birthday, for it is their very being that is important.

This idea is also connected to the idea of *teshuva* and Elul, which are focused on the inner life, on the general direction in which to proceed, on one's dreams and aspirations. The goal of Elul is to attain a human image, and what distinguishes a human is not the number of mitzvot or transgressions one has performed or the number of pages of Gemara one has studied, but the transformation of one's inner life. The purpose of Elul – and all *teshuva* – is thus to transform the essence of one's life and inner being into holiness and prayerfulness, beyond one's various acts and achievements. During Elul, one should focus not on externals and external actions, but on turning and directing one's inner life toward holiness.

That is what constitutes the human image, that is what constitutes life, and that is the goal of *teshuva*.

PRAYER AFFECTS A HALF

Teshuva constitutes the resolve to return, to change one's direction and life. Something substantive happens as a result of the aspiration for holiness alone.

Ḥai Elul is a holiday of Hasidim. How can a regular person be called a "*ḥasid*"? Our sages say that *ḥasidut* (loving devotion) is the highest spiritual level![5] The answer is that the moment a person resolves to attain the level of a *ḥasid*, the moment he dreams of achieving holiness, at that moment, although he is not yet a *ḥasid*, his aspiration already does something to him. Whether or not a person succeeds in becoming a *ḥasid* depends on the grace of God. But the will itself and the fact that he begins the path to the realization of his dream accomplish something real; already now he deserves to be called a *Hasid*.

The Midrash states: "Prayer affects a half."[6] The very prayer, the very will, and the very supplication themselves already advance a person half of the way to his destination. Every good wish and every good intention become part of a person's reality, and in themselves already constitute the beginning of the journey. The very determination to reach great heights, and certainly the genuine readiness to set out on the path one has decided upon and dreamed about, change the person himself and make it possible for him to actually get there, even though great persistence will yet be required.

---

5. *Avoda Zara* 20b: "Thus, R. Pinḥas b. Ya'ir said: 'Torah leads to carefulness, carefulness leads to diligence, diligence leads to innocence, innocence leads to detachment, detachment leads to purity, purity leads to holiness, holiness leads to humility, humility leads to fear of sin, fear of sin leads to loving devotion, loving devotion leads to *Ruaḥ HaKodesh* (the holy spirit), *Ruaḥ HaKodesh* leads to resurrection; and loving devotion is the greatest of them all, as it says, "Of old, You spoke to Your devoted ones in a vision" (Psalms 89:20).'"
6. *Vayikra Raba, parasha* 10.

The limits of possible achievement in this regard depend solely on the person's will. The place that a person wants to reach will mark the limit of his ability.

Thus, setting a goal, an objective, provides the opening for reaching it, the possibility of real life, life with direction – a human life.

ASK OF ME AND I WILL GRANT IT

In Elul, one should direct himself to the path of spiritual uplift, and one should begin to ascend it. Usually, however, a person aims no higher than to become a decent *ba'al habayit* (layman). Since that is the maximal level that one strives to attain, what becomes of him in the end is a not so decent *ba'al habayit*.

A person must aspire to become no less than an angel. This does not mean that he ultimately will *be* an angel, but at least he will be something closer to that level; at least he will have a chance of resembling an angel!

A person must aspire to ascend higher and higher, and he must dream great dreams. Although he will likely not reach the supreme goal, the main thing is that, as far as he is concerned, he has already begun to ascend heavenward. If he should fall short, God will "join intention to deed"[7] – God will reward him for his good intention as though he actually reached his goal. If, however, his dream remains earthbound, he will remain rooted in this world and never uplift himself from it.

Determination is the key factor; one must truly want to reach heaven. The point of Elul is to decide where it is I want to get to, and the greater and higher my aspirations, the more I will succeed.

In Psalms, it is written: "Open wide your mouth, and I will fill it;"[8] "You are My son… Ask it of Me, and I will make nations your estate."[9] God says to everyone: My child, do not be content. Ask of Me; request everything. When one asks of the One who has the power to give, it is worthwhile to ask for the greatest things one can think of. The wider we open our mouths, the more they will be filled.

7. *Tosefta Pe'ah* 1:4.
8. Psalms 81:11.
9. Ibid. 2:7–8.

The verse, "Why didn't the son of Jesse come to the meal yesterday or today?"[10] is expounded as follows: Why does the son of Jesse – the Messiah – not come? The answer is that on the two days of Rosh HaShana (yesterday and today), man asks for bread and sustenance ("to the meal"), but nothing beyond that, and so that is also what he receives. He could have asked for the son of Jesse, and yet he did not; hence, the son of Jesse does not come.

Why does man not ask for the son of Jesse? Because he is a minute creature, a small person, who is incapable of uplifting himself – even in his aspirations – above the level of reality.

In all that pertains to mitzvot, the fear of God, and good deeds, one must not content himself with little, as though saying, "What further obligation is there for me?"[11] In such matters, not only is it a great sin to content oneself with little, it is contemptible. In the service of God, there is no such notion as "sufficient" and no such grade as "passing."

In all that pertains to serving God, one must always go further still and aspire to much more. It has been promised in the Torah, in the Prophets, in the Writings, in the Mishna, and in the Gemara that whenever someone tries to ascend, the way is opened for him – one need only decide and make an attempt. No one is forced to advance through those open doors, but one must never rest on his laurels, content with what he has already achieved. Only in material matters is being content with little a virtue; in spiritual matters, there is no end to what a person should desire.

Our sages say: "Everyone must ask, 'When will my deeds reach those of Abraham, Isaac and Jacob?'"[12] Obviously, not everyone can be like Abraham, Isaac and Jacob. What is the point of asking, "When will I reach their level?" The answer is that everyone must at least aspire to this, work at it, dream of it, and set out on the path, even if it is unattainable in reality.

Persistence in and preservation of the path and the idea are not sufficient; one must do more. One must build his commitment so that

10. I Samuel 20:27.

11. Cf. *Sota* 22b.

12. *Seder Eliyahu Raba* 23.

it will last and live on over the long haul, consolidating the idea so that it can endure for thousands of years and can continually create.

The Psalms refer to the "House of Israel," the "House of Aaron," and "those who fear God;"[13] there is no mention of the "House of those who fear God." One of the Hasidic Masters explained that "those who fear God" have no ordinary, stationary, and static house. Rather, they have the "House of Jacob," which is continuously growing and renewed.

A person must not remain stationary; if one does not ascend, one actually descends. Success is not measured by whether or not one falls, which transgression he committed, or which mitzva he performed. The question is: Did I ascend higher today? Is today a better day than yesterday? And if the answer is "no," then I am descending. In order not to descend, I must do greater and bolder things.

This is not a requirement to live in perpetual instability, but to establish something stable that lives, progresses, and renews itself. A person must ask, "When will my deeds reach those of Abraham, Isaac and Jacob?" and he must at least touch their level, living in his own world while following their example. He must not compromise or be content with little; he must aspire to the highest attainments.

SEVEN TIMES A TZADDIK FALLS AND GETS UP

Whoever takes this upward path must be willing to absorb falls along the way – "Seven times a *tzaddik* falls and gets up."[14] A person's decision to follow the way of the righteous, to reach for heaven, includes the awareness that all sorts of things can happen on the way. No one is immune to failure, and everyone is liable to fall. But the *tzaddik* is not broken by problems; rather, he gets up. He moves on, not like creepers in dust or like cringing, stooped, pitiful creatures, but like a human being. In spite of everything, he remains on his course and continues in his direction.

The decision to follow the way of the Patriarchs is the spiritual work of the month of Elul. Elul is the time to decide where I am headed and to begin marching in that direction. Ultimately, I may not reach my destination; but I, for my part, have at least begun marching. If God

13. Psalms 115:12.
14. Proverbs 24:16.

grants me strength and time, I will get there – perhaps sprinting, perhaps walking, perhaps even crawling.

A person can undergo radical change at any age, young or old. Even at the age of seventy, a person can change the direction of his life. He can say, "Master of the universe, if You let me live until one-hundred-and-twenty, I will be able to accomplish something. If You do not let me, at least I can say that I, for my part, made that accomplishment my goal." A person should not, at any age and at any station in life, allow himself rest – not in his actions and not in his dreams.

TESHUVA – ESTABLISHING A COVENANT

There is another important aspect of *teshuva* that anyone who wishes to attain a human image must know – something of this process must remain forever and ever. The *teshuva* must indelible, like a *brit mila* (circumcision) is permanently engraved on the flesh. A regular contract can be invalidated with the help of a few capable lawyers, but a covenant in the flesh cannot be disavowed; what was cut remains cut. Once a covenant is established, it remains forever significant and unforgettable – and so must *teshuva*.

When a person does *teshuva* in this way, whenever he recalls the decision that he made, he will get the shivers, which will give him no rest and not allow him to carry on as usual. His decision to do *teshuva* will push him again and again to advance further.

This is simply a matter of taking the leap and making the decision. A person can study and pray a great deal, but as long as this does not stem from a genuine decision and the establishment of a covenant, all his study and prayer is just a collection of particulars that will ultimately evaporate without leaving a trace.

Our sages teach that there is one type of *ba'al teshuva* (penitent) whose willful sins are turned into merits.[15] How does this happen?

If a person sins and then desires to return to God, his sins give him no rest; they are ever present in his consciousness and continually torment him. He understands that someone like himself, someone who has sinned and transgressed, is obligated to do much more than others

15. *Yoma* 86b.

in order to draw near to God. Thus, the sinner's past and sense of loss serve as fuel for doing more and reaching higher. If a penitent is doubly energized to act as a result of his sins, he is a true penitent – and those sins are transformed into the merits that they inspire.

A person who simply became "religious," who always does the minimum, fulfilling the mitzvot and the halakhot, but does not feel compelled to go further – such a person cannot elevate himself. He is, in fact, not a penitent; he simply became a "religious" person, and on that level he will remain.

A person must enter the path of *teshuva* in the manner of Abraham, Isaac and Jacob. The mitzvot should be performed in such a way that they cannot be erased from memory, from the heart and from the mind. Once he begins on this path, it will never give him rest; his past will always remain with him and urge him on to more and more.

TUNNELING UNDER THE THRONE OF GLORY

Entry into the world of *teshuva* requires readiness for work and effort. One must knock his head against the wall until he breaks through. That is how the gates of Heaven are opened before us.

The Book of Kings recounts the story of King Menashe, who committed almost every possible sin and who was totally wicked in every respect. The Book of Chronicles relates that at the end of his life, "in his distress, he entreated God his Lord and humbled himself greatly before the God of his fathers. He prayed to Him, and He answered (*vaye'ater*) his prayer, heard his plea, and returned him to Jerusalem to his kingdom. Then Menashe knew that God alone is the Lord."[16]

Our sages interpret the Hebrew word "*vaye'ater*" as "*vayeḥater*:" "This teaches that the Holy One, blessed be He, made Menashe a kind of *maḥteret* (tunnel) in Heaven, in order to accept him in repentance, on account of the attribute of Justice."[17]

Some people are unworthy of reaching Heaven by the highway; the gates of Heaven will not open on their behalf. Yet they are not rejected absolutely; God is willing to dig for them a special path by which

16. II Chronicles 33:12–13.

17. *Sanhedrin* 103a.

they can reach Him. They must go through a secret tunnel, entering the Palace from beneath the Throne of Glory. Their only way to reach Heaven is to dig and tunnel through until they succeed in breaking a way through to God.

God allows everyone to reach Him – our task is to take advantage of the small opening He offers.

TO BRING THE DAYS OF THE MESSIAH

In Elul, a person must begin his way forward. To do so, he must first know the desired end. The goal is to bring redemption to the world and to make the world ready for the coming of the Messiah: "'All the days of your life' – to include [literally, to bring] the days of the Messiah."[18] That is our task all the days of our lives – both the days and the nights, the mitzvot and the transgressions. Everything we do is in order to bring the days of the Messiah; we must not settle for less.

The whole point of Elul and *teshuva* is to direct ourselves to the goal of the redemption and not to be content with little – to think of the truly great things. We must build ourselves – body and soul – so that we become the track on which the Messiah will come. We must not be content with anything less, and must not desire anything more.

18. *Berakhot* 1:5.

Teshuva – Return to the Source

THE COMMON CONCEPTION OF TESHUVA

People talk a lot about *teshuva* throughout the year, and all the more so in the month of Elul and the Ten Days of *Teshuva*, the traditional period of *teshuva*. Yet, despite all the talk about *teshuva*, one senses feebleness and a lack of truthfulness in the matter. We speak theoretically about *teshuva* and what it entails, yet we sense that it is merely fine talk; it certainly cannot actually be implemented according to its fundamental intention.

The fact that *teshuva* is not taken seriously does not stem from a failure to evaluate our sins and character defects properly. Many people recognize their shortcomings and wish to rectify them, and yet *teshuva* remains for them purely theoretical.

This strange state of affairs – in which everyone agrees that *teshuva* is necessary, and yet it is not taken seriously – proves that there is something unsuitable and unrealistic in the common conception of *teshuva*, as a result of which *teshuva* becomes mere rhetoric.

When people think of *teshuva*, the basic idea associated with it is that of sin and leaving the way of God. When a person sins, he leaves the Holy One, blessed be He, and when he has remorse for his sins, he returns to his Creator. This idea is contingent upon the basic assumption that man's place is with God, and that attachment and closeness to

God is man's natural and innate state. *Teshuva,* then, is nothing other than the return to the holy, which has been forsaken.

This view, though it appears to be the simplest and most fundamental of all, is not considered plausible by most people. Even if they profess their belief in it, deep in their hearts, they do not think that their true place is beside God. Even the religious and the impassioned do not generally experience their own existence as being identical with God's existence.

Only one who can say, like Elijah, "As God lives, before whom I stand,"[1] can feel the pain of separation and detachment from the holy. Since most people do not feel that their natural place is beside the holy, the natural consequence is that they cannot fully experience the idea of *teshuva,* which is based on that assumption. A person cannot truly return to God if he does not feel deep inside that he was once beside Him and that his true place is at God's side. Most people therefore sense in the usual discourse about *teshuva* an internal contradiction between themselves and their words, with which they cannot fully identify.

As long as this is the notion, the conception of *teshuva* has no leg to stand on; it cannot be real and vital in people's hearts.

MAN'S RETURN TO HIMSELF

Does this understanding of *teshuva* truly comprise its entire essence? Isn't the concept of *teshuva* broader than simply returning to God after we have distanced ourselves from Him and fallen into sin? To pose the question more radically: Is it necessary to sin in order to return in *teshuva*? Does *teshuva* really depend exclusively on the feeling of intimate closeness to divinity?

An ancient *midrash* lists the things that were created before the creation of the world, and among those elemental things is *teshuva.*[2] If *teshuva*'s origin is before the creation of the world, is cannot possibly entail only repentance for sin. *Teshuva* is something basic and essential for the world in its totality; it is more essential and fundamental than actual sin or even the ability to sin. *Teshuva* is not an accident or an epi-

1. I Kings 17:1.
2. *Pesaḥim* 54a.

sode; it is one of the consummate essences of life, which builds life and is not just a by-product of life.

What, then, is this original *teshuva*, the *teshuva* that preceded the world? How can we even begin to understand the concept of *teshuva* when sin does not yet exist and there is no possibility of deviating from divinity?

The truth is that there is reason to return, even if we have not sinned; there is reason to come back, even if we have not drifted away. In such a case, we cannot return to a former path, nor is there an assumption that the former path is the better path; it is not necessary to return to any specific path of life. It is possible to return to something much more intimate and basic – namely, to ourselves.

A person's true self, like the essence of every creature in the world, is immeasurably deep and broad, and underlying every essence and transcending it is divinity itself. To return to the divine essence means to be more independent, to deepen one's self-awareness, understanding, and perception of one's essential nature. Clearly, then, we are not necessarily speaking about a religious return, about becoming more religious, about performing more mitzvot, good deeds, and the like.

If *teshuva* is return to one's true self, return to the divine essence, the way a person returns to divinity is defined as the way that he becomes himself. In other words, *teshuva* is indeed a return, but is not more than return. The basis of *teshuva* is not the attempt to go beyond what is inside ourselves; on the contrary, it is the attempt to come closer and closer to our own true selves, to be more ourselves.

Hence, *teshuva* is not based on the performance of good deeds, on more mitzvot, on more prayer, on more devotion, on greater scrupulousness and conscientiousness, unless these also constitute a return to one's essence. If they do not, they do not constitute *teshuva* at all. Endeavoring to become closer in general to divinity is obviously not a bad thing, but that is not included in the concept of *teshuva*. To be better or greater than oneself constitutes an effort to grow, an attempt to ascend, but *teshuva* is both simpler and deeper than that.

The key to *teshuva* is return to the right place, the correct and fundamental condition suited for each person from his very inception. *Teshuva* is achieved by returning to what is required and demanded of a person as one who is apart, distinct, and different from all other people, as one who has his own unique destiny in his own life.

Thus, it is told in the name of various *tzaddikim* that they would say: "When I go up to Heaven and stand before the Heavenly Court, and they ask me, 'Why were you not like our forefather Abraham?' I will have an answer. But if they ask me, 'Why were you not as you could have been?' – to this question I will have no answer at all." The great test and trial lies not in the demand that we be giants, but in the demand that we be what we are meant to be and are capable of being – ourselves.

THE TEST FOR COMPLETE TESHUVA

How does one determine the path of returning to himself? If the test is to revert to self-awareness and self-perception, complete lawlessness might result; "returning to oneself" could imply virtually any wildness or villainy, which one could justify as "being myself." There are numerous factors, situations, and moods that may lead a person to conclude that to be himself, he must act in an unrestrained manner or gratify his vulgar desires.

But, here, too, there are limits. These limits do not so much restrict as teach; they teach the right path and the progress that ought to be made on it. The returnee must be aware that he is going to the place where he ought to be, where he was destined to be from his very inception; he must not give in to factors that seem so natural, but are actually ephemeral.

Returning to oneself entails perceiving and recognizing oneself as one comprehensive essence, which constitutes a human being. We seek here not only the person, but his innermost nature – not what he is, but what he ought to become.

The most profound test of return to oneself is the recognition that within my essence, within my being, there is a deeper essence – the divine essence. The divinity that is the foundation of all foundations and the essential point of every human being is like a distant light that always shows the direction.

If "to be myself" entails contradicting and opposing that tiny point that connects me and God, it is an internal contradiction. To sever the bond with the exalted, supernal spark that gives me life, or at least the meaning of life, entails fleeing from my essence; escape from that bond is nothing but an escape from myself.

Everyone aspires to advance in certain realms. Often, one is confident that he has discovered the goal of his *teshuva,* and when that *teshuva* does not succeed, he is left perplexed, and even depressed.

One who advances in specific points cannot and will never succeed in reaching the level of complete and true *teshuva. Teshuva* means returning to the true path of the "I," to one's destiny as it is; it entails disregarding and trying to forget all the secondary and peripheral points. The inner and true point of *teshuva* is the longing to connect again and again precisely with something essential and basic.

Teshuva is not the attempt to be more religious, nor even the attempt to be better; it is the profound attempt to be "me."

ROSH HASHANA – THE DAY OF TESHUVA

TOWARD ORIGINALITY

On Rosh HaShana, the day of *teshuva,* we say, "This day is the beginning of Your works." This day of Rosh HaShana is a beginning; it is a new creation of a new year. All of creation returns on this day to the inception of the world, its root and origin. The *teshuva* of man corresponds to the *teshuva* (return) of all of creation. Over and over again, I must try to find, amidst all the peripheral things, the essential and elemental "I" within me.

Every person loses his way many times. A year or perhaps several years are wasted on things unrelated to one's destiny, things that are not the goal, not the essential purpose of life. In such cases, one must, most importantly, leave the path of wickedness. For wickedness is not merely an incidence of sin in the usual sense, but a whole path leading to evil; it is deviation and sin (חטא) in the sense of missing (החטאה) life's essential objective.

The self-reckoning of Rosh HaShana need not be like a peddler's reckoning of small sums, a reckoning of mitzvot and transgressions. Indeed, for this very reason, sins are not mentioned at all on Rosh HaShana. The *teshuva* of Rosh HaShana is not *teshuva* for sin, but a reckoning of one's life in its totality – an accounting of one's guiding principles, of one's path and direction in life. Will these lead me to my essence, within which lies the divine essence, or will they lead me away from it?

Teshuva, whether great or small, must always seek to uncover the inner person, what lies hidden deep inside him. The purpose of *teshuva* is to bring forth and reveal those hidden things, to bring to light all that is concealed and hidden of what is most precious in every person.

Teshuva Preceded the World

TESHUVA TOWARD GOD

The *Zohar* writes that in the future rectification of the world, the Messiah will "lead the *tzaddikim* to *teshuva*."[1] In the days of the Messiah, those rare individuals who are true *tzaddikim* will merit to attain a higher level – that of *ba'alei teshuva* (penitents).

But how can a *tzaddik* do *teshuva*? How can one who has not committed any transgressions repent?

In truth, however, *teshuva* is not essentially connected with sin. The term *teshuva* denotes "return," returning to one's place, returning home. Indeed, *teshuva* appears on the Gemara's list of things created before the creation of the world;[2] it clearly does not depend on a preceding transgression, but, rather, stands on its own.

The *teshuva* whose origin is before the creation of the world is the return, or the turning, to God. In this sense, *teshuva* is not the reverse side of transgression, but rather the reverse side of ordinary reality. In a certain sense, the creation of the world and its existence cast God's creatures into exile, into a condition of being distant from God. Through

1. *Zohar, Raya Meheimna*, 3:153b.
2. *Pesaḥim* 54a.

the process of creation, God, as it were, distanced us from Himself. But He provided the balm before the blow – He created *teshuva*. *Teshuva* is the possibility of traveling the distance back to God. It is the remedy for the world, the ability to emerge and return to the original Source.

Teshuva means, first and foremost, "Return to Me"[3] – regardless of whether a transgression has or has not been committed. Even someone who has never transgressed, one who has done only what is good and right in the eyes of God and man – even he must return.

Sin, in its innermost sense, results from forsaking, neglecting, and losing the connection with God, and this can occur even without committing actual transgressions. Transgressions may add a certain bitterness or urgency to the will to return, but they are not connected with the essence of sin.

Nevertheless, as a rule, the motivation for *teshuva* is somehow related to transgressions committed. R. Menaḥem Mendel of Vitebsk, in his work *Peri HaAretz*, cites the image of a swing: The more the swing moves to one extreme, the more it is able to move to the other extreme. This is also the relation between transgression and *teshuva*. If a person committed a serious transgression that weighs on him and breaks his spirit, the path of *teshuva* for him is simpler and clearer. For a person whose transgressions are minor, it is much harder to return in *teshuva*, and even if he does return, his *teshuva* will not attain the level, intensity, and resonance that characterize the *teshuva* of someone who committed a serious transgression.

GOD IS NOT IN OUR MIDST

In essence, we must return in *teshuva* for leading private lives, ordinary "civil" lives. One may be an observant Jew, but his consciousness, as a whole, is generally ordinary consciousness, without real feeling of God's presence.

It is the goal of many people, and religious ones in particular, to treat God the way many families treat elderly parents. A person sends his father to a home for the aged, as luxurious as he can possibly afford, and he tells him, "Father, I love you. I will come to visit you every day,

3. Malachi 3:7.

I will even bring the kids with me. But I have one request: Don't come to my home."

That is what we would like to do with the Holy One, blessed be He. We are ready to build Him a home, even an expensive one, on condition that He will stay there and not come to our homes, for we want to live our lives without Him. We are ready to give God a percentage – of our money, of our time, even of our convenience – provided that there will be a fundamental separation between His domain and our domain.

This separation does not necessarily mean that we want to be adulterers, thieves, or consumers of *treif*; it means that we want to lead "normal lives" like other peoples. Indeed, this is precisely the model that others follow: They build cathedrals of unparalleled beauty, sometimes spending centuries on their construction, but the cathedrals stand apart from the people; they do not reach the individual. Everyone has his own private home.

The allure of leading such a life is not the product of sin, nor is it the outcome of the character defects of any particular person. It is the allure of the reality of the world as a world. The world (הָעוֹלָם) is concealment (הֶעְלֵם) of the divine countenance, and for that reason it offers the possibility of leading a life whose core and essence depend on all sorts of things other than God.

It is for this that one must return in *teshuva*. Even if one commits no transgression, one must do *teshuva* for ordinary, daily life itself – for forgetting that the sense of God's presence is the central point of our being Jews.

The basic difficulty of Jewish life stems from the fact that God does not give us a minute's break. The *Shulḥan Arukh* begins with detailed instructions about what a person must do from the moment he wakes up, and the precise instructions continue to guide how he is to go to sleep. The halakha guides our lives twenty-four hours a day, every day of the year. It begins even before birth and continues until one is dead and buried. The Jew is in a constant state of interaction with His Creator, who enters every moment and every place, leaving no place entirely empty of Him or His intervention. This difficulty is far greater than any specific problem that exists with the performance of any particular mitzva.

Still, Jews are always trying to turn this system into a limited, bounded system, with beginning and end, which can be separated and isolated from "life."

Perhaps we do not pay attention to what we say in our prayers, which are replete with far-reaching declarations about drawing near to God and attempting to be united and bound up with the Master of the Universe. For in practice, we are always trying to do just the opposite – to disengage and distance ourselves. We do not do things that are intentionally contrary; we just keep ourselves as neutral as possible. This neutral stance requires return in *teshuva*; it is not a result of one specific problem, but of the reality in which we all live, into which we all are born and in which we all grow.

CHANGE OF DEFINITIONS

Teshuva is not meant to move us to fulfill one more mitzva or to buy a more beautiful *etrog*. Its purpose is to bring about a change of our conceptions regarding substance and truth in all that pertains to the question of what is truly important and what is not. To make a change, one must do more than beat one's breast in contrition. What is needed is *teshuva*.

To affect this essential change, one need not do anything extraordinary. One need only do one thing, which is the essence of *teshuva*: turn around. For, basically, the root of transgression is: "But they turned their backs to Me, and not their faces."[4] A person who faces west will go west all his life; but if he should want to go east, all that he needs to do is turn around.

This turning, however, is a most difficult matter. It is an inner turnaround that entails a truthful definition of what is truly important to me. The whole world – its objects, noises, voices, music, sights, beauty, charm, and allurements, among which one was raised and one continues to live – constantly distract us from this point. The goal of *teshuva* is to find it once again.

In other words, *teshuva* involves a change of identity: How do I identify myself? Where am "I" found? There may be many details that

4. Jeremiah 2:27.

are unknown to me, but the minute I determine my "I," I reach a different place and become a different being.

Teshuva, a different definition of one's identity, can change one's whole world. R. Tzadok HaKohen spells this out sharply in his work *Tzidkat HaTzaddik.*[5] In his opinion, even someone who knows nothing about Judaism attains an exceptionally high level from the very fact that he calls himself a Jew. R. Tzadok adduces proof for this assertion from a Talmudic discussion[6] regarding a proselyte who converted while he was still among the gentiles. Such a proselyte not only does not know details of the mitzvot, he does not even know basic halakhot. What, then, transforms him into a proselyte? Presumably, the very fact that he calls himself a Jew makes him a different person.

This transition from one form of being to another is supremely difficult, but it is a requirement that is set forth every day before every person, good and bad alike. The Gemara speaks of "a tree that stands entirely in a pure place but whose branches extend into an impure place."[7] When does the tree decide to move to another place and to build the center of its life in a different sphere? The question posed by *teshuva* is: Where is my essence rooted? Where is my "I"?

The world is like a veil, a place where external reality is apparent but God is hidden. According to the laws of the universe, there is no point of exit; the world's laws chain us to a framework of cause and effect, a framework that is not necessarily good or evil, but that restricts us to a certain kind of life simply because we are part of reality. To transcend this reality we must somehow transcend the world.

Returning in *teshuva* is not a necessity; it is "only" a possibility. But that possibility, the ability to extricate oneself from the laws of the universe, is the theoretical, theological, and metaphysical basis of *teshuva.* Our sages stated that *teshuva* can act retroactively to transform willful sins into unwitting sins, and even into merits.[8] *Teshuva* makes it possible to turn left into right, to rewrite the past and make it new.

5. *Tzidkat HaTzaddik* 54 (This teaching was omitted in the first edition of that book.).
6. *Shabbat* 68b.
7. *Kiddushin* 40b.
8. *Yoma* 86b.

Obtuseness of the Heart Which Impedes Teshuva

HOW TO PREPARE FOR TESHUVA

Our sages delved deeply into the matter of *teshuva*, and they maintained that the concept of *teshuva* is not necessarily connected to sin; *teshuva* is possible even when there is no transgression. However, all agree that *teshuva* is impossible without a sense of deficiency. A person who does not sense any deficiency in himself, who considers himself perfect, is as remote as can be from *teshuva*.

Of all the communities in *Eretz Yisrael* and elsewhere, the community that senses most strongly its virtues and its particular eminence is undoubtedly the religiously observant one, in all its segments and levels. It seems that there is no other community that holds so strongly to the opinion that all the defects of the present reality stem from other parties, whereas it has achieved the highest state of perfection.

Various events – some shockingly joyous, like the aftermath of the Six Day War, and some shockingly tragic, like the aftermath of Yom Kippur War – had an impact, even if only for a short period, on Israel's entire population. To be sure, the awakening was not deep or long-lived, but people felt a need for change, for rectification, for reexamination of values. The only community that largely remained crowned in its self-perceived halo throughout those jolting events was the religious community.

This phenomenon of self-satisfaction is a well-known phenomenon among the religious community as a whole, but one can say that it generally pertains to the religious individual as well. He, too, feels that he is part of an entire community; except for a few minor exceptions he, too, thinks that if there are defects in the present reality, the defect should be sought in someone else.

When there is no feeling of deficiency, there is no real ability to do *teshuva*. Neither the month of Elul nor the Ten Days of *Teshuva* can solve the problem, for a person must be *shav miyediato*[1] – that is, he must do *teshuva* out of awareness of his deficiency, whether it is a deficiency that stems from sin or the deficiency of not attaining the exalted goals and aspirations that he should have attained.

"WE HAVE NO WORTHY DEEDS"

The factors that create this smug self-satisfaction are essentially two primary causes of damage, which can be designated as "the principle of closed spheres" and "the principle of relativism."

Almost every segment of the religious community (and surely almost every member of this community) chooses – consciously or unconsciously – spheres within Judaism regarding which it declares a moratorium, releasing itself from their binding force.

To be sure, theoretically speaking, an observant Jew is defined as one who considers himself obligated by all aspects of Judaism. However, this is a completely abstract definition and is fit only for external use. In respect to the essential religious experience, as it actually appears in life, every person chooses the spheres regarding which he, as it were, serves notice from one Yom Kippur to the next; he does not take them upon himself, neither in general nor in detail. They are essentially "closed spheres."

Each segment of the religious community has its own division of these spheres. One segment excludes interpersonal mitzvot from Judaism-in-practice. Another segment excludes all the problems relating to

1. *Shabbat* 69a et al.

the pains of the community as a whole, shouldering only the problems of its limited circle. Other segments of the religious community exclude from Judaism several other basic mitzvot – e.g., Torah study, the prohibition of the menstruant woman, certain forbidden sexual relationships, the daily afternoon prayer – all according to their interest and will.

When transgressing these excluded mitzvot, one does not even feel that he commits an offense. This is not even a case of "If a person commits a sin and repeats it, it becomes to him as though it were permissible"[2] – for from the very outset, there is no sense of transgression. The offense is considered completely permissible, for in regard to these excluded spheres, the offender feels as though he was never obligated to observe these mitzvot to begin with.

Another primary cause of damage is the principle of relativism. Relativism is the inner justification for every deficiency and for every defect. It is based on constantly looking outward, at people who are "worse than me" in one way or another. Values are not assessed in and of themselves, but always in comparison to others. In our generation, it is always possible to find other people who are much further from Judaism than we are; the sense of satisfaction and contentment from the very fact that "He has not made me a secularist" thus suffices to atone for all sins.

The fact that some other person violates the Sabbath serves the religious person as a never-failing source of general atonement for himself. Since he himself keeps the Sabbath in his own way, he is not wanting in any respect. All he needs to do is to look at his neighbor to see how he is, in fact, full of goodness and blessing!

It is told in the name of one of our luminaries that man was created in such a way that he would always be able to look upon his fellow man from the standpoint of his material state. He would then give thanks to God for his own more fortunate condition and be content with his own lot. In the spiritual realm, in contrast, he can look at those who are superior to himself and recognize his own deficiency through comparison. Man, however, tends to do the opposite: He looks at the other's material wealth and is grieved that he himself has not reached

2. *Yoma* 86b.

that bracket, whereas in the spiritual realm he looks at those who are inferior to himself so as to be satisfied with his own lot!

WE HAVE BEEN GUILTY

For these reasons, a person can recite the whole order of the "*Ashamnu*" confession, and it is as though he skipped it entirely. He can recite the whole list of the great "*Al ḥet*" confession, the confession of Rabbeinu Nisim, and the *Tefilla Zaka* of Yom Kippur eve, and it is as though he did not recite them. For to each one of these, there is an addendum that he silently adds; he "vows with his lips and nullifies the vow in his heart."[3] When he reaches one sin, he declares: For me, such-and-such is not considered a transgression, for I am not the type of Jew who is bound by the prohibition or who takes it upon himself. In the case of another transgression, he says to himself: Why, this is the transgression that my neighbor so-and-so commits, and for that reason my own private world is actually the height of perfection! All I have left to do is complain about the sins of the generation, of its leaders and rabbis, for they are the ones who are afflicted with all the shortcomings.

Before thinking about *teshuva* in any particular point or detail, it is necessary first to make an overall reckoning, to remove the aforementioned "primary causes of damage" from the community as well as from the individual. Then it will no longer be necessary to search for ways of *teshuva* or to listen to sermons on the topic. For from a true sense of one's own deficiency, one can come to the rectification of all that is required.

3. *Kalla* 1:16.

You Shall Return to God[1]

BELIEF IN THE ABILITY TO CHANGE

All forms of *teshuva*, however diverse and complex, have a common core – the belief that human beings have it in their power to cause inward change.

Many factors lead to stagnancy and routinism and many factors conspire to distance a person from his Creator – beginning with the training one received and ending with habits that one has acquired.

The rule that "transgression begets transgression"[2] is not just an assumption about the existence of supernatural elements that direct a person, but a sober view of reality. There is a causal connection between things; one cannot extricate oneself all at once from both the inward and outward consequences of one's actions. For this reason, one transgression creates a situation in which a second seems logical, natural, and almost inevitable.

A way of life remote from religious observance not only makes

1. The translation of this chapter is greatly indebted to the original translation by Michael Swirsky, which appears in Adin Steinsaltz, *Teshuva. A Guide for the Newly Observant Jew* (New York: The Free Press, 1987), pp. 3–7.
2. *Avot* 4:2.

such observance difficult, but also, by its own inner logic, makes it progressively more difficult. Yet, despite this natural causality, *teshuva* remains above these behavioral laws; it expresses the ever-present possibility of changing the direction of one's life.

According to our sages, this possibility of altering reality, which we should regard as one of the mysteries of all being, is one of the things that were created before the creation of the world.[3] *Teshuva* existed before the laws of nature came into existence. "Before the mountains were born,"[4] a principle even more fundamental and more exalted was proclaimed: that change – *teshuva* – is possible.

THE ESSENCE OF TESHUVA

Many books and articles have been written about *teshuva*, providing detailed analyses of the various stages in the process, from start to finish. Yet, for all its manifold aspects, a few fundamental principles underlie all forms and levels of *teshuva*, whether its starting point is exalted or lowly and whether it aims at a high level of spiritual perfection or at more modest objectives. Two basic points are found in every kind of *teshuva*: leaving the path of past sin and adopting a better path to be followed in the future.

If we were asked to summarize the subject and point to *teshuva*'s starting point, we would say that *teshuva* is rooted in the point of transition from the past to the future. It is the point at which one leaves the path of the past and turns to a new path. As expressed by the very meaning of the word, *teshuva* is simply a turning – be it a complete, total change of direction or a series of many separate turning points of unequal significance.

Three times a day, a Jew petitions for *teshuva* and forgiveness, and each petition indicates the possibility of *some* kind of turnabout. As a rule, the more settled and tranquil a person's life, the less sharp a turn he is likely to take. Often, however, it is only in retrospect that a person realizes what the truly important turning points in his life were, even though he did not notice them at the time.

3. *Pesaḥim* 54a.
4. Psalms 90:2.

FEELING THE NEED FOR A CHANGE OF DIRECTION

As we have stated, two factors make this turning possible – the recognition that the past, whatever it may have been, is imperfect and in need of correction and the decision to change direction, to go a different way in the future. Indeed, most of the *teshuva* literature deals with the details, the precise formulation, and the possible consequences of this turning.

The recognition, the feeling of the need to change, does not always come in the same way. Sometimes, one is overcome by a sense of sinfulness and defect, of defilement that burdens the soul, and this results in a powerful desire to escape this condition and to purify oneself of the blemish and sin. But the desire for a turnabout can also come in more subtle forms – in feelings of imperfection or unrealized potential, which lead to a search for things of another kind or of a different nature.

As a rule, the more acute the initial feeling of past inadequacy or blemish, the sharper the turnabout is likely to be, sometimes to the point of extremism and complete reversal. Conversely, when the feeling of uneasiness or imperfection about the past or present is more subdued, the resulting turnabout will generally be more moderate, both in the pace of the change and in its sharpness.

But whatever the initial feeling about the past, the desire to do *teshuva* always springs from a clear sense of unease about the status quo and about the past.

OBTUSENESS OF THE HEART

The greatest obstacle in the way of *teshuva* – an obstacle that affects everyone, wicked and righteous alike – is self-satisfaction. A person who is pleased with himself feels that he has done well, that "everything is okay" as far as he is concerned; If reality is flawed, the flaws are common to the world as a whole, to all human beings, to society, to the family, to God, and so forth.

Spiritual and moral complacency is not necessarily related to one's objective condition. A person may appear to others to be a sinner and a criminal, yet he himself may have no awareness of his failings. Such a person will never attain *teshuva*. Conversely, even if someone appears to others to be blameless and upright, if he himself is aware of a personal failing, the way of *teshuva* is open to him.

One great sage termed the great obstacle to *teshuva* as "obtuseness of the heart."[5] Obtuseness of the mind is easily recognized as an impairment of cognitive functioning. Obtuseness of the heart, however, is more insidious. It is a condition in which a person's emotional sense of his own deficiencies and problems is blocked. Even if one is filled with wisdom and understanding, even if he intellectually knows everything, this will have no effect on his actual behavior if he has no emotional sense of deficiency.

In many cases of *teshuva,* the pace of the turnabout intensifies from a certain point onward, creating an "opening of the heart" – the initial block to feeling one's own deficiency is overcome. The breakthrough of this initial openness leads to a deeper awareness, and thus to a stronger response.

These observations apply universally. They are true of those who have remained distant all their lives from everything involving holiness, and who therefore feel no lack in that area, as well as those who lead pious lives with which they are so satisfied that they cannot see how far they are from perfection.

This discerning and spiritual awakening is the first point of "confession." When a vague sense of unease turns into a clearer recognition that something is lacking, and when this recognition is expressed in words spoken either to oneself, to God, or to another person, the first step in the turnaround has been taken. This is the stage of *teshuva* that relates to the past, to one's life and character before the turnaround.

COMMITMENT FOR THE FUTURE

The second component in *teshuva* is called "commitment for the future" – the resolve to change one's direction from now on. In a certain respect, this component is the natural continuation of the first step in the turnabout, and its force, direction, and staying power largely depend on the clarity and strength of one's initial feeling about the past.

One who feels uneasy and characterizes his uneasiness and himself with the words "not good" (or any other more complex and intel-

5. *Tanya,* ch. 29.

lectual formulation that essentially expresses the same thing) does not necessarily come to the decision to change, let alone change in practice.

On the other hand, the fact that a person regrets his actions, is sorry about something that happened to him, and feels his inadequacy does not necessarily lead to the desired outcome either. Instead, it can lead to a deepening sense of despair, the loss of hope, and a fatalistic resignation to the status quo, without any attempt to change the situation. Such despondency, which is regarded by many as one of the most serious afflictions of the soul, not only does not produce positive results, but sometimes is itself the cause of a person sinking further in his defects and deficiencies.

A person may come to feel so sunken and lowly (morally, religiously, or from any other perspective of himself and his lot in life) that he decides to blot out the source of his degradation from his consciousness. Such repression is usually accomplished by choosing to lead a life of instinctual pleasures or other pursuits whose common denominator is their ability to dull the senses, temporarily or permanently. The purpose of this escape is to relieve the person of his feeling of depression. Turning to alcohol, drugs, sex, or other forms of "entertainment" is an attempt to blunt a feeling of unease and dissatisfaction, but it solves nothing. Such indulgence only creates a false sense of relief from pain and the illusion that one can carry on without changing direction.

Thus, remorse in itself, for all its decisive initial importance, must be accompanied by another aspect – the element of hope and belief in the possibility of change. In this sense, the principle that at all times and from any starting point, no matter how low, it is possible to return in *teshuva* is one of the foundations of man's hope and reawakening. The awareness that the door is always open and that there is a way to *teshuva*, that there is no situation from which there is no return – this awareness itself can serve as a stimulus that creates the possibility of *teshuva*.

A PATH BOTH LONG AND SHORT

Resolutions, of course, are not always carried out. The obstacles and impediments that lie in man's way are very great. Routine and habit, the factors that often bring a person into a certain state, usually continue to operate, regardless of the fine resolutions in his heart. Nevertheless, the will to change and the decision itself are an important step, even when this decision is not immediately carried out. As long as the decision to change is not mere talk or self-deception (one is just as liable to speak words of deception to oneself as to others), every such decision, no matter how small, is important.

In some cases, of course, the great turn in a person's life is made suddenly, at a sharp angle and at high speed. But usually such a turn is preceded by many less dramatic and often concealed stages – small decisions that are not always implemented, wishes never carried out. Yet when the time comes, all the small decisions accumulate and coalesce into a single essence.

In short, *teshuva* is a world unto itself, embracing two apparent opposites.

On the one hand, it is an exceedingly lengthy path which, in fact, has no end point. When a person wants to attain *teshuva,* whatever his starting point, each subsequent moment of change throughout life becomes the fulfillment of that initial inner resolution to make the turn.

On the other hand, *teshuva* is a tiny point, a turnabout in miniature. *Teshuva* is a moment of reflection, remorse, and thought of change, a flash of insight that instructs a person to change and improve.

These two aspects of *teshuva* are not contradictory, but complementary. In one respect, there is nothing more difficult than doing *teshuva,* because *teshuva* means transforming oneself, fashioning a new nature. In another respect, there is nothing easier than *teshuva;* a split second of turning is already considered *teshuva.*

The *ba'al teshuva* (penitent) is thus like a person following a certain course who in an instant decides to change his direction. From that point onward, he no longer goes the old way, but follows a different path. Yet the new path, like the old one, is long and unending.

Bibliography

GENERAL JEWISH SOURCES:

Babylonian Talmud
Bible
Jerusalem Talmud Tractates *Berakhot, Megilla, Sukka*
Maimonides, *Commentary on the Mishna*
Mishneh Torah: *Hilkhot Teshuva, Hilkhot Mamrim, Hilkhot Mikvehot, Hilkhot Yesodei HaTorah*
Minor Tractates: *Kalla, Derekh Eretz, Semaḥot*
Mishna
Passover Haggada
Rashi's commentary to the Torah and the Talmud
Shulḥan Arukh (Code of Jewish Law)
Siddur (Prayer Book)
Tikunei Zohar
Tosefta
Avot
Tur
Zohar
Zohar Ḥadash
Zohar, Idra Zuta

Zohar, Raya Meheimna

MIDRASHIC LITERATURE:

Mekhilta DeRabbi Yishmael
Mekhilta DeRashbi
Midrash on Proverbs
Midrash on Psalms
Midrash Raba: Genesis, Exodus, Leviticus, Numbers, Deuteronomy, Esther
Pirkei DeRabbi Eliezer
Seder Eliyahu Raba
Sifra
Sifrei Bemidbar
Sifrei Devarim
Yalkut Shimoni

OTHER BOOKS:

Ben Porat Yosef – Hasidic work by Rabbi Ya'akov Yosef HaKohen of Polnae
Ein Ya'akov – Collection of all the Aggadic sections in the Talmud
HaYom Yom – Daily study calendar, added to the Chabad prayer books, which includes special Chabad dates
Keter Malkhut – One of the most important Jewish religious-philosophical treatises, written in beautiful poetic form by R. Shlomo Ibn Gabirol (1020–1058)
Keter Shem Tov – Collection of commentaries to the Torah attributed to R. Israel Ba'al Shem Tov, founder of the Hasidic movement
Likutei Torah – Commentaries to Leviticus, Numbers and Deuteronomy by R. Schneur Zalman of Liadi, founder of Chabad (1745–1812)
Ma'amarei Admor HaZaken – some 25 volumes of collected teachings of R. Schneur Zalman of Liadi, founder of Chabad
Sefer HaIkarim – Major philosophical treatise by R. Yosef Albo (1380–1444)
Sefer Yetzira – One of the most ancient Jewish esoteric texts, attributed to our Patriarch Abraham
Sha'ar HaKavanot – A philosophical-devotional book by R. Ḥayyim

Vital (1543–1620), the most important disciple of R. Yitzḥak Luria, founder of Lurianic Kabbala

Shulḥan Arukh HaRav – Code of Jewish law, edited and updated by R. Schneur Zalman of Liadi, founder of Chabad

Siddur Admor HaZaken – Chabad prayer book with commentaries by R. Schneur Zalman of Liadi, founder of Chabad

Siḥot HaRan – Collection of some 300 teachings of R. Naḥman of Bratslav (1772–1810)

Tanya – The most basic book of Chabad Hasidism and one of the most important Hasidic works, by R. Schneur Zalman of Liadi, founder of Chabad

Tanya, Iggeret HaKodesh – A section of the *Tanya* which is a collection of letters that R. Schneur Zalman of Liadi, founder of Chabad, sent to his disciples

Tanya, Sha'ar HaYiḥud VeHaEmuna – A section of the *Tanya* that deals with God's unity

Teshuva: A Guide for the Newly Observant Jew (New York: The Free Press, 1987), by Rabbi Adin Steinsaltz

The Book of Beliefs and Opinions – Major philosophical treatise by R. Sa'adia Gaon (882–942)

The Tales of Rabbi Naḥman of Bratslav, "The Seven Beggars"

Tiferet Yisrael – Philosophical book by the Maharal, R. Yehuda Leib b. Bezalel of Prague (1520–1609)

Torah Or – Commentaries on Genesis and Exodus by R. Schneur Zalman of Liadi, founder of Chabad

Tzidkat HaTzaddik – Collection of sayings and writings of R. Zadok HaKohen of Lublin (1823–1900)

About the Author

Rabbi Adin Steinsaltz was a teacher, philosopher, social critic and prolific author who has been hailed by *Time* magazine as a "once-in-a-millennium scholar." His lifelong work in Jewish education earned him the Israel Prize, his country's highest honor.

Born in Jerusalem in 1937 to secular parents, Rabbi Steinsaltz studied physics and chemistry at the Hebrew University. He established several experimental schools and, at the age of twenty-four, became Israel's youngest school principal.

In 1965, he began his monumental Hebrew translation and commentary on the Talmud, and completed it in 2010. The Rabbi's classic work of *Kabbalah, The Thirteen Petalled Rose,* was first published in 1980 and now appears in eight languages. In all, Rabbi Steinsaltz has authored some sixty books and hundreds of articles on subjects ranging from zoology to theology to social commentary.

Continuing his work as a teacher and spiritual mentor, Rabbi Steinsaltz established a network of schools and educational institutions in Israel and the former Soviet Union. He has served as scholar in residence at the Woodrow Wilson Center for International Studies in Washington, D.C. and the Institute for Advanced Studies at Princeton

University. His honorary degrees include doctorates from Yeshiva University, Ben Gurion University of the Negev, Bar-Ilan University, Brandeis University, and Florida International University.

Other works by Adin Steinsaltz
available from Maggid

A Dear Son to Me

Biblical Images

The Candle of God

The Essential Talmud

In the Beginning

The Long Shorter Way

The Soul

Strife of the Spirit

The Sustaining Utterance

The Tales of Rabbi Nachman of Bratslav

Talks on the Parasha

The Talmud, The Steinsaltz Edition: A Reference Guide

Talmudic Images

The Thirteen Petalled Rose

Teshuvah

Maggid Books
The best of contemporary Jewish thought from
Koren Publishers Jerusalem Ltd.